D0499347

IN THE FOOTHILLS OF MEDICINE

Dear Lauren —

Thanks for coming
to the talk!
Enjoy the read!

— Peter c Mcheese —
4/08

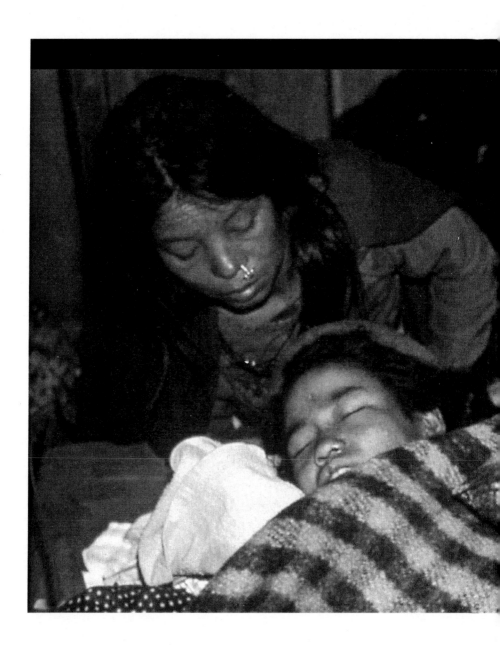

ROBERT C. McKERSIE, MD

IN THE FOOTHILLS OF MEDICINE

A YOUNG DOCTOR'S JOURNEY FROM THE INNER CITY OF CHICAGO TO THE MOUNTAINS OF NEPAL

iUniverse, Inc.
New York Lincoln Shanghai

IN THE FOOTHILLS OF MEDICINE
A YOUNG DOCTOR'S JOURNEY FROM THE INNER CITY OF CHICAGO TO THE MOUNTAINS OF NEPAL

Copyright © 2005 by Robert Crosier McKersie

All rights reserved. No part of this book may be used or reproduced by any means, graphic, electronic, or mechanical, including photocopying, recording, taping or by any information storage retrieval system without the written permission of the publisher except in the case of brief quotations embodied in critical articles and reviews.

iUniverse books may be ordered through booksellers or by contacting:

iUniverse
2021 Pine Lake Road, Suite 100
Lincoln, NE 68512
www.iuniverse.com
1-800-Authors (1-800-288-4677)

ISBN-13: 978-0-595-36368-1 (pbk)
ISBN-13: 978-0-595-80805-2 (ebk)
ISBN-10: 0-595-36368-7 (pbk)
ISBN-10: 0-595-80805-0 (ebk)

Printed in the United States of America

CONTENTS

ACKNOWLEDGMENTS

There are many people who have helped with this book whom I would like to thank. First and foremost, my patients, not only those whose lives have been shared in the pages of this book, but also the ones I have not written about. All have made me a better doctor.

Early drafts of this book were read by Robert and Nancy McKersie, Edward Eckenfels, Dr. Richard Norton, Annelise Robey, Eric Schreiber, Robert Silverman, and Alison McKersie. Each gave me immensely helpful feedback. In addition, and most important, Drs. Catherine M. Creticos, Alan L. Jackson, and Richard Warren (specialists in HIV, cardiology, and hematology/oncology, respectively) read parts of the book for medical accuracy. Also, I am fortunate to have had three astute editors, Jean Eckenfels, Steve Bridge, and Nancy McKersie, without whom this book would never have made it into print.

During medical school and residency training I was fortunate to have had many fine medical mentors: those who deserve particular acknowledgment are Drs. Maria Brown, Frederick Richardson, Steve Rothschild, Paul Luning, Mark Loafman, and Mark Gideonson. They have been wise and generous role models and have guided me in my preparations for a career in medicine. Several of my close friends and colleagues during my medical training also deserve special mention for their friendship and support: Drs. Rebecca Ratcliff, XinQi Dong, Robert Matthew, and Felix Meza. And most particularly, I wish to thank Drs. Geeta Maker-Clark and Gary Hsin for their compassion and steadfast friendship throughout our medical training.

Very special thanks also to Mr. Anil Parajuli and the Himalayan HealthCare staff in Nepal for the great humanitarian work they accomplish under trying circumstances and for inviting me to be a part of it.

Finally, I would like to thank my mother, father, and sisters, Liz and Alison, for their understanding and loyal support. Special thanks go to my brother, Bill, who offered me buoyancy during my times in rough water. Although their help often goes unacknowledged, each has been a key influence in my life.

Robert McKersie
September 2005

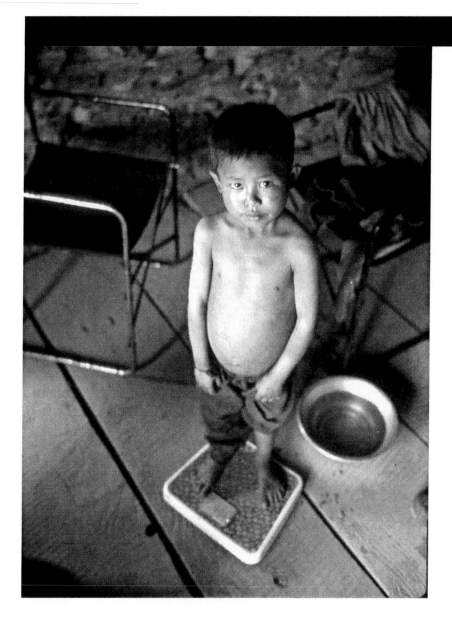

A young boy suffering from malnutrition has his weight checked at the Sertung medical camp.

Into the Mountains

March 25–27
Chicago to Kathmandu

After helping my intern sign out our five ICU patients to the incoming intern and my fellow senior resident, I eagerly jumped into a cab waiting at the hospital and headed for O'Hare Airport to begin a two-day flight to Kathmandu, twelve time zones and half a world away from bitterly cold Chicago. As a second-year family medicine resident, I had chosen to head to the mountainous "Shangri La" of Nepal for an elective rotation in rural and international medicine under the auspices of Himalayan HealthCare. The year was 2001.

I hoped that this medical trek into the mountains of Nepal would refresh me. The U.S. medical system over the last two years of my residency had taken its toll. My continual attempt to get our inequitable healthcare system to work for both my uninsured and insured patients had exhausted me. The constant struggle to find affordable medicines for all of my patients, the battle to get referrals authorized by healthcare insurance companies for my few insured patients, the inability to get timely radiological exams at the local community hospital for my uninsured patients, and the late night pleading with specialists to see my patients free of charge had become maddening. I was demoralized by my inability to arrange timely and proper healthcare for a number of seriously ill patients. I envisioned that the complexities of our U.S. healthcare system would not be present in Nepal, and that this trek would reaffirm for me one of the reasons that I had entered medicine, namely, to have a relationship with my patients that would be pure and unencumbered by the many aggravating hurdles that I had been navigating in our healthcare system back home. I wanted the relationship to be based only on the patients' need for care, not on their ability to pay—a relationship, if you will, where nothing would come between us except my stethoscope.

The two-week trek into remote Nepal would be self-contained. We would carry everything on our backs and only have the bare essentials in medical instruments and supplies: a few blood pressure cuffs, our stethoscopes, a small microscope, and a limited amount of basic medicines. With these simple tools we would care for the people in two villages in one of the poorest countries in the world. Without a lab or X-ray machine, this trek would force me to hone my clinical skills; there would be no modern medical technology to help confirm a diagnosis. I did not know at the time that the serious conditions of some of our patients would force me to draw on all the critical care skills that I had learned several months earlier during my intern year.

As I stepped onto the tarmac at the Kathmandu airport that March morning, I was greeted with a blast of thick, muggy air. Despite an elevation of 4,400 feet, the temperature was already 90 degrees. After customs, I proceeded out of the airport into the bright, high-altitude sun and was welcomed by several dozen sign-waving Nepalese all encouraging me to stay in their guesthouses. Through the maze of placards and people, I spotted my name held aloft, and I headed toward it. I was greeted by two small Nepalese boys, each grabbing one of my two overstuffed duffle bags. Without a trace of effort each boy swung one of the large bags (equal to his weight) onto his back, hooking the webbed handle snuggly across his forehead. After seeing this, I had no doubt that these two could be sherpas on Everest in a few years.

As we walked to the car I met Kul, a short, pleasant-looking gentleman who would be our tour guide for the medical trek. Upon arriving at the car, the young boys in unison dropped the bags, stuck out their hands and said in near-perfect English, "ten dollars." I looked at Kul, a person who I had known for a mere two minutes for some honest consultation on this fee; he held up one finger signaling the proper amount to tip. After getting into the car, I learned that one of the other doctors, lacking small bills, had earlier tipped these same boys ten dollars, a day's wage for the most experienced sherpa, and a week's wage for a porter. I reconsidered my notion that these boys would need to climb Everest to make a decent living.

As we pulled out of the airport, the sights, sounds, and smells of Kathmandu enveloped us. Our tiny car, sputtering thick black smoke like so many other vehicles on the road, was instantly folded into the daily bustle of this city of two million people. We meandered through many narrow alleys clogged with cars, locals, bicycles, and shopkeepers selling their wares. The smell of spices mixed with incense, cow dung, and burning garbage wafted through our car window. Our driver, continually using his brakes and horn, was forced several times to make a slalom course out of the pedestrians, bikes, and free-ranging cows, giving only the animals, bestowed with sacredness by the Hindus and Buddhists, a wide berth. Killing a cow in Nepal is punishable by incarceration.

After settling into a comfortable hotel, I met the other participants on the medical trek. Anil Parajuli, the director of Himalayan HealthCare and our trek leader, is a sturdy Nepalese gentleman of forty years with a quick laugh and gentle smile. He has led treks in Nepal for over twenty years, the first ten years as a guide for wealthy hikers; then after some soul-searching, he founded Himalayan HealthCare, a nonprofit, nondenominational, nongovernmental organization that works to enable rural Nepalese to achieve their own economic and social development. Through this organization in the last ten years he has led scores of medical treks for doctors from around the world who have given untold amounts of humanitarian aid to the poorest of the Nepalese people. The other three participants were doctors: an emergency room attending from North Dakota, a pathology resident from Tennessee, and a family medicine resident from New Mexico. We were a diverse lot with a common purpose.

After a quick briefing of the trek's itinerary in the hotel lobby, I headed across the street for a traditional Nepalese dinner of rice and lentils called *daal*. Having gone two days without sleep and knowing that I would soon be testing my lungs and legs, I turned in early.

March 28
Kathmandu to Parvati Kund

Anil, Kul, and we doctors left Kathmandu for our medical trek in the early morning, heading northwest out of the smog-laden Kathmandu Valley. Our long, winding full-day drive would be into the remote and seldom trekked mountain region of north-central Nepal. Along the way we passed many charming but extremely poor villages. Kakani, Trisuli (the village that we would walk out to at the end of our hike), Kalikasthan, Ramche, Dhunche, Shyabru Besi, and Rasuwagadi were several of the many villages that gave my uncoordinated American tongue trouble. Several of these villages had checkpoints where we had to show our passports—some for our personal safety (trekkers often get lost) and others for national safety (to make sure that we were not Maoists).

After nine hours of hard, bumpy driving and having gained 4,000 feet in elevation, we pulled our dusty vehicle into a lovely camp at Parvati Kund, the disembarkation point for our hike the next day. This campsite, made up of several weathered wood buildings, looks out onto the Ganesh *Himals* (mountains) to the north. With peaks reaching up into the clouds at 21,000 feet, the Ganesh Himals are part of the Himalayan Range that is bordered by Everest to the east, the much-trekked Annapurna Range to the west, and Tibet to the north. All these mountains are snow covered and magnificent. At this 9,000-foot-high campsite, we were met by the 41 porters, 6 cooking staff, and 5 staff members who would be our guides and friends for the next 15 days. The porters ranged in age from 15 to 50 years old, and each would receive about two to three U.S. dollars for every back-straining workday they were about to do. The cooks, many having graduated from being porters, carried less weight and were compensated at a higher rate, approximately four to five U.S. dollars a day. Their cooking skills, which I soon learned were superb, were cultivated through apprenticeship and observation. After our formal greeting, we were served a five-course meal on a table made up with place settings and a tablecloth. Something told me that we were not going to be "roughing it" on this trip. We retired early to the sound of barking dogs and the glow and smell of the wood fires in the local village huts.

March 29–30
On the trail

We awoke early this morning and were greeted by the grand views of the Ganesh Mountain Range and the sweet taste of *chai* (tea) brought to our tents by the cooking staff. After a breakfast of tea, hot cereal, corn cakes, and omelettes, we closed up the one small daypack we were expected to carry and started our trek.

The cooking staff was split into two groups: one that would leave early in the morning each day to prepare our hot lunch on the trail, and another group that would stay behind to cook us breakfast and then clean up after we started to hike. This second group would inevitably pass us on the trail long before lunch and would be at the next campsite to prepare our dinner. The porters all carried about 40 kilograms (90 pounds) in large baskets (*dokos*) on their backs, supported only by a long strap that was strung across their forehead. No shoulder or waist straps held these massive loads, only the porters' sturdy necks. Some porters will carry up to 220 pounds in this manner!

Our hike over the next two days would take us through some of the most beautiful landscapes in the world. This morning, as we ascended higher and higher, we walked through many pine and rhododendron forests. The day was clear, our packs were light, but our pace was slow due to the elevation and the relatively easy existence that the three other doctors and I have lived at sea level. We stopped for lunch today at 12,000 feet. This flat clearing in the woods overlooks the valley and last evening's campsite that we toiled three hours to rise above.

Near the end of lunch it started to hail—a reminder that we were in the mountains—and the afternoon's hike took us up a steep, icy climb through sleet and more hail. The ground underneath was wet and slick, our breathing labored. After an hour of hiking we reached Khurpu Pass at 13,000 feet. There was still snow here, attributed to the long and tough winter. This was the first time that this medical staff had hiked in snow in its ten-year history.

At the pass we took a break and met seven Nepalese porters, four women and three men, all from the same family. Since leaving camp our group had been playing a "tortoise and hare" game with this family, our group catching and passing them on the trail and then in turn being caught and passed while we rested. We were clearly the hare; our fast and eager start after each resting spot soon slowed to a sluggish walk and even another rest stop soon thereafter. The Nepalese family, slow and methodical under their Goliath-sized loads, used its knowledge of the mountains to hike an even pace, rarely stopping even for water. They were also heading to Tipling, but would do the three-day hike in two days, each carrying over 120 pounds. As both our groups rested on the pass, I was struck by the refreshing simplicity of this family, all of them squatted in a resting position, their thick, leathery bare feet planted firmly in the icy mud, their short, thin bodies clad in homemade woolen cloth and nourished only by cold, cooked rice, eaten with weathered hands. The complexity and stress of my urban life and family medicine residency were starting to ebb away.

Once over the pass we descended for two hours through a rich green valley, moist with rain, and entered the village of Somdang at 10,500 feet. This small community is a lead-and zinc-mining town located on a river that is formed by the merging of two mountains. That evening we set our tents among the village huts and enjoyed a delicious fresh chicken curry made from one villager's bounty. We had walked nine hours—our first day out!

The following morning after breakfast we started our long ascent to Phangsand Pass. We climbed for five hours up through a rhododendron and alpine forest and then crossed a series of steep ridges on a narrow path. One step to our right was thick, soft mountain grass. One step to our left was a 1,000-foot drop into the valley below. We broke for lunch at the pass which still had a dusting of snow and was quite cold and windy; we needed to put on extra layers.

The pass is at an elevation of 14,000 feet and has a line of *mani* stones (Buddhist prayer sites) that mark the edge of the trail. Strung between these ten-foot monuments of neatly piled stones are several Buddhist prayer flags that snap loudly in the brisk wind. Behind us are the Ganesh Himals; looking westward over the pass are the remaining Ganesh Himals that divide the

Everest and Annapurna ranges. And as far as one can see down the valley is the village of Tipling, our first medical stop another day and a half away.

After a hot lunch we napped next to the mani stones protecting us from the wind and under the prayer flags protecting us from evil spirits. The remaining part of the day was spent on a steep and rocky three-hour descent into the valley of Mar Melung at an elevation of 9,000 feet. Here we camped for the evening in a grassy meadow shared with local herdsmen grazing their cattle. It rained most of the evening; the higher elevations would be blanketed with snow. I dozed off to the patter of rain on my tent and the softening clang of cowbells as the herdsmen made their way home.

March 31
Our first clinic stop

We left camp this morning at our usual time of 7:30 A.M. We descended for three hours through more rhododendron and alpine forests, passing an increasing number of villagers as we neared Tipling. At mid-morning we took a long break, resting at the outermost edge of the terraced fields of wheat, rye, millet, and oats that—like an offering of goodwill—mark the entrance to the village of Tipling. An additional hour's walk through these lush fields brought us to the Tipling health post at 8,000 feet. The clinic lies 1,000 feet above the town on the south side of the valley. (At the bottom of the valley, 4,000 feet below, is a river that we followed westward when we left Tipling.)

The medical clinic consists of two long buildings, one above the other on consecutive terraces. The exam rooms, all rather rudimentary but adequate, have a wood examining table without a mattress. The room's light comes from a sheet of translucent fiberglass that has been placed among the tin slats of the roof. A bowl of water tinged blue with potassium permanganate is the disinfectant used to sanitize our hands.

We were supposed to have the afternoon off, but word of our arrival spread down the valley and into the village of Tipling a day before our arrival. When we entered the Tipling Medical Clinic we were greeted by approximately fifty villagers waiting to be seen. We quickly unloaded the half-ton of medical supplies into the clinic's pharmacy, ate a hurried lunch, and started to see patients. The patients came fast; my first two were so sick that I would have admitted them to an ICU if I were in the United States.

The first patient was a distraught woman who was carried in by her husband. She was three weeks post-partum and her legs and lungs had filled with water, making walking painful and breathing difficult. In addition, she had a fever and a heart murmur. I consulted the other three doctors, and we surmised that she had dilated cardiomyopathy, endometritis or endocarditis. Dilated cardiomyopathy is a rare condition in which the heart expands, making it inefficient and increasing the potential of heart failure. Endometritis is an infection of the lining of the uterus and not as serious if treated with antibiotics. Endocarditis, a very serious condition, is an infection of one or more of the heart valves. We did not have an echocardiogram to help confirm our suspicion of the life-threatening dilated cardiomyopathy or endocarditis, and we were left trusting our clinical skills. We gave her Lasix to help draw the fluid off her lungs and legs and a course of antibiotics to treat the possible infection in her uterus or heart valves. We instructed her to come back the following day to be checked again.

The second patient I saw, also carried in by her husband, was an elderly woman who had been prescribed a number of heart medications by a cardiologist in Kathmandu some years earlier. She informed me that she ran out of her medications three weeks ago and had not urinated in three days. She, too, would have been admitted to a hospital in the United States. I refilled her medication and instructed her to come back in the morning if she had not urinated, knowing full well that there was a good chance that she walked two days to get to the clinic and would now start her return trip home, putting complete faith in the western medicines that I had just placed in her hands.

April 1
Medicine in the mountains

On our first full day at Tipling Medical Clinic, when I awoke and ventured out of my tent to watch the sunlight slide down the snow-capped mountains to the north, I noticed a tall white gentleman with a lone Nepalese porter waiting at the clinic door, some 100 yards from our tents. I walked over to him and found out that he had been trekking for the last several days with a group of Christian missionaries in a remote area north of Tipling. The previous evening he had developed a very sharp pain in his abdomen that was not relieved with antacids. His wife, a nurse by training, had urged him to come down to our clinic to be seen. He had departed his campsite at 4 A.M. and hiked down to our clinic with his loyal porter. Upon examination it was determined he had acute appendicitis.

The question now was what to do with him. He certainly could not walk the three days out of the mountains to receive the care he needed. He was also too heavy to carry, and even if we could find the four or five porters that would be needed to transport him, his condition was too tenuous to have him away from immediate medical care during a three-day journey. We were left with no option but to try to fly him out of the clinic to Kathmandu.

Unfortunately, because of an ill-advised government regulation that only "major mountaineering expeditions" could carry two-way radios, we were left with no immediate way to communicate with a rescue team in Kathmandu. While we sorted out our dilemma, we put him into a tent, started an IV drip for hydration, and gave him a dose of IV antibiotics in case his appendix ruptured.

Getting a helicopter into remote parts of the Himalayas is no easy task. First, you have to call the helicopter, which for us meant sending our guide on a run to the closest phone, a VHF solar phone four hours away. Second, solar phones, needless to say, only work during the day, giving us a limited window when a rescue can be initiated. Third, the cost of the helicopter rescue (roughly $1,500) has to be guaranteed by a third party before the helicopter will take off from Kathmandu—this can take several hours in itself. Finally, because the area is remote and maps are poor, most pilots have never flown into the Tipling Medical Clinic and certainly would not fly in at night.

The spring days are long in Nepal, but we were up against a time constraint. Nevertheless, we sent Dal, our fastest guide, running for the phone, and we had the cooking staff draw an 8-foot "H" (for hospital) with baking soda on the terraced field just below our clinic. We continued to see patients that morning, periodically checking in on our sickest one, and waited for the helicopter.

At about noon we heard the beat of the helicopter's blades against the sky and left the patients we were examining to watch. The pilot, not seeing our 8-foot signal, had a difficult time finding us. It was only after a second pass that he located us by spotting our bleached white undergarments hung out to dry. He then made a perfect landing on the "H," kicking up a dust storm of dry dirt and baking soda. After numerous photos of the pilot and Dal with all of the doctors and medical staff, the helicopter picked up and whisked the patient and his wife down the mountain to Kathmandu as two hundred wide-eyed villagers watched.

The rest of the day was uneventful except for a woman who was carried into my examining room by a relative I assumed was her son. She looked about seventy years old and was thin as a bone, weighing no more than sixty pounds. Her face was drawn, she had a large mass under her left jaw, and she lay lifeless on the wood examining bed. After talking to her family through two translators (Tamang to Nepalese and Nepalese to English), I learned that she was not seventy, but thirty, and she had a three-year-old child. She had been losing weight for about two years and withered away to her present emaciated state. We suspected tuberculosis (TB), which is quite prevalent here, or the worst case scenario, cancer. I consulted the pathologist who immediately took a biopsy of the mass under her jaw and then examined it under the microscope. Thankfully, the biopsy did not show the malignant cells we feared. At this point we assumed that she had disseminated TB, which has a good prognosis, if treated.

This case has interesting medical and ethical aspects. Earlier in the day, the pathologist had taken a biopsy of a sixty-three-year old woman whose right breast had been hard and painful for over a year. This hardness and discomfort had spread around to her right underarm and back. Unfortunately, this patient's biopsy showed metastatic breast cancer. The question then was what to do. Should this woman, who had already lived five years beyond the average life expectancy of a Nepalese woman, be encouraged to walk (or even be carried) the three-day journey to Kathmandu for cancer treatments that, at best, would be only palliative and not curative? These questions were answered for us by the fact that Himalayan HealthCare could not afford to fly her to Kathmandu. In addition, our patient was in no shape to walk or even be carried. Finally, as our sage leader, Anil, said several times during our trek, "sometimes you have to play God." With this advice the decision was made to give her medication to ease her pain and to let her live out her remaining days in her home in Tipling. I was struck by how different this decision would have been in the United States.

What to do with our thirty-year-old woman with potentially curable TB and a three-year-old child was not as difficult to decide; she needed to be seen by a specialist in one of the teaching hospitals in Kathmandu. Her family was handed some traveling money by Anil; they wrapped her in a blanket, sat her in a porter's basket with the back cut out allowing room for her legs, and hoisted her onto her husband's sturdy back. They then departed the clinic for the three-day trek out of the mountains.

April 2
Common ailments

This day was uneventful compared to the last two days. I saw close to forty patients all with the typical complaints of "stomach ache," "whole body hurts," "headache," "worms," and "diarrhea."

Tamangs, the major ethnic group in this region, are a very hearty population. They eat a low-fat diet consisting of wheat, barley, millet, and oats with various roots and greens. Their protein consists of eggs and an occasional chicken. In the mountainous region where they live, they get an enormous amount of exercise, carrying 200-pound loads over 14,000-foot passes and working for hours in the fields. Consequently, the prevalence of heart disease is low. But, because of their enormous amount of physical activity, many of the older villagers have arthritis. In addition, the population is plagued by gastritis and diarrhea.

April 3
Tipling to Sertung

After a busy morning clinic, we packed up our supplies and left the Tipling Medical Clinic in early afternoon. In three full days of clinic we had seen three hundred and fifty patients. As we descended through the town, many of the villagers came out to greet us, and, true to their custom, many of the Nepalese children ran alongside us and shouted, *Namaste*, the traditional Nepalese greeting. When we came to the village's western border, there was waiting a lone woman with her child. She placed a string of white rhododendron flowers around our necks and presented to each of us the traditional hard-boiled egg. The string of flowers was a thank you; the egg, a symbolic gesture of food for our continuing trek.

After this touching sendoff, we hiked down a steep ravine into a gorge 2,000 feet below and crossed a rickety old wood bridge that spanned a crystal clear river. In the glow of the late afternoon sun we had a refreshing dip in the river and then continued our hike up the steep and treacherous northern slope of the ravine. As the evening light faded, we crested the top face of the gorge and walked onto the flat terraces that surround the village of Sertung. As I regained my breath, I remarked to one of the other doctors how lucky we were to get out of that steep gorge while we still had light. Little did I know what this comment foreshadowed.

We came into the village of Sertung an hour later and set up camp in front of the dilapidated four-room schoolhouse that (much to the delight of the village children) would be our clinic for the next three days. The school's walls were fieldstones held together with decaying mud, straw, and yak dung. The roof was a patchwork of mismatched sheets of corrugated tin. The windows, wood slats with hinges, could be swung open to let the air in or closed to keep the dust out. The classroom's blackboards were uneven pieces of slate taken from the mountains and cemented into the stone walls. The building had four rooms, one of which we converted into a pharmacy and stocked with the eight remaining porter-loads of medical supplies. Two of the remaining rooms were each divided in half by blankets hung from the rafters, making four semiprivate exam rooms. Each room was given a wood examining table, a towel, and a bowl of blue-tinged disinfectant water. This would be our medical clinic for the next four days.

April 4–6
An ICU at 7,000 feet

We awoke each morning at the Sertung medical camp to the beautiful view of the snowcapped Ganesh Himals to the north and our customary cup of hot chai brought to our tents by our Nepalese cooks. Each morning, after a hot breakfast, we would leave our tent area, ascend the 20 feet to the adjacent terrace, find our two translators, and start to see patients.

Over the next three days we would see more than five hundred patients, but only one of them will forever stand out in my mind. She was an 18-year-old Tamang woman who was carried into the clinic by her husband and mother on our second day. She arrived wrapped in a blanket and was laid on the wood examining table in my room. She was pale, her hands were trembling, and in between bouts of vomiting she moaned something unrecognizable even to her family. The history we received was vague and incomplete, largely due to the language difficulty of a double translation. What little we learned initially was that three weeks prior she had suffered a spontaneous miscarriage and since then had not gotten out of bed, taking only a little food and moderate liquids. It was only in the last few days that her condition had deteriorated to her present state. What further complicated the story was that the person who witnessed the miscarriage was not present, so we did not know if our patient had delivered both the fetus and the complete placenta.

Proceeding with only this information, we took her vitals—normal except for an elevated heart rate of 120. Her physical exam was also relatively normal for someone who looked as sick as she did. The only part that was suspicious was her pelvic exam. It showed that she had cervical tenderness, but no discharge. At first glance we suspected endometritis, pelvic inflammatory disease (a more serious uterine and ovarian infection), or pyelonephritis (a bladder and kidney infection). All three of these could have been caused by bacteria that had entered her genital or urinary system after her miscarriage.

We started her on the only two IV medications we had, neither of which would completely cover all of the possible pathogens that she may have had. We also started an IV to rehydrate her. We checked on her periodically, and after the last patient of the day, I went to see her, and she communicated through her mother that she felt better. She indeed looked better and her tremors, which we attributed to nervousness, had resolved, and her blood pressure was normal. But she still had vague abdominal pain and a repeat pelvic exam still elicited cervical tenderness. In addition, she had developed a fever. I made the choice at this point to send her back to her hut with antibiotics that she could take orally. In hindsight, I should have kept her at the clinic overnight to be watched.

Our dinner that evening was interrupted by one of our Nepalese cooks who urgently informed us that one of the young women that we had treated earlier that day was now being prepared for death by a shaman medicine man. As we grabbed our stethoscopes and ran to the hut, I could not recall any Tamang woman we had sent home to die.

After a breathless run up the trail, we pushed our way into a crowded, dark, smoke-filled hut. Our gas lantern cast a swath of light that fell on a young woman lying on the dirt floor in her mother's arms. She was in a tremulous state and barely arousable. We instantly recognized her as the young Tamang woman we had seen earlier that day who had suffered a miscarriage. She had a high temperature by touch, her blood pressure was 80/60, and her pulse was weak and very high. She was in septic shock. The story relayed to us was that she had thrown up her medication shortly after returning home. She had then tried to walk across the room and collapsed. Her tremors came soon after. The family, convinced that she was going to die, summoned the shaman.

We bundled her in a blanket and raced her back to our makeshift clinic. We placed two large gauge IVs, ran two 500 cc bags of fluid into her wide open, and placed a Foley to collect and monitor her urine output. Her condition worsened soon after and she started to throw up large amounts of green and yellow bile. We did not have any way to prevent her from aspirating her own vomit into her lungs, so we did our best and manually wiped her mouth out after each emesis. After she received 1.5 liters of fluid, her systolic blood pressure came up to 90, enough to keep her perfused. However, we quickly learned her blood pressure would drop if we decreased the rate of her IV fluids. The IV fluid was keeping her alive.

With her IV fluids wide open, we took a quick break and searched our few available IV drugs, our collective brains, and two books for help.

Needless to say, we were not in a good situation. We did not have the proper antibiotics to completely cover all of the different bacteria that may have been causing her septic shock. We also did not have any way to protect her airway and no way to suction her mouth. Nor did we have any cardiac medications in the event she went into cardiac arrest. Finally, the only thing keeping her pressure up was the IV fluid, which at the present rate would run out before the first light of morning, the earliest time that we could have a helicopter land. With little to be optimistic about, we did our best at creating an ICU at 7,000 feet and hoped for the best.

I informed Anil that we would not have enough IV fluids to make it until morning. Anil, without hesitation, made the decision that two of his guides would return to the Tipling Medical Clinic for more fluids. This trip from Tipling to Sertung, two days prior, had taken us four hours. What Anil was now asking the guides to do was to leave Sertung, descend 2,000 feet into a treacherous ravine in the dark, climb up the other side, and then ascend another 1,000 feet to the Tipling Clinic. They would have to return by the same route and do this total round trip in four hours and with only a flashlight to see the trail. I paused when I heard this plan, remembering the difficulty in cresting this ravine two days prior in the fading light of dusk.

The Nepalese people are a tough, proud, and strong lot, living in a country with numerous social and geographical barriers, many of which they continuously confront. They are also some of the most genuine, gentle, and humble people I have met. These two guides were no exception. With nary a hint of apprehension or reservation, Kamal, a medical assistant, and Tullu, a literacy teacher, knowing the potential danger of the trip, quickly and quietly grabbed their packs, said goodbye, and headed out the door.

As the two guides ran through the darkness of night, John, the other family medicine doctor, Som, a medical assistant, and I stayed with the patient. We took her vitals every 15 minutes and read, under the dim glow of a propane lamp, our two medical books for any information that would be useful.

The fluid we were administering intravenously was helping, but the lack of the proper antibiotics was a cause for concern. We had given her a series of IV antibiotics that covered a broad range of potential pathogens, but we were missing one that would cover anaerobes, an important group of pathogens that very well could have been causing her present septic shock.

Earlier in the day, when our patient first arrived at our clinic and again when we first rushed her back to our makeshift ICU, I had asked the staff what IV antibiotics we had with us. Both times the staff had diligently reviewed with me all the available antibiotics, none of them being broad spectrum enough to cover all of the potential pathogens she might have had. As we sat there taking her vitals and worrying if we were going to lose her, I said jokingly, to break the tension, "I would give $1,000 for Imipenem," a drug with a very wide spectrum of coverage. Anil, taking one last look through the box of haphazardly arranged medications, suddenly stopped, smiled, and held aloft a vial. It read, "Imipenem." My mouth went slack as my eyes carefully traced over each letter. How we had twice overlooked this medication is anybody's guess. As we drew up the chalky-white medication into the syringe and administered it into her thigh, a feeling of hope entered me for the first time since finding her comatose on the dirt floor of her hut. All we had to do now was to protect her airway and keep her blood pressure up with our dwindling supply of IV fluids.

At 2:30 A.M., three hours after Kamal and Tullu left, they returned with two backpacks full of the much-needed IV fluid. These two guides had run through hazardous terrain the equivalent of a fifteen-minute mile nonstop for three hours, at 7,000 feet elevation in the dark!

At 5 A.M., one hour before dawn, we sent Dal, a medical assistant, running down the valley to the closest solar phone.

At 8 A.M. Dal returned with news that he had made phone contact with the medical helicopter. We had our cooking staff again make a large "H" with baking soda on the terrace below our clinic.

At 10 A.M., with our patient hemodyamically stable and afebrile for the first time in sixteen hours, we heard, for the second time this trek, the welcome beat of the helicopter blades against the sky. We all ran out of the clinic, and saw the pilot set down perfectly on our "H," raising the familiar cloud of dust and baking soda that momentarily engulfed the helicopter. The patient, carried in a blanket by six guides, was halfway to the helicopter before the pilot opened the door. The guides laid her on the floor of the helicopter and fastened her IV to a strap on the roof. Her husband and Som jumped in and straddled her with their feet. Her distraught mother shoved a handful of soiled money into her son-in-law's coat pocket as the door closed. The helicopter picked up, hovered momentarily as if deciding where to go, then turned to the north and headed down the valley to Kathmandu. When the dry dust of the field kicked up by the helicopter had settled, one of the Nepalese guides, in typical humble Nepalese fashion, thanked me for saving her life.

After hearing this compliment, my mind drifted back to an ICU nurse named Pam who had taught me the basics in fluid management ten months earlier when I was an intern. In all honesty, I did not save anyone's life; I did what anyone in my situation would have done. I gave the patient all the medication and IV fluid we had. The real heroes were Kamal and Tullu, the two Nepalese runners.

The remaining two days of clinic in Sertung were routine with most of the patients' complaints being the typical, "stomach ache," "headache," "worms," and "diarrhea." There was, though, one other case of interest.

He was an eight-year-old boy with severe malnutrition (see photo preceding Prologue). His mother had died giving birth to him, leaving him with his father. A combination of his father's alcoholism and lack of money contributed to the young boy being improperly cared for. At eight years of age he weighed only 40 pounds and had the classic moon face, swollen belly, and emaciated appendages, all typical of protein malnutrition.

We referred him to the Kathmandu Nutrition Rehabilitation Center. His medical condition, being of a chronic nature, did not necessitate a helicopter evacuation. Rather, he and his father would hike the four-day trek out of the mountains with us after we finished our medical camp.

Our second medical camp ended after dusk on April 6 under the glow of fluorescent lamps powered by the generator the porters had carried over two mountain passes. The line of patients waiting to see us this day had formed early and stretched a good way down the path leading up to the clinic. The patients today, as in all the clinic days, waited patiently for hours to be seen. To not disappoint them, we held clinic well into the evening until the last patient was seen.

After dinner we were invited back to the clinic where we were greeted by close to one hundred villagers all standing in a circle. They had assembled to give us a thank you celebration. The women formed half of the circle and the men formed the other half. The children of the village made up the inner circle. Several of the adults had brought the traditional Nepalese drums, which produce a melodic sound more reminiscent of a sharp moan than a tympanic drum beat. The entertainment for the evening was the village women singing a traditional Nepalese song to the rhythm of their drums and then slowly fading their voices as the men would start their song to the same beat. This serenading between the men and women continued for some time, and, being the honored guests, we were all encouraged to dance. After some embarrassing but joyful dance steps, the singing ended, and Anil made some heartfelt remarks. We, in turn, had an opportunity to thank the Sertung villagers for allowing us the opportunity to serve them. The evening was perfectly delightful!

April 7–10
Descending back to earth

We left Sertung in the early morning of April 7 to a gracious send off by the villagers. The villagers, as did the lone woman standing at the Tipling village exit several days prior, presented us with a necklace of woven white rhododendron flowers and the traditional hard-boiled egg. The villagers also place *tikas* (a mixture of vermilion powder, rice, and curd) on our foreheads for good luck. Our collective group (grown in size with the addition of several patients we were taking with us to Kathmandu for referrals) hiked up and out of the village with high spirits and a special fondness for the people of Sertung.

We would spend the next two days following the Ankha River south as it meandered towards the fertile plains of Nepal. With the magnificent Ganesh Mountains to our backs, we walked alongside many terraced fields of grain and through numerous villages of stone huts and thatched roofs. All along the way we were escorted from village entrance to exit by smiling and inquisitive Nepalese children. We spent the night of April 7 on a grassy terrace in the village of Jharlang, pitching our tents next to a Buddhist shrine. We had the good fortune to hike up to a seldom-visited village in the mountains above our campsite. Our journey to this remote hamlet was for the purchase of the famous Gurka knives, known around the world for their craftsmanship and strength. The knives are worn decoratively on Army soldiers' belts, and are indispensable tools for the villagers as well. We didn't find any knives but had an enjoyable meeting with the villagers who looked at us with curiosity—perhaps their first glance at foreigners.

The four-day hike out of the mountains was a good time for getting our legs back in shape, as well as affording us many moments
to reminisce about our two medical camps. Our thoughts were on
the accomplishment of having seen more than nine-hundred
patients and having made a positive contribution to two desperately poor villages. My mind was also on our young Tamang
woman who had been evacuated by helicopter. I was looking forward to visiting her in the hospital, although I had uneasy feelings
not knowing her condition or even if she had survived.

This was also a time of concern by our guides for our safety. The
Maoist guerillas, with significant support in the rural areas of
Nepal, had in the year prior to our medical trek escalated their
terrorist attacks. Although they mainly target police stations, foreign tourist spots have also been targeted. An earlier medical
trek this spring had been cancelled because of an explosion in a
tourist area of Kathmandu. Thankfully, no one was injured.
However, upon our arrival in Kathmandu two weeks earlier, we
were greeted with the news that the Maoist guerillas had massa-
cred twenty-one police officers in the western part of the country.
Our trek, being of humanitarian nature and sharing at least one of
the demands of the Maoists ("Health care for all"), was reason for
us to believe, at least on one level, that we were not obvious targets for the Maoists. Reality was, however, that we were four
Americans and four very obvious targets for their anticapitalist
rhetoric. Our leader, Anil, ever mindful of our safety, led us
through the mountains with a guide on each side and a keen eye
on the trail behind and ahead of us.

Even with this vigilance, we twice almost came into contact
with the Maoists. The first was at the second campsite after we
left Sertung, in the village of Khaniyabaas. The Maoists had
planned a rally in this village for the same night we had expected
to camp there. (So much for advance reservations!) With the typical "Sickle and Hammer" emblem prominently displayed around
this village, we decided to move our camp that night an additional hour down the trail.

Our only other close contact with the Maoists was along the
trail. Several times during our last few days we heard their eerie
whistles (their method of communicating) echoing down the val-

ley as we hiked out. No job is completely without risks, and any job where you are delivering humanitarian aid to people in politically volatile areas has its potential for injury or worse. Thankfully, none of us were injured and the staff did a masterful job of keeping all of us healthy and safe during the entire trek.

The four-day hike out was not easy by any means. We were dropping to lower elevations each day, but the walking was on "Nepalese Flat," as one of the guides liked to joke. "Nepalese Flat" is not flat at all, but consists of many ascents and descents throughout the day that ultimately progresses to a lower elevation. In addition, the heat and humidity at the lower elevation was high (90 degrees). The porters themselves preferred walking up into the cool thin air of the mountains as opposed to down into the muggy, hot valleys. Nevertheless, after two weeks of hiking, our team emerged from the mountains and ended our trek in Trisuli Bazaar. Some had sore feet, others a little diarrhea—but we all harbour great memories.

April 11–13
Rounding on the patients

Even though the trek was over and two of the other three doctors were heading home, John (the other family doctor) and I would spend the next few days checking on the patients we had referred to several Kathmandu hospitals. I was looking forward to having a tour of three Kathmandu hospitals: one private, one public, and one church affiliated.

The first patient we visited was among the first that I had seen in Tipling, the 30-year-old emaciated Tamang woman we suspected of having TB. She had been carried out of the mountains successfully by her family and taken to the Kathmandu Medical Hospital, one of the city's private teaching hospitals. We met with three of her doctors, and their diagnosis at the time was abdominal TB. Cases like these, rare in the United States, are not that uncommon in areas like Nepal where TB is prevalent. This patient's TB had caused so much inflammation in her abdominal region that it had obstructed her stomach and intestines from emptying properly. The result of this bowel obstruction was the vomiting, poor appetite, and weight loss that she had been experiencing. Over the two-year period of her disease, she had lost about forty pounds, one-third of her body weight. In all probability, her TB would be treated successfully with twelve to eighteen months of TB medications. If she had no complications, she should have had a full recovery.

The second patient we visited in Kathmandu was the severely malnourished eight-year-old Tamang boy whom we had examined in Sertung. This child and his father had hiked out of the mountains with us, and the child was admitted to the Nutrition Rehabilitation Center in Kathmandu. The center is a well-funded private clinic that admits malnourished children and their parents for treatment and education. The children and their parents receive three to five nutritious meals each day; in addition the parents are educated about proper nutrition and cooking techniques. Children will stay at this center until they reach a healthy target weight, on average about three months. It was very encouraging to see our little patient eating. Once at a healthy weight, he would be enrolled in a Kathmandu school, sponsored by Himalayan HealthCare. In addition, his father was to receive help with his alcoholism. It is heartening to see that a country with such poverty is able to provide important healthcare and education services.

The third hospital we visited was the Christian-affiliated Patan Hospital, which was of particular interest to me because it was the medical facility that accepted the two patients evacuated by helicopter. The gentleman with acute appendicitis had been discharged after a successful appendectomy, but the 18-year-old Tamang woman who had gone into septic shock was here, still alive.

We had the opportunity to discuss her case with the head nurse, and she related that the doctor's working diagnosis was indeed pelvic inflammatory disease. Her blood cultures had not grown any specific bacteria—not surprising since we had administered several antibiotics to her prior to her blood being drawn in the hospital. The doctors were treating her, as we had, with a series of broad spectrum antibiotics. The nurse reported that her condition had improved, and that she was now taking food and even sitting up in bed. We had the good fortune of being able to visit her and her husband in her room.

Many language barriers existed between us American doctors and our patients during this trip. In Nepal there are thirty-seven different ethnic groups with an equal number of distinct languages, not to mention Nepalese, the national language. There were several times during this trip when, regardless of how accurate the translations were, the language barrier between the patient and doctor slowed, or even misguided, the medical diagnosis and care. Today, however, when John and I entered the hospital room of the young Tamang woman, we did not need a translator to help us understand each other. We stood there and were able to communicate across a room of silence just what the moment meant to each of us. Two doctors, early in training, and one young Tamang woman, early in life, each having shared a critical and intimate time with the other, were now in the same space, time, and thought—without words.

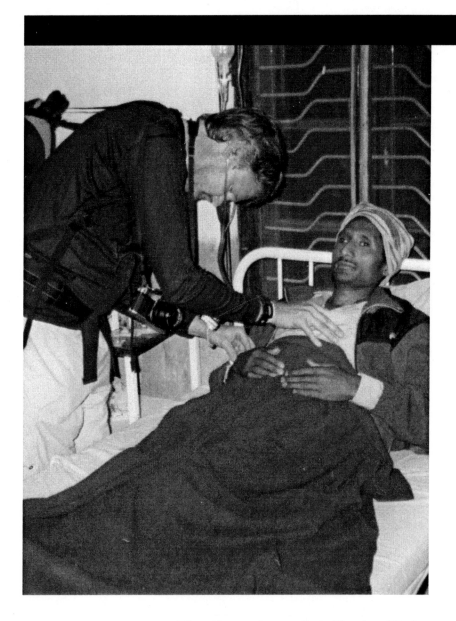

The author examines a patient with endocarditis at the Ilam hospital. (October 2002 medical trek in northeastern Nepal)

Like a post-term baby coming into the world days after its expected arrival, I entered the profession of medicine late. I was not one of your traditional medical students who had known since a young age that they would be doctors. I was accepted into medical school at the ripe age of thirty-two, after nine years of working as a children's theatre actor, a youth volunteer, and a high school and middle school teacher.

Because of these life experiences, I never felt that I was the conventional "programmed" medical student or resident. Doctors in training, as a result of the competitive nature of medical school acceptance, have had to be extremely disciplined and focused for many long years. But for many of them, the narrowly focused premedical curriculum and the pressure to start the long years of medical training as early as possible have robbed them of the opportunity to take courses outside of the sciences and the chance to have other life experiences. It is interesting to note that many medical schools do not require an applicant to have a college degree to be accepted; all that is required is the completion of the premedical curriculum, which can be accomplished in two to three years. In addition, there are a number of combined college-medical school academic programs that grant a bachelor's and medical degree after seven years of study, effectively eliminating one year of academic life. This academic and career mindset, although it may help these students master the basic science courses needed for admission to medical school, does preclude many from having broader and more diverse experiences outside of medicine.

I clearly remember my first day at Rush Medical College. The younger students in our class seemed edgy and restless, as if they wished to be somewhere other than medical school at that moment. A couple of these students even commented to me that they wished they had taken a year or two off in order to see

the world before entering medical school or had had employ-
ment that would have given them an experience other than
medicine. The older students appeared more relaxed—unfortunately, grayer—and like me, they seemed to be wondering
more if they would be able to get their atrophying brains
around the enormous amount of material we had to learn, and
further, if they would have the physical stamina to finish medical school and residency. At that moment, we were not looking
to travel the world or have jobs outside of medicine, for many
of us had already had these experiences and some had even
had several prior careers. We were here because we had chosen to be. My life experiences, expectations, and hopes would
profoundly influence the way I viewed every aspect of my medical education.

I did not enter medicine for the money. I was living adequately at the time on my teaching salary. I also did not go into
medicine to satisfy a large ego—the innumerable theater and
film audition rejections I had received during my four years as
an actor in Chicago had gone a long way towards humbling me.
I became a doctor for two reasons. The first—and incidentally
one that is found on almost all medical school applications—
was my desire to help heal people. Learning the skills that
could help cure or lessen a person's physical and mental ailments and thereby relieve his suffering and despair was—and
still is—important to me. These medical skills could also be
used universally, and the idea of having a career that filled a
global need intrigued me.

The second reason I became a doctor, one that, on account of
the conservative environment of medical education, is rarely
seen on medical school applications, was my desire to use the
profession of medicine to effect social change. Doctors are
given an enormous amount of respect in our society—when
physicians speak up for the human condition, it can have a
powerful influence on others. In this arena, during my course of
study, my idols became Dr. Albert Schweitzer and Dr. Quentin
Young on the international and national levels, respectively. On
the local level were my advisor and mentors, Dr. Maria Brown,
Dr. Fred Richardson, and Ed Eckenfels. Each was profoundly

concerned with the human condition and dedicated to social justice; each took considerable professional risks challenging society's and their own institutions' prejudices while championing progressive causes. These doctors, and many not mentioned, have courageously used the power of their profession not only to call attention to the inequities of the world, such as racism, sexism, and lack of affordable healthcare, but also to begin the important task of righting these wrongs. I was fortunate to find these altruistic professors and mentors while in medical school who helped me strengthen my resolve to try to effect social change.

I had become interested in medicine several years after college while working with inner-city youth in Chicago and eighth-grade students in East Palo Alto, California. Through them, I witnessed the paucity of available healthcare for disadvantaged students and their families. During these years, I spent a good amount of time outside the classroom "patching up" injured students' scrapes, bruises, and sprains with my emergency medical technician (EMT) skills. For many of them this would be the only medical attention they ever received. I noted other more serious injuries, such as displaced fractures and lacerations, and chronic conditions, such as asthma, obesity, and depression, all of which went unattended. It was sobering to come face-to-face almost daily with the lack of preventive medical care available to these youths, and the need for healthcare workers in disadvantaged areas became increasingly evident to me. At this point I set my sights on medical school.

From my work as a teacher, I was schooled in the belief system that education, like other social services, is guaranteed for all. From my work in both private and public education, I was keenly aware that vast inequities in educational opportunities exist in this country, but that even with these disparities, a minimum quality of education is guaranteed through high school for all.

I entered medicine believing, perhaps naively, that healthcare, if the providers were available, would be available to all. However, my intern and residency years awakened me to the vast discrepancies in our country's healthcare system and, more important, to the fact that healthcare, unlike education, is not available to all.

In fact, America is the only industrialized nation that does not cover all of its citizens with health insurance, and this lack of insurance has been detrimental to Americans' health. For example, our country's infant mortality rate, which has been shown to be a good marker of the health of a nation, is the highest of all industrialized nations; seven of every one thousand infants born in this country die before reaching their first birthday.[1] When we compare our infant mortality rate with that of other countries (Japan with four, and the United Kingdom, Germany, and Canada with five for every thousand infants born), we see the strong connection between health insurance and health outcomes. As Drs. Himmelstein, Woolhandler, and Hellander have noted in their book, Bleeding the Patient: The Consequences of Corporate Health Care, the U.S. has the lowest prenatal care rate of any developed nation; 18% of all pregnant women and 28% of pregnant black women fail to receive prenatal care during their first trimester (no other wealthy nation has a rate higher than 10%). The number one reason for this delay in seeking prenatal care cited by women who know they are pregnant is their lack of health insurance or money.[2]

And despite the fact that we spend two times as much per capita on healthcare in this country as compared with Germany, Canada, France, and Japan, our country's health has dramatically worsened. Dr. Himmelstein and his colleagues observe that between 1960 and 1997 our infant mortality rate ranking, compared with 29 other industrialized nations, dropped from 12th to 24th place. During this same time period, our women's life expectancy slid from 13th to 20th place, and our men's life expectancy fared equally poorly, falling from 17th to 22nd place among these same 29 nations.[3] The physical consequences of being uninsured are very real: the mortality rates for uninsured people have been shown to be 25 percent higher than those for insured people.[4] This equates to roughly 18,000 adults dying each year because they are uninsured and cannot obtain adequate healthcare.[5] Finally, as the authors of Bleeding the Patient note, the irony of our healthcare system is that there are no uninsured legislators. However, 12 percent of all healthcare workers (including doctors), 7 percent of teachers and university professors, and greater than 10 percent of the clergy are uninsured.[6]

I wrote this book primarily to educate. Growing up in a household that had a reverence for education and teaching, from my first formative years until I emerged from graduate school, I was continually immersed in the importance not only of obtaining a good education but, more notably, of striving to be a good educator in the profession I chose. Commencing with my grandmother, an elementary school teacher, through my father, a college professor, and down to my siblings, who are educators, I have been surrounded and nurtured by people in the field of education. These life experiences, some as mundane as daily dinner conversations as a child and adolescent, to the many opportunities to learn from my students when I was a teacher, have left an indelible imprint on me of the importance of conveying information to others.

This primary desire to educate led me, during the final part of medical school and the intern and second year of my family medicine residency, to write home and share with my family the experiences that are in this book. I would be less than forthright if I did not also admit that during these years I wrote for my own mental health. Medicine is a complex profession; its body of knowledge is vast and detailed, covering everything from the subatomic particle to the multifactorial causes of the diseases of the body and mind. As well, it exposes its caregivers to all the glories and tragedies of life, yet it seldom offers these same caregivers the simple time or space to process or debrief after these experiences. Writing home was a chance for me to start to make sense of all that I experienced as an intern and resident.

This book is not an attempt to tell my experiences as a typical doctor, as many others have done; this is not my place in life. Nor is this book my effort to record, in an anthropological manner, my story as a doctor who came to medicine later in life, for this, too, has been articulated by other doctors. Rather, this book, since it was originally a series of letters that I wrote home, is my endeavor to tell my story as a doctor from a very personal point of view. My professional and personal experiences, many of which happened before matriculating into medicine, while others happened while I was in training, have allowed me, for better or for worse, to look at the profession of medicine from an angle not ordinarily seen. This viewpoint, I hope, will be both informative and interesting for the reader.

Starting with Chapter One, which relates an event that happened during my fourth year of medical school and helped confirm my desire to be in primary care, and continuing with cases encountered during my intern year and second year of residency—these writings are mostly about my patients. It is my hope that their lives, and my experiences with them, can offer a window into the training of a doctor, the profession of medicine, and a glimpse at our nation's healthcare system.

Author's Note:

Residency programs, the long, hard years of specialty training after medical school, vary in length. Family medicine residency training takes three years. Regardless of where you train, the first year (internship) in family medicine is spent predominantly in the hospital on inpatient care. This year comprises one-month rotations (some repeated more than once) in the following major areas: family medicine, obstetrics and gynecology, pediatrics, surgery, intensive care, and emergency medicine. Some residency programs, such as mine, combine the obstetrics and gynecology and pediatrics rotations into a single maternal-child health rotation. Interns are also in the outpatient clinic one-half day a week.

After the initial intern year, the family medicine resident spends the next two years rotating for one month periods in many of the other specialties such as: ophthalmology, dermatology, endocrinology, pulmonology, cardiology, and pediatric emergency medicine. These years of residency training also require an increasing number of outpatient clinic days.

The goal in the training of family physicians is to produce doctors who are able to care for the whole family as well as treat the vast majority of human ailments. I completed my three-year family medicine training at West Suburban Hospital in Oak Park, Illinois. I chose this particular family medicine training program for its strong emphasis on maternal-child health (obstetrics and pediatrics) and the opportunity to work on the West Side of Chicago in an impoverished community with a predominantly minority population, many of whom had chronic medical conditions that had gone untreated for years. Some who read this book may think that I have "stacked the deck" by illustrating our healthcare system's woes with stories predominantly about patients who have been marginalized by society. However, there has been no "sleight of hand" here; the stories in this book are a broad representation of the patients that I was exposed to during my training. And our struggle (both my patients' and mine) to obtain care for them is similar to the struggle that most healthcare providers around this country go through daily to secure adequate care for their patients, regardless of the patients' socioeconomic level.

To facilitate the flow of each chapter, I have placed the detailed descriptions of many of the diseases and medical terms used throughout this book in the section entitled, "Glossary of Terms." In addition, with an acknowledgment to the importance of being gender-sensitive, but with an interest in brevity, I have used either the masculine or feminine pronoun.

ER entrance of Ventura County Medical Center, Ventura, California.

ONE

A Letter Home

December **22, 1998**

At about 4 P.M., while getting ready to leave Ventura County Medical Center for the day, a "Code Green" call came over the intercom notifying the ER staff that a trauma case was on its way to the emergency room. The on-call resident and I ran down to the ER to prepare for what in many "Code Green" cases is a person injured in a motor vehicle accident. These patients, because of the added safety factor of airbags, typically are more frightened than injured.

What we got word of, seconds before the first of two people was wheeled in, was that there had been a hostage scene in town for the last ten hours, and the whole incident had ended very badly. The first person to arrive was a white male in his late thirties. He had twelve gunshot wounds to his chest and arms. One paramedic was giving him chest compressions while the other administered oxygen. We quickly transferred him to the ER bed and placed EKG leads on his silent chest; his heart showed no electrical activity. The ER doctor, knowing he had been pulseless for over twenty minutes, pronounced him dead. It was disquieting to gaze at this lifeless man covered in gunshot wounds and tattoos, one of which read "Gone Forever."

The second person to arrive was a thin, white female in her mid-thirties with multiple knife wounds to her chest. She was alert and talking to us, which was a good sign. We transferred her to the ER bed, placed an oxygen mask on her, quickly examined her, inserted two IV lines, took a chest X-ray, and started to clean and suture her wounds. When the chest X-ray came back, it showed her left lung had collapsed from one of the knife wounds. We inserted a chest tube to help reinflate this injured lung and took another X-ray to confirm our tube placement. We then took an ultrasound of the woman's heart and were relieved to see that none of the knife wounds had entered her heart. The woman's blood pressure and pulse were normal, and everyone in the ER was confident that she was going to make it. The woman's three young daughters then came into the ER to spend a few comforting moments with her, and she assured them that she would be all right.

After the daughters left the room, we waited and watched the woman's blood pressure and pulse for any sign of internal bleeding. The two hospital surgeons came down and evaluated her for possible exploratory surgery to determine if the knife had severed any major organs or vessels. They were fairly certain, given that her blood pressure and pulse were normal and the ultrasound reading was reassuring, that she was out of the woods and would be sent up to the ICU for close observation.

Before going to the ICU to get her admitting paperwork ready, we were informed by one of the police officers as to what had happened. The man, who was dead on arrival, was the ex-boyfriend of the woman with the stab wounds. He had had a long history of drug abuse, scrapes with the law, and domestic violence against this woman. Just yesterday he had bailed himself out of prison, where he had been sent for repeatedly threatening and stalking her. And even though she had a restraining order on him, he had gone over to her house today at 6 A.M., cut the phone lines on the outside of her house, broken in, and then barricaded the two of them in the bedroom. For ten hours he held the county SWAT team at bay, and then something happened. All we know, since the police officer stopped giving us details at this point, is that the police stormed the house with tear gas and shot him to death, but not before he was able to attack her with the knife.

After finishing her ICU admittance orders, I stopped by the ER to see her again before heading home for the evening. When I came into the room she was still lying there comfortable and alert. I went to her bed and smiled at her. Although her long dark hair was matted and bloodied, and she had just been through a horrific event, her delicate facial features and large oval eyes conveyed to me that she felt safe. I felt good that she was doing well, and even thought to myself for a few seconds that justice had been served to her lousy ex-boyfriend. I wondered about how she was going to try to cope with this violent event, and how it would affect her and her three daughters. I was happy that she was going to live and that she would now be out of harm's way. I walked out of the ER to go home.

I wish this were the end of the story, but sadly it is not. Before I could get out the door, one of the surgeons shouted, "Her pressure is dropping!" I ran back to her and looked at the monitor, her blood pressure had dropped to 80/60 and her pulse was now 160 beats per minute. I spoke her name and shook her; there was no response. I looked at the surgeon, whose face was ashen; something was very wrong. He said that he was taking her to surgery right away.

The two surgeons, the resident, and I raced her gurney up to the operating room where the anesthesiologist and surgical assistant were waiting. We slid her onto the operating room table, and before we were barely able to strap her down and expose her chest, her blood pressure dropped to 50/20 and her heart rate rose to 200. The anesthesiologist shoved the ventilator tube into her throat and anesthetized her as the surgeon made a long and deep scalpel cut under her breast, opening her chest wall. The surgeon then placed a metal retractor between two ribs and ratcheted it open, exposing her lung. From my little amount of experience in surgery, I have learned that there is something that you never want to hear in the OR and that is, "There is a hole in the heart." But, that is exactly what the surgeon yelled when he lifted her lung and exposed her heart. The hole was on the front side of her heart continuous with one of the stab wounds that were initially not thought to be that deep. With the tough fibrous covering of the heart and rib cage now cut away, there was nothing to hold back the surge of blood from this wound, and with each heartbeat her blood pulsed out.

The next forty minutes involved a frantic effort to suture this hole. Suturing live tissue is hard enough, but when it is moving live tissue it is nearly impossible. The surgeon alternated between attempting to close this hole and compressing her failing heart with his fingers. But every time he closed the hole, the pressure in the heart built up and forced the hole open. Throughout this ordeal the anesthesiologist, who continued to watch her blood pressure and pulse, kept yelling, "I have no pulse! I have no blood pressure! I need more blood! I need more Epinephrine! I need more Atropine!" He yelled this over and over again as if this mantra would will her a normal blood pressure and pulse. Word circulated in the hospital that something "interesting" was going on in the OR, and more people were needed. Several other surgeons and nurses came in to help. People ran for blood; people ran for Epinephrine; people ran for fluids. The two surgeons were desperately trying to sew this one hole. The anesthesiologist continued to put syringe after syringe of potent stimulants into her heart to keep her pressure and heart rate up. The resident and I pumped blood into her as fast as we could. This whole symphony of movement took place with us hanging blood, passing drugs, holding retractors, sewing tissue, cutting sutures, compressing the heart, and collectively holding our breath. But every unit of fresh blood that we transfused flowed out the hole in her heart, down onto the table, and then onto the floor.

After a dozen cardio-conversion attempts and thirty minutes with no pulse or blood pressure, the surgeons called it and walked away. We had pumped ten liters of blood into her, and it all went onto the floor. I had never felt such utter futility in my life.

The resident and I stayed around to sew and clean her still and lifeless body so that her family could see her for the last time.

I had so many emotions at that point that I needed time before I was able to write about this experience. The surgeons, who had tried their best, walked out of the OR saying, "It was an interesting case." The resident and I, having never seen anything like this before—and hoping we never would again—did not say a word; we just stood there and sewed, washed, and wondered.

Now able to distance myself somewhat from this "interesting case," as the experienced surgeons had done, I wondered why this situation had to end so violently, so explosively. As I write, I think about the many places that intervention might have prevented her tragic end—interventions such as good parenting of the abusive boyfriend when he was a child; prisons that rehabilitate and not debilitate; laws that keep stalkers in prison; parole officers who have smaller case loads, enabling them to be more effective; police officers and SWAT teams that do not aggravate a tense situation. I also wonder about the effectiveness of restraining orders.

This woman had done everything she possibly could to protect herself legally from this man. She had taken out numerous restraining orders. She had the courage to testify before a judge, which ultimately placed him in jail, so she and her daughters were out of harm's way. She had even asked for and been given a special phone with a direct line to the police if he came after her again. And just yesterday, the day he was bailed out of jail, she had asked the police what she should do to protect her children and herself. The police told her to lock herself in her house, and that is what she did.

I wonder about two other things as well. The first is the woman's children. How can they begin to understand their mother's death? Just an hour before they were talking to her in the ER, and now she is gone from them forever. My one hope is that it does not perpetuate itself with them. Second, I wonder where I stand in all of this. What should my role be?

During the frantic race to keep her alive, I stood at the end of the OR bed and manually pumped blood into her. Like most people in medicine, I also stood at the end of the line of this sad story. Preventionists and interventionists would have stood anywhere but at the end of either the OR table or at the end of this woman's life. They, by the nature of their profession, would have been involved earlier and could possibly have been effective at averting the tragedy. It is something for me to think about. I know the power of preventive medicine from my work in medical school. I just need to figure out where I belong. I know that doctors are privileged to stand where they do in people's lives, but being at the end is not where I want to be.

TWO

The First Day of Residency

July 1, 1999

My first day of internship found me awake at 4 A.M. trying to decide what I was going to put into all of the pockets of the trademark long, white jackets residents wear in the hospital. Attendings, the top of the physician pyramid, pride themselves on having nothing in their pockets, thus displaying to *all* that they have *all* of the information in their heads. Interns, on the other hand, put our egos aside, cramming our pockets full with every book that we might have to reference during the day. We often look like overstuffed hippopotamuses waddling down the hospital's corridors attempting to keep pace with our less-encumbered attendings. Interns often live by the motto, "No factoid of information shall be more than an arm's length away." I decided on a heavy informational load for my pockets.

My stomach churned with apprehension as I drove the thirty minutes from my apartment to the hospital. Along the highway were many exits, and as I approached each one, I thought about taking it, turning back, and going home. It seemed like the proper thing to do. At this time of year, many new interns, including me, have fears that it is a complete fluke or mistake that we are doctors. We surmise that maybe in fact we are just fakers or actors and nobody has found us out yet. Our fears make us forget about the countless hours of studying during the four years of medical school just finished; we irrationally convince ourselves that we do not know enough to be doctors.

But I did not turn off at any of the exits and parked next to the hospital. As I entered, the security guard looked up and said, "Good morning, doctor!" I turned around to see who that doctor was, but all that was behind me was a long empty hallway. And all that was before me was a hospital full of sick and vulnerable people, the unknown, and my own fears.

■ ■ ■

Baby X was the first patient assigned to me on my first day on the Maternal Child Health ward; it was her twentieth day of life, all of which had been spent in the hospital. She arrived as a thirty-two-week premature infant, weighing just over two pounds, born at home—into a toilet. Her mom, perhaps not realizing that she was pregnant at the time or that the child she had just given birth to was still alive, tried to flush her down the toilet. The paramedics, called to the house by her eight-year-old son, found Baby X lying in the toilet. She was blue, had stopped breathing, and had a pulse of forty. They rushed her to our hospital, and here she has been for the last twenty days. I found Baby X in an incubator sleeping quietly. Her arms and legs were as thin as sapling twigs. Her skin was loose and looked as delicate as tissue paper. Her face was drawn and her eyes were shut. I stood there for quite some time peering at her through the transparent incubator, pondering her cruel start in this world. I wondered if I had it in me to take care of this fragile creature barely larger than my outstretched hand. Instinctively, I put my hand into my pocket to find a book to reference, but quietly realized that there was not a book in the world that I could hide behind now. I hesitated. And then I put my hand into the incubator. I touched her warm, transparent skin and felt her labored breathing. I moved my fingers down her tiny body and found her femoral pulse; then I laid my stethoscope onto her thin chest and listened to her heart, and thus began my internship.

■ ■ ■

July 11

It is the second week of internship, and Baby X is still with us. Our nurses mark this tenuous soul's days by recording every three hours her temperature, respiration and heart rate, amount of formula eaten, and number of diapers changed. Baby X's days end the same way they began, in an incubator, but hopefully one ounce heavier and a little bit stronger. I mark my days by the numerous patient encounters I have, the enormous amount of busy paperwork I have to do, and the many high-risk births I assist, holding my breath and hoping no disaster happens on my shift. I end my day hoping I have learned something and breathing a sigh of relief that I "did no harm."

Baby X and I are different in every respect: she, an underprivileged, two pound, premature, African-American female born into a toilet and left there to die; I, a middle-class, white male born into a world that has given me numerous privileges and allowed me to be where I am now. If not for her physical fragility and my medical training, our lives would never have crossed. We would have continued to live in two completely separate and different worlds. But it is because of her tenuous physical being and my assumed medical knowledge that we have met. And there is commonality between us.

This commonality might seem like a curious reflection. What would a premature, African-American female infant and her white, male physician have in common? How would two people from drastically different opportunities and spheres in life find mutuality? The answer lies in nurturing.

Baby X nurtures me. Even though she has not opened her eyes to look at me, does not turn her head when I speak to her through her incubator window, or does not respond to my warm touch when I listen to her heart, she nurtures me. She nurtures me due to our commonality.

This commonality is our shared fragility. Baby X's fragility is her struggle to gain an ounce of weight each day. My fragility is my intellectual struggle with trying to figure out the best way to keep her going as well as my physical struggle in managing a floor of high-risk pregnancies.

The first birth I assisted—on my first night of call—involved an African-American teenager, pregnant for the first time. As is common with the patients we see on our labor and delivery floor, she had had no prenatal care. When asked why she had not found a doctor to care for her and her unborn child, she said that she did not have any health insurance, an all too common occurrence in this country. Lack of prenatal care not only puts the mom and her baby at risk, it creates a trying experience for the labor and delivery team who have to manage the delivery with minimal prenatal information, the most important of which is the gestational age of the fetus. Knowing how old the fetus is helps us decide, in the event that the patient is having uterine contractions, if we should attempt to pharmacologically stop the contractions or proceed with the delivery. And if delivery is inevitable, having knowledge of the gestational age helps us predict if the fetus will be viable and able to be resuscitated. In addition, it is important to know the baby's position in the womb and if the pelvis is large enough to deliver the baby vaginally. All of this vital information about our patient was unknown.

This young mother came to us in active labor, giving us little time to determine her pelvic dimensions or the size and age of her fetus. Determining these dimensions in the first pregnancy of a patient with no prenatal care is something of a guessing game. Estimations of the fetus's size can be made by ultrasound or palpating the woman's abdomen, and determination of the mother's pelvic dimensions are made by pelvic exam. These "guesstimations" were hastily done at the bedside with our teenage mom screaming and thrashing about with each intensifying contraction.

One of the most important responsibilities of the doctor performing the delivery is to determine if the baby will actually fit through the birth canal; if the pelvis is too small or the baby too large, a relatively safe cesarean section can be performed, putting the baby and mom at far less risk. We also want to know as early as possible if a cesarean section is required, preferably before the baby descends deep into the pelvis, and definitely before the baby's head delivers. We estimated at this time that the baby would fit through the birth canal.

As quickening waves announce to the shoreline that a bow approaches, each of our patient's heightening contractions heralded her to bear down and inch her baby closer to dry land. Forty minutes into pushing, with the senior doctor continually coaching, the baby's head crowned. At this point the head is normally just a few pushes from emerging, and the rest of the baby's body, in most cases smaller in diameter, follows without difficulty. But this birth was not normal. As the next contraction crested, she bore down once more and delivered the head up to the neck. Now the body, I thought. Having mastered the technique, she patiently waited for the next wave to crest and bring her newborn to shore. But, when she pushed with this contraction the baby's head did not move. Nor did it move during any of the next several pushes. It quickly became obvious that the baby's anterior shoulder was wedged behind the mom's pelvic bone.

The medical term for this condition is "shoulder dystocia." When the baby's body is tightly wedged, inevitably the umbilical cord is compressed and in only one to two minutes the baby can start to asphyxiate. A relaxed and smooth labor can turn into a frantic rush to get the baby out when there is a shoulder dystocia, and that is what this delivery became. On the sixth push, still with no head movement, the fetal heart monitor pierced the rising commotion in the room warning that the baby's heart rate was dropping. A fetus's heart beats normally between 120 and 160 times a minute; this baby's heart rate had dropped to sixty.

There are several maneuvers one can try to dislodge a shoulder dystocia. One of these (McRobert's maneuver) is to flex the woman's hips, bringing her legs as close to her chest as possible, the hope is that this will change the angle of the pelvis and create enough pressure to free the baby's shoulder. Another maneuver is to put a lot of pressure, just above the pubic bone, on the woman's abdomen to try to dislodge the baby's shoulder from behind her pelvis. Other more drastic maneuvers are to try to rotate the baby in the vaginal canal, or break one or both of the baby's collar bones to help dislodge the shoulder.

The doctor who was running the birth and putting a lot of downward pressure on the baby's head (with the hopes of freeing the shoulder) asked for the McRobert's maneuver, which the nurses and I did without success. He then asked for suprapubic pressure, which I tried multiple times also without success. The shoulder was still stuck, and it had been several minutes. The fetal heart monitor wailed its warning signal and showed the baby's heart rate, now in the fifties. Several other doctors had come running into the room. To save the baby, the doctor increased the downward pressure on the baby's head, and the anterior shoulder finally dislodged. The rest of the baby quickly followed. We clamped and cut the umbilical cord, took the seemingly lifeless and blue baby girl to the warming table, and started to resuscitate her. After a couple of long, agonizing minutes the baby pinked up and started to cry.

The unforgettable part of this case was not apparent until two hours later when we realized that the baby was not moving her right arm. The arm lay still and lifeless, and it was cool to the touch. In the rush to get the baby out, the senior doctor had put enough pressure on the baby's head and neck to dislodge the anterior shoulder, but it was also enough pressure to damage the brachial plexus, the branch of nerves that exit the cervical spinal cord and innervate the arm. Sadly enough, this injury (Erb's palsy)—as severe as it appeared—usually does not heal, and this baby will likely not have use of her right arm for the rest of her life.

I looked at this baby for a while and watched her squirm and move for the first time outside of the close confines of the womb. With each twist of her body and movement of her extremities she seemed to delight in exploring her new spacious world. I watched her left arm's arrhythmic and erratic motions that are normal for a newborn. I looked at the right arm lying still and motionless and was caught off guard by a deep sense of sadness that overcame me. To avoid showing anyone in the room that I was anything less than the strong, composed doctor that I was trained to be, I excused myself from the room.

I found myself walking back to the nursery to see Baby X. Her regulated warm incubator, her daily one-ounce weight gain, and her strong and steady heartbeat were a comfort from the uncertainty, anxiety, and occasional sad outcome of the labor floor. Baby X nurtures me. From our shared fragility, she nurtures me.

THREE

Baby X Goes Home

July 18

In medicine, one learns the etiquette of the profession by following the example of senior residents and attendings. And these well-trained senior doctors undoubtedly had learned it by following the lead of their senior residents and attendings. Thus, the culture of medical etiquette training is handed down through training, with little change, from generation to generation of doctors. The teaching of these lessons, done predominantly during the last two years of medical school and throughout the residency years, takes place in many forums, but the patient's bedside during morning rounds is the most common. Some of these lessons are explicit, such as not allowing one's personal belief system to interfere with the treatment that the patient is entitled to and deserves. Other lessons are more implicit, such as learning to keep emotions in check while working with patients, lest your professional judgment become clouded. Personally, perhaps because of my training in theater, I have never been able to keep my emotions and feelings artificially in check. This conflict between what I feel and how I have been trained by the traditional medical establishment is something that I continue to examine. I have seen attendings coldly leave a patient's side when some comforting gesture would have been more appropriate. At times, I have followed their lead, but I regretted doing so.

Why it is hard for doctors to bridge that gap between their reserved professional demeanor and a warmer, more open manner is not entirely clear to me. Perhaps it is the long and arduous hours that, as many doctors joke, "grind the life out of us." Or perhaps it is all of the pathos that we see that either dulls our more humanistic side or forces us to protect a more vulnerable emotional self. Regardless, some doctors—and I am in this group—rely inordinately on social workers to take care of the patient's bereavement and counseling needs. Many of us justify ordering a social worker consult for our patients by telling ourselves that we are too busy to be concerned with the psychosocial aspect of our patients' care. Undoubtedly, we feel more comfortable with the cool, emotionally removed predictability of the medical knowledge that we have spent years learning, opting to steer clear of the potentially variable and emotion-laden interactions that arise when we take care of the whole patient.

However, the very philosophy of family medicine is to treat the whole person as well as the whole family. Our training, the breadth sometimes daunting, is steeped in biosocial and psychosocial philosophy. By nature we are generalists, trained to examine and care for anyone who walks into our examining room. Family physicians offer comprehensive care for the vast majority of human ailments, and we pride ourselves on the continuity of care that we provide. (A number of older family medicine doctors recall with satisfaction that they have birthed and buried some of their patients.) We do not limit our examination and care to one area of the body but are concerned with the whole body, which most definitely includes the patient's psyche.

So, when I find myself, like one of my more emotionally detached fellow doctors, exiting a distraught patient's room and ordering a social work consult, I struggle with my conscience, knowing that I have not made the right choice, for it goes against everything that we have been taught in our formative years and now as family physicians.

In medicine, one edict that we all live by is that through repetition one improves, even despite the fact that each case is unique and challenging. Whether it is mastering a history or putting a catheter into a patient's vein, through repetition one starts to master the task. And that holds true for learning the difficult task of interacting with patients and their families during their time of need.

With this as background, today was the day that Baby X's mother was to take her home, and it was also to be the first time I would meet her face to face. So, instead of ordering a social worker to take care of the discharge details, which would have effectively shielded me from a good portion of our interactions, I made most of the arrangements myself.

Baby X had arrived in our ER a little less than two months ago—blue, not breathing, and weighing just over two pounds. She would leave tonight healthy, forty days older, two pounds heavier, and up to date with her immunizations.

Her mother was scheduled to pick her up in the afternoon, as we had arranged over the telephone. I was both eager and nervous to meet Baby X's mom. I was eager because I wanted to learn more about the dynamics of this family and, I hoped, understand the circumstances around this delicate baby's sad beginning. As a zealous intern, I also wanted to try to impart to the mom some of my newly acquired knowledge of how to care for a premature infant. I was also nervous, because I was not sure how I would react to Baby X's mom. I wondered if I would be able to ignore the lingering doubts I had about her story as to what had happened at Baby X's birth, thus allowing my more rational and medically appropriate side to prevail. Or would the unease I felt about the whole event be apparent in my interaction with her? Would I come out and ask her what the circumstances were around her decision to try to flush her baby down the toilet, or would I show a certain amount of goodwill and forgiveness, giving her an accepting look, conveying that everything is OK now?

I was also feeling insecure—should not such a delicate encounter be handled by someone more experienced than I? (If, indeed, there was anyone experienced in talking with people with this unique situation.) With my mind alive with questions, I sat there with wet palms and bated breath waiting to meet her. But I never got the chance. She did not arrive at the hospital until midnight, long after I had given up waiting and gone home.

Several of the nurses the next morning voiced their opinions that the mother was again being neglectful with her tardy arrival. What I believe happened was that Baby X's mom did not want to "suffer the slings and arrows" of our medical staff's stares and comments. Who knows what was going through her head two months ago when she tried to erase any sign of her baby's life, and who truly knows what was going through her head now? To her credit, though, I do think that she very much wanted Baby X to come home; during the time I cared for her baby, she had called the nursery daily inquiring about Baby X's weight gain and progress. For some, this might not be proof enough that she should have custody of her child, but it was one of the reasons the Department of Children and Family Services (DCFS) found Baby X's mom was fit to care for her child. DCFS also believed Baby X's mom when she told them that she did not know she was pregnant at the time or that her baby was alive when she was born. In addition, DCFS said that there were no eyewitnesses to the mother trying to flush Baby X down the toilet, even though the mother's eight-year-old son had called and reported the event to the police and that the paramedics had found Baby X in the toilet. And so Baby X was released to her mother. That was the last we saw of Baby X as her mother did not come for any follow-up appointments at our clinic.

I cannot put into words the many thoughts and emotions that I experienced while working with Baby X. What I can say is that I imagine that the guilt and shame that Baby X's mom carries must be immense: immense enough to have kept her away from the hospital during Baby X's entire recovery period, immense enough to have her come to the hospital in the cloak of night to face no one but her baby. No one knows what the interactions between the mom and her baby were when she saw her for the second time—perhaps moments like these should be private, but I am curious about what she was thinking. Did she stand there and look at her baby for some time, as I had done that first day of internship? Did she pick up the tiny body and hold her with care, as the nurses had done for all those days? I suspect few words were said between the night nurse and the mom, and the mom left quickly after having Baby X officially signed out by the sleepy resident on call. I do not know very much about what happened after I left, but I do know that Baby X's mom left behind many fears and concerns for her baby's safety.

■ ■ ■

As I reflect on Baby X and her mother, I am struck by my conflicting feelings about not having met her. I felt oddly relieved but also frustrated. These feelings were similar to the ones that I had in college when one of our crew races was cancelled. In crew, as in medicine, training consumes many long hours. The event in crew is a 2000 meter race rowed at a pace that exhausts every fiber in the rower's body. Rowers, who regularly push themselves to their physical limit, have been known to vomit or even pass out at the end of a race. The pain experienced in a crew race is immense, and the body and mind remember. Rowing to the starting line in a race was always a time of unease for me, knowing that I was about to endure an enormous amount of physical discomfort. More than once I thought to myself, while floating on the starting line and waiting for the starter's countdown, *wouldn't it be better if we just cancelled the race and agreed to a tie*? And on one extremely windy day I got my wish—the official called the race off because of inclement weather. An initial feeling of relief overcame me, but it was soon replaced by one of frustration from not having had the chance to perform the event for which we had trained so hard. The "event" in medicine, for me at least at this moment, was meeting Baby X's mom. It was not as physically demanding as a crew race, but it was equally angst-ridden. I had not taken the easy route this time of having the social worker be the lead person to interact with the family, and I felt that I had prepared my emotions well. The missed opportunity to "perform" in this situation left me feeling disquieted. I do wonder how I would have performed in my meeting with Baby X's mom. But, as I would soon discover in the coming months, there would be ample opportunity to test these skills.

FOUR

Pam the RN

August 19

It needs to be stated, because regrettably it is rarely acknowledged, that nurses are the unsung heroes in medicine. Consistently underappreciated, they are the backbone of our healthcare system. They are underpaid and, unfortunately, too often disrespected by the other medical professionals, including doctors. There is no doubt that on rare occasions the life of a patient of mine has been put into jeopardy by a novice nurse's inattention or reporting erroneous vital signs, but in the vast majority of cases the skilled, well-trained, and compassionate nurses I have worked with have offered excellent professional care and have more than once saved my patients (and me).

One of those memorable nurses was Pam, whom I met on my first night of call in the ICU. Pam, a wiry and energetic RN in her late thirties, had worked in critical care since graduating from nursing school fifteen years earlier. With these many years of experience in the ICU, there was little that she had not seen or done. She was always willing to teach and very adept at bridging the awkward, and potentially precarious, authority gap that exists between novice residents, who have the power (and believe they have the knowledge), and experienced nurses. In the three years that I worked with Pam there were several times that I saw her gently and skillfully educate a resident about the best way to manage a difficult medical problem. Pam worked hard, often moonlighting at another hospital to fill out a six-day work week. But her mind was clear and sharp as a razor, even in the middle of the third shift, which she preferred so that she could spend her afternoons with her two children.

We first met during the evening that we cared for V.J., a sixty-six-year-old African-American man who was brought to the ICU after undergoing surgery to remove part of his cancerous pancreas. V.J.

arrived in our busy ICU late in the evening, wheeled up from the OR recovery room by the surgical assistant and the anesthesiologist, who was manually assisting his respirations. The surgeon had scrubbed out and gone home, leaving the anesthesiologist with the verbal order that V.J. should go to the ICU since he was "critical." The surgeon's written orders were minimal and barely legible. The anesthesiologist attached V.J.'s endotracheal tube to the respirator in his ICU room, looked at Pam and me, smiled and said, "And there you are," with a tone of a wine steward at a fine restaurant offering us a rare bottle from his special stock. Yes indeed, *and there we were*: a resident on his first night of ICU call, an overflowing, understaffed ICU, a patient that was "critical," and thankfully, a seasoned nurse.

Night call in the hospital starts at 5 P.M., at which time the on-call residents, including one of the interns on ICU service for the month and the senior who rotates in for the evening, are given a brief description by the departing residents of each patient's medical condition, medications, and any other information that would be necessary for care during the night ahead. Night call ends at 7:30 AM, when the on-call residents update the returning residents regarding the patients who were signed out to them fifteen hours earlier as well as any new patients who were admitted during the evening. Night shifts in the hospital are traditionally understaffed, both with nurses and with residents. During the day, the twelve to fifteen ICU beds that are the family medicine residents' responsibility are covered by at least two and often three interns, one senior resident, and one or two attending doctors. At night our ICU staff was reduced to two doctors: an intern and a senior resident who was responsible for the general medical floors and was often called to other floors.

Our teaching hospital never had an attending doctor in the ICU or on any of the general medical floors at night, leaving crucial medical decisions to the resident and intern. The ICU, frequently full, made ICU night call a hectic and trying time for the medical staff. One of the expressions an on-call intern quickly learns in the ICU is "Keep them alive to eight-o-five." That is, the intern's major task during the night was to keep the critically ill patients alive through to the morning light when returning residents and staff could help with the workload. To realize success at this endeavor, it is imperative for the patients' safety that the residents and nurses work together. And so it was on this night, when V.J. came to the ICU floor, that his good fortune was to be placed with the extraordinary Pam.

After the anesthesiologist left, Pam and I pulled down V.J.'s bed sheet, exposing his large abdominal girth, which looked like a blimp tethered to its mooring with so many tubes attached to him. I started by placing my stethoscope on his chest as Pam inventoried verbally and in writing the innumerable tubes and lines entering and exiting him.

> "Number eight endotracheal tube taped at twenty-two centimeters. NG tube to intermittent suction, fluid yellow with coffee ground appearance. Two 8-gauge IV lines, one in each cubitus, right with LR running at 125 cc/hour, left with dopamine at 18 mcg/kg/min. Rectal tube, 60 cc's brown fluid, no blood. Foley catheter, scant output, dark yellow, no blood. Four JP drains, drain number one and three with 10 cc's serosanguineous fluid, drain two: 5 cc's serosanguineous fluid, drain number four..."

As I listened to Pam, her voice calm and confident, and felt my heart pounding against my chest wall, I started to realize that I had little to no knowledge of how to take care of a post-operative patient in critical condition. I had not taken a four-week critical care rotation in medical school, and, with essentially no orders from the surgeon, I was left on my own. My unease started to mount. Pam finished her inventory noting the color of the drainage on the abdominal dressing covering his incision. She announced that his blood pressure was 90/50 and he had had less than 10 cc's of urine output in the last three hours, my cue to intervene.

"What do you want to do?" she asked looking up at me while I listened to his lungs.

I want to do everything and nothing, I thought to myself. Everything that will help get him through this night and nothing that will kill him before the other interns returned to help.

An experienced nurse can read a doctor's mind, or in this case his body language. My slumped shoulders, worried eyes, and silence had unmasked my inexperience.

"We need to get his pressure up," she said. This I knew, so I asked about his dopamine level.

"We don't have much room to move on that," she said. "Can I bolus him?" It was a statement subtlety disguised as a question.

"Yeah, 500 cc's normal saline," I said with a hint of gratitude in my voice.

My pager went off and the number was the extension at the other end of the unit. As I left V.J.'s room I asked Pam to let me know if the bolus helped. I then said, as confidently as I could, for her to let me know if she needed any other orders. Instead of picking up the phone right outside V.J.'s room, I walked the length of the ICU to the extension itself, my not-too-subtle way of escaping, shamelessly obvious to Pam I thought at the time.

At the other end of the ICU I met two nurses that were waiting by the phone for me to return their page. These nurses, one as experienced as Pam and one hired within a year, were working with five of my eight assigned patients, and each nurse had more than a few questions about each patient's care. The less experienced nurse had been assigned two uncomplicated patients, one a diabetic who had just had his right leg amputated because of a gangrenous infection. His blood sugars were high and she wanted an order for insulin. I had cared for many diabetics during medical school and also at my outpatient clinic. I quickly wrote the orders and was on to the next patient. She was a suicidal teenager who was under observation after an overdose of Tylenol. The nurse wanted to know which labs to draw and what type of IV fluid to administer. I wrote an order for the fluids and told her I would give her an answer about the labs once I had consulted the poison hotline.

The more experienced nurse had three patients. The first was a middle-aged woman with diabetes who had developed pneumonia. She had stopped taking her insulin two days earlier when her appetite waned, thinking that if she was not eating she should not be taking her insulin. She was half right. When a diabetic is consuming fewer calories, the insulin regimen should be adjusted, but only by half the dose, not by stopping altogether. Her daughter had found her at home in a stupor with rapid respiration and had shrewdly observed that her mother had a fruity odor about her. As the daughter was experienced at using her mother's blood glucose meter, she pricked her mother's finger and analyzed a drop of blood. When the home glucose meter blinked its warning sign that the glucose reading was above its upper limit of 500 mg/dl, she called 911. Her mother was brought to our hospital where she was quickly diagnosed with diabetic ketoacidosis, a metabolic complication that arises from lack of insulin.[1]

Clinically the patient is dehydrated, is sometimes in a stupor or coma, breathes deeply in an attempt to expel the body's excess acid through the lungs, and commonly, as her daughter noted, has a fruity odor, the source being one of the excess acids. The fruity smell on these patients' breath and their lethargic, confused state has resulted in some diabetics, when found collapsed on the street, being taken to the police station to "sober-up." Without proper medical attention, they can die.

This patient's lab work at admission showed that she had a blood glucose level of 820 mg/dl and was indeed in ketoacidosis. Although this medical condition sounds daunting, managing it is straightforward, and something that I had done several times in the past. She needed to be well hydrated and have her blood glucose brought down slowly with the help of insulin under our watchful eyes. I answered the nurse's several questions about the management of this patient without having to reference a medical book or call a hotline, a much needed, although admittedly insignificant, confidence builder.

Her second patient was a thirty-two-year-old white male asthmatic and heroin addict. He had developed respiratory distress after going on a heroin-smoking binge. It is a tribute to the compelling obsession users have for this drug that many of them, especially those who have a life threatening disease like asthma, will repeatedly risk their lives to get high. This patient was receiving continuous albuterol and atropine aerosolized treatments to help dilate his bronchial tubes. In addition, he was now several hours beyond his "high," and he was starting to withdraw. Patients who are addicted to heroin tell me that withdrawal is very painful.

The signs and symptoms are well described, "The eyes start to tear, followed by a runny nose and profuse sweating, and then goose bumps form on the skin (the term 'going cold turkey' comes from this). Next chills, shivering, nausea, vomiting, diarrhea, and severe abdominal, back and leg cramps and spasms develop (hence the term 'kicking the habit')."[2] The patient can also develop hypertension and tachycardia. All of these symptoms can last up to ten days, which is why most addicts find themselves seeking another high before the first of these symptoms commence.

Heroin addicts do not die from withdrawal, even though the symptoms make them think they might. They are usually treated by administering enough methadone to stop the withdrawal symptoms and stabilize their condition. If the patient is too incoherent to take the orally administered methadone, then intravenous or intramuscular injections of morphine are used.

Over the next several days the patients on morphine are then weaned and started on methadone. After release from the hospital the patient is sent to an outpatient methadone clinic where methadone is administered on a daily basis. These clinics have the difficult task of eventually weaning these patients from methadone, sometimes over years. In Chicago, as in many urban areas, the number of addicts seeking treatment is far greater than the resources available. The number of available methadone treatment clinics has diminished so much that only pregnant women who are withdrawing are guaranteed a place after leaving the hospital. Regrettably, this patient will find himself on the street and using heroin again within twelve hours of being discharged.

Heroin withdrawal combined with respiratory distress (due to an asthmatic condition) has killed many heroin addicts. Our patient would need to be monitored very closely throughout the evening and at some point would probably need to be intubated. In addition to his respiratory treatment, we gave him Clonidine, a central nervous system medicine that would help ease his increasing anxiety and elevated blood pressure.

The final patient was an eighty-eight year old Asian man who had suffered a massive cerebral hemorrhage earlier in the day.

The CT of his brain showed that the bleeding and subsequent increase in intracranial pressure had caused his brainstem to herniate. He was brain dead and being kept alive on life support. His children were coming from the West Coast to pay their final respects before, at his wife's choosing, we removed him from the ventilator. His care would be minimal, but answering the family's many questions would take time.

As I sat with these two nurses and discussed each patient's care, their management seemed fairly straightforward, whereas V.J.'s tenuous condition and the care he would need seemed complex and forbidding.

With the numerous very ill patients we had on the floor, in addition to five new admissions during the evening from the ER, our meager staff was kept busy throughout the night. My patients, having increased to a total of ten during the evening, were so demanding that I had little time to stop by V.J.'s room to check on his condition or progress. Pam, however, frequently ventured over to the rooms of my sickest patients, where she found me at their bedsides. On each visit, in a comprehensive, yet succinct summation that would impress an attending, she would give me an update on V.J.'s progress, reciting his vitals, physical exam, urine output, level of dopamine, boluses of fluid given, and labs drawn. She would then, with an acute awareness of the hierarchy in medicine, respectfully let me know what she thought should be done next, and then deferentially ask if I agreed. Since all of the decisions she had made appeared to be stabilizing V.J., and since I really did not know what needed to be done, I readily agreed with her.

I must admit that several concerns crossed my mind during the evening. The first was that I had misgivings about not having more knowledge of fluid management for the critically ill. It is not an easy subject, and one that I touched on only lightly in medical school. My dearth of experience in this area, as I now sat on the front lines of a busy ICU, was disconcerting. If the ICU had been quieter, I would have gone to the library and done a "quick read," but that luxury was not available. My second concern had to do with putting V.J.'s medical management in the hands of Pam, who was not a doctor. If any of the medical decisions about V.J.'s care had caused him harm, even though I was quite removed from his care, I would have been held accountable, for I was the doctor on the floor. Putting a patient's care in a nurse's hands—to the extent that I did—would have been frowned upon by many of my peers. Some of them would worry, just as I had, about the legal ramifications of such a decision, while others would object on the grounds that nurses do not have the training to make these types of medical decisions. There is no doubt that definite knowledge differences exist between doctors and nurses in certain areas of medicine, but in many areas a nurse's knowledge and experience is invaluable to the recovery of the patient. Sometimes the difference a nurse makes in a patient's care is subtle; other times it is more obvious, but rarely is it acknowledged by the physician.

As morning light reached the ICU and the returning interns and residents arrived at the hospital, Pam took me aside and went through all of V.J.'s medical orders that *we* had executed during the evening and that she wanted me to sign. She had a dozen order forms with over thirty orders written across them in neat and accurate handwriting that seems to go with the territory of nursing. Before me she next placed her nursing notes. Starting at V.J.'s arrival and continuing throughout the night, every fifteen minutes she had recorded all she had done. During the next half hour, with a clarity and articulation that one does not usually witness in a person at the end of a long, hard shift, she diligently reviewed what *we* had ordered, why *we* had ordered it, and what the results were. As we slowly flipped though her meticulous and copious notes she detailed why she had given boluses of IV fluids at certain times, while other times she had chosen to adjust V.J.'s dopamine level, impressively highlighting the connections between her interventions and his vital signs. She finished by saying that *we* did a nice job and that V.J., who had now been weaned off of dopamine, had a stable blood pressure and normal heart rate, and was now making urine.

I signed each one of Pam's orders and thanked her for the good work that *she* had done. It does need to be said that what benefited V.J. (and saved me) was my luck to be on call with such an accomplished nurse. She had managed a very difficult patient's care, and she had taught me the basics of fluid management of the critically ill. This knowledge would be not only invaluable to me throughout the rest of my residency, but also essential on the trek in Nepal.

I cannot help but think that in some ways Pam was the Cyrano de Bergerac for this patient's care. I was the front man, the supposed all-knowing doctor, who gives the orders that are followed by the nurse, when in reality, I was just the front man for Pam's experience, knowledge, and skill. Even though the nurse's notes and orders do not portray this, Pam and I know the truth.

I now have a heightened appreciation for the integral and indispensable part that nurses play on the medical team. And as aptly demonstrated by Pam, they are on the front line when patients are in need of vital medical care. Nurses are the ones that feed, change, talk with, and comfort patients. They are also the ones that are there for the patients and their families when the patients are dying.

■ ■ ■

How doctors relate to and interact with nurses, other members of the medical team, and even patients is learned during the years of medical school and residency, usually by following the example of the senior residents and attendings. Unfortunately, these examples are too often good illustrations of bad technique. Medicine has a strict pecking order that does not allow anyone to question superiors even if they have been disrespectful to a patient or a fellow healthcare worker. This system often leaves the more sensitive and caring medical students and residents feeling that they are in the minority and powerless.

An example of this was Sarah, who was on my surgery rotation during our third year of medical school. Sarah was from a poor family, had worked her way though college, and was fortunate enough to receive a well-deserved scholarship to medical school. She had experienced the paucity of pediatricians in her impoverished neighborhood and had decided early in life that she wanted to be a pediatrician and work with the underserved. She was very talkative and highly opinionated, often driving away our fellow medical students during lunch with her endless but astute observations about the numerous injustices in the world. She was a staunch liberal and often confronted our more conservative classmates, residents, and attendings, about the many inequities in medicine, goading them into arguments that they found difficult to win.

Sarah ran into the "wall of hierarchy" one morning during our daily surgery rounds. She had noticed for several days during these rounds how uncomfortable the patients, especially women who had had mastectomies, felt when all eight of us (four medical students, three residents, and the attending) barged into their rooms without a word of greeting, pulled back their bed sheets exposing the women's chests, and then inspected the incisions, never acknowledging that the patients were anything more than manikins. Sarah, to her credit, would sit and talk with the patients after each one of these encounters while the rest of the surgical team continued on rounds. Our chief surgical resident, noticing her continual lag behind the team, ribbed her about her behavior, suggesting that she go into psychiatry.

Sarah, her outspokenness not to be suppressed, boldly suggested to the team that only one or two of the team go into each room, affording the patient some privacy. She even suggested that the residents and surgeon be more mindful of how they exposed the patient, offering the utmost dignity possible. Both of these suggestions were soundly denounced by the chief resident, and quickly seconded by the all-too-eager-to-please other surgical residents. The chief announced that anyone who was not interested in learning could remain outside the patient's room with Sarah. Unfortunately, none of the other medical students— or I for that matter—spoke up for Sarah. We shamelessly stood by in silence and let Sarah be humiliated.

Regrettably, I behaved like the vast majority of medical students and residents: remaining silent and not questioning authority. This behavior is due, in part, to the consequences that many doctors in training feel will result if they do question authority. Every medical student and resident knows that a poor evaluation on a rotation could keep him from being accepted into a competitive residency or fellowship program. Consequently, there is enormous pressure—not only within oneself but also within the medical training environment—not to speak up. Sarah's verbal chastising and public embarrassment was her punishment. It takes a strong-willed person to be able to step away from the servile mentality that many medical trainees adhere to and be able to question authority. Whether it would have made a difference if I had spoken up in Sarah's behalf is not clear. Perhaps I, too, would have become a resident's joke, but, in the end I would have given my view on an important issue.

Sarah made the best of a difficult situation. For the remainder of her rotation she continued to come into the patients' rooms with us, and she continued to sit with the patients after the team had left, and, unfortunately, she continued to hear the same disparaging comments from the surgical residents. I imagine that she did not receive a good evaluation on her surgical rotation. But she was accepted into a prestigious pediatric residency on the West Coast, and I am sure that she continues to practice compassionate medicine. I hope that she also continues to be outspoken.

Having been a teacher before entering medicine, I have a perspective on the education process that some of my fellow medical students and residents may not have. Creating an environment that is conducive for learning is of paramount importance in education. Whatever the educational setting, if the environment is one where the student feels safe, if there is respect between the teacher and student, and if there is a mutual sharing of ideas, then the student will undoubtedly thrive. It is also indispensable in education for the teacher to be a good role model, for a student's learning is dependent on following the lead of the teacher. Unfortunately, medical education too often does not create such an environment. Perhaps the long hours and the pressure of making life and death decisions leave a diminished reserve for civility. Or perhaps the inordinate amount of respect and praise doctors garner from society plays to our egos to the point that we become blinded to relationships among members of the medical delivery team. Medical education needs to strive continually to create an environment that is advantageous, not only for learning, but also for being respectful of each other, whether it be a nurse or a rare medical student who has the courage to speak up against insensitivity.

FIVE

Daphne Williams

September 2

Some doctors have a superstition about walking through emergency rooms. They fear that their presence, even momentarily, will somehow offend the gods and instantly bring a deluge of bad luck on them, mainly in the form of extra admissions and more work. A few doctors are so superstitious that on their morning rounds, with residents and medical students in tow, they have devised intricate and circuitous ways to navigate the hospital without setting foot in the ER. During medical school one of my attendings took our medical team up three flights of stairs, across a ward, and back down another three flights of stairs to avoid walking even a few meters though an ER.

I try not to believe in such superstition and would regularly walk through our ER on my way to and from my outpatient clinic. As I walked through our ER this day, a doctor spotted me and called me over. He knew that I was one of the new family practice residents with a wide open outpatient schedule who could accommodate a follow-up appointment for the patient who he was examining.

Daphne was a sixteen-year-old African-American female without insurance who had come to the ER with the complaint of abdominal and back pain and nausea. Her history revealed that her last menstrual cycle was in late April, and her physical exam was normal except for a uterus that was the size of a large grapefruit. A urine pregnancy test diagnosed what this doctor already suspected, and the ultrasound showed the fetus to be approximately eighteen weeks old.

The ER doctor's plan, at Daphne's request, was to have her visit Planned Parenthood and discuss the option of having an elective termination. She was then to follow up with me for her outpatient care. I looked into the examining room and was struck by how young she looked: her petite features, her constant nervous fidgeting, as well as a small teddy bear she held for comfort, made her appear to be much younger than her sixteen years.

When I greeted her, she did not make eye contact, but sat in silence and held her bear. I asked her several questions about the pregnancy, all of which she answered quietly without lifting her gaze from the floor. Although her affect was of some concern, I was reasonably satisfied that she was handling the news of her pregnancy calmly and with resignation. I took the time to write out directions to Planned Parenthood, and when she asked in a helpless way, "I have to take the CTA?" I gave her a few dollars for the trip. I told her I looked forward to seeing her in a week. To this she raised her shy gaze slightly and thanked me for the train fare. She then gathered her belongings and left.

One half of all pregnancies among American women are unintended.[1] One half of these (approximately 1.5 million) will end in abortion each year, with 90 percent being performed in the first trimester (before 13 weeks) of pregnancy and less than 1 percent of the total being performed beyond 21 weeks of gestation.[2] As Dr. Stanley Henshaw observes in A *Clinician's Guide to Medical and Surgical Abortion*, it is revealing that in most developed countries a higher percentage of abortions are performed at an earlier gestational age because these countries provide universal health insurance that covers abortion services. By contrast, in the U.S., gaining access to abortion services and acquiring the money to pay for the procedure makes obtaining an elective termination more difficult, thereby delaying the procedure.[3] Although a surgical abortion is relatively safe (0.6 deaths per 100,000 performed),[4] the earlier the procedure is performed the safer it is. It is important to note that a surgical abortion is more than 10 times safer than carrying a pregnancy to term and delivering.[5] The U.S. maternal mortality rate in 1999 was 9.9 deaths per 100,000 live births.[6] Knowing that few doctors perform abortions beyond the gestational age of 22 weeks, and also knowing Daphne's pregnancy was now at 18 weeks, it was important that she visit Planned Parenthood as soon as possible.

My first clinic visit with Daphne came two weeks later when she was, to my surprise, still pregnant. Over the next hour she told me her life story. She was born to a teenage, single mom on the West Side of Chicago and abandoned at the age of six— left on a street corner by her mom whom she never saw again. She spent the next ten years in a half-dozen foster care homes and attended as many schools, dropping out by the ninth grade.

She had had one previous pregnancy at the age of thirteen which she ended with an abortion. She did not want to talk about that pregnancy which made me suspect that it was rape. She also did not want to talk about the father of her present pregnancy, other than to say that, "the relationship is not good." She denied any drug or alcohol use but stated that she smoked a couple of cigarettes each day. Her past medical history did not reveal any diseases, and she said that her mood was "OK." She lived with a female friend at her friend's mother's home, and this is where part of the complexity of her life became apparent. She indeed had gone to Planned Parenthood, but when she returned home after the initial informational visit, her friend's mom told her that if she went through with the abortion she would "kick her out onto the streets." I imagine that for someone carrying the scars of being abandoned at the age of six, the thought of losing one's emotional support and housing was too much. She never went back to Planned Parenthood. She told me this story with a steely face that belied her inner turmoil. She said rather fatalistically that she was carrying the baby to term.

I did her initial exam and ordered her labs. I encouraged her to stop smoking, referred her to our social worker for support, and told her I would do everything I could to find her housing.

The next several days became a concerted effort to find her a different place to live. With the help of the social worker, over two dozen possible living arrangements were explored, but all were either not available or were inappropriate.

At the next visit I told Daphne that we were as yet unable to find housing, but we still had one more week before she was too far along with the pregnancy to terminate. She told me that she appreciated the effort, but that she had decided to keep the baby. When I asked her if she would go though with the abortion if we could find her a place to live, she shook her head and replied, "The pressure is too much." To this I gently reminded her that the decision was hers to make, and that I would be willing to do whatever I could to help her find a place to stay, even if it meant admitting her to the hospital in the interim. Daphne contemplated this offer for a few moments and then said, "No." Although I was disappointed, there was nothing I could do to change the course of her care. At this point, I chose to focus my efforts entirely on her pregnancy. I reviewed with her the labs and cultures from the prior week and encouraged her again to stop smoking and to continue taking her prenatal vitamin. I told her I would see her in one week.

Daphne's decision to take her pregnancy to term worried me. Research done at the Alan Guttmacher Institute and the National Abortion Federation has shown that, "If a teen gives birth and keeps the baby, she will be much more likely than other young women to drop out of school, receive inadequate prenatal care, rely on public assistance to raise her child, develop health problems, and have her marriage end in divorce."[7] In addition, these teenagers' children, Daphne having been one herself, are more likely to become pregnant and have children themselves when they are teenagers, as Daphne had done.[8] It has also been shown that the psychological distress for a woman who decides to get an elective termination appears to be greatest before the abortion, not after, contrary to the erroneous information that pro-life groups disseminate.[9] In fact, "relief" was the most common emotional response felt following the procedure.[10] In addition, I have seen from my own experience with other cases that these women regain a sense of hope. For all of these reasons, I offered Daphne, as I do all my patients, comprehensive family planning services. And for women who desire an elective termination, I do all I can to help them obtain these services.

Over the next four months I saw Daphne every other week for her prenatal care appointments. Normally, a doctor sees pregnant patients once a month, but due to Daphne's unique circumstance, I wanted to keep in close contact. During our many appointments, Daphne slowly began to relate to me, and she went through a surprising transformation. In the beginning, Daphne would lie quietly on the exam table, her mind elsewhere, as I laid the measuring tape along the circumference of her growing abdomen. And when I would listen to the baby's heart with the fetal heart rate amplifier, she would turn her head away and stare at the wall. To ease her dissonance, I would turn the volume down. Several weeks into her care with me, however, her mood and demeanor started to change. First, she stopped bringing her teddy bear to clinic. At the next visit she announced proudly that she had stopped smoking. This development was followed by her starting to make eye contact with me. Soon after she began to take an interest in listening to her baby's heart beat. But, by far, the most significant change came when she stopped referring to her fetus as "the baby," and started calling it "my baby."

I do not have an exact answer as to what helped Daphne transform from an introspective child in a cocoon into a young soon-to-be mom. Observing her transformation, I was reminded of a time when as a small child I tried to befriend a timid, stray puppy. With time and a constant presence, trust develops and overcomes the barrier of fear. What brought Daphne and me together, but more important Daphne to her pregnancy, was not anything specific that I did, but rather, as I have learned from working with teenagers, it was the security of just being there that made the difference.

In early December, Daphne, two months before her due date, went into preterm labor on account of two sexually transmitted diseases that she had contracted from the father of her baby. Thankfully, the maternal child health team at the hospital was able to stop her contractions and treat her infections, and she was released three days later, healthy, and still carrying her baby. Since her initial cultures three months earlier were negative for any sexually transmitted diseases, these diseases were a clear indication that the father of her baby was involved with someone else and continuing to have intercourse with Daphne. Daphne took the news with real heartache, but after some discussion she said that she was ready to move forward in life without the father of her baby. She appeared to be relieved and happy still to be pregnant.

In late December I saw Daphne at our clinic for her regular prenatal visit, and all seemed well. This visit became the last time I saw her before she delivered because, uncharacteristically, she missed her next two appointments.

In the early morning of January 26 I received a page from the on-call intern working on the maternal child health service. He told me that Daphne (now 39 weeks pregnant) was in active labor and her cervix was dilated four centimeters. He told me that everything appeared normal and that he would page me again when she had progressed to seven centimeters, allowing me the time to drive to the hospital before she was complete and ready to push.

Delivering the baby of your own patient is always a thrill both for you and for the patient; it is a memorable moment in a patient-doctor relationship. I had especially looked forward to delivering Daphne's baby. She and I had developed a good relationship over the preceding five months, and being at her delivery was very important to me. I knew it was important for her as well, for she had asked me on each of her clinic visits if I would deliver her child.

The next page from the on-call intern, however, was from her delivery room, where she had just given birth. The good news was that she delivered a healthy seven-pound, two-ounce baby boy. She had progressed to complete in a third of the time we expected, and her precipitous delivery gave the intern no time to page me. Although I was frustrated I did not make it to the delivery, I was delighted she had had a healthy baby. I asked the intern to put the phone up to Daphne's ear and I told her how happy I was for her and that I was coming into the hospital to see her—to this she said nothing.

When I arrived at the hospital her disappointment was apparent. I surmised that she was angry with me. I apologized for not making the delivery and told her again how happy I was that she had a healthy baby. Though at that moment she was not ready to forgive me, I could understand her feelings and was not concerned; her disappointment with me, I told myself, would pass with time and subsequent interactions. What I was concerned about, however, was her lack of interest in her new baby boy. The beautiful infant lay sleeping quietly in the warmer next to her bed, yet during the next hour as I examined him and spoke with her, she did not look at him once. I tried at one point to direct her attention to him by asking if she had chosen a name. Without looking up she shook her head. As I left I told her to page me if she wanted to talk. On my way out of the hospital, I wrote an order for our social worker to see her.

Although in retrospect it is apparent that Daphne's demeanor could wholly be attributed to the pressure she felt from being a new mom, I still regret not making her delivery. But, as I told Daphne, there are times when plans and best intentions go awry. These words, as innocent as they appeared at the time, foreshadowed the coming events.

By the time of her first clinic visit, one week after the delivery, Daphne had had two evaluations for postpartum depression, one with our outpatient clinic nurse and one with a visiting nurse; neither turned up any signs of postpartum depression. Under the parent-infant interaction section of their paperwork, however, the only box that was checked was "talks and sings to infant." Left blank were the boxes, "holds infant," "touches infant," "kisses and cuddles infant."

Postpartum depression is seen in approximately 10 to 15 percent of women and can last up to several months. Interestingly, depression is also seen in some women who adopt children. The causes are generally unknown but are thought to include changes in the woman's estrogen and progesterone level following delivery, socioeconomic stress, and a genetic predisposition for depression. The signs are similar to those of other types of depression: sadness, tearfulness, fatigue, lack of enjoyment in activities that used to be enjoyable, sleep disturbance, labile mood, and weight loss or gain to name a few. The risk factors that Daphne had for postpartum depression were many: history of depression during the pregnancy, family history of depression, early childhood loss, an unwanted pregnancy, socioeconomic stress, and an unsupportive social system. The treatment is to have the mom get proper sleep and rest; in addition psychotherapy can be helpful. If needed, an antidepressant can also be prescribed. I addressed the first two treatments with Daphne, although she refused the therapy. I neglected to prescribe her an antidepressant. There are rare cases when postpartum depression can sink into postpartum psychosis, a condition in which the mom can have thoughts of hurting her child—and act upon them.

During this first clinic visit Daphne expressed her frustration with her infant. She desired more time off than the one to two hours per week she was presently getting when he was watched by her landlady. She also said that she was seeing the father of the child but the relationship was not going well. In addition, she had started smoking again. I offered some suggestions of ways she could have additional time off from the baby. I also made her promise to page me directly if she ever became so frustrated that she thought that she could harm her infant. I noted in my chart that she stated that she had no intention of harming her baby.

Daphne brought her baby into our clinic two more times in the next six weeks. The first visit was for a regular check up, and the second visit was for a simple cold. During both visits Daphne and her baby were seen by other doctors since I was not in the clinic at the time. Both progress notes documented that her infant was gaining weight and developing appropriately. Neither of the notes mentioned that Daphne showed any frustration with her son, or that the doctor had any concerns with the way mother and infant were bonding.

In late February I received the page I hoped I would never get. The same ER doctor who had introduced me to Daphne six months earlier, when she was first diagnosed with her pregnancy, informed me that Daphne had just brought her infant into the ER, and he was not breathing and had no pulse. The ER team was performing CPR and his initial arterial blood pH of 6.45 did not look hopeful. Life usually cannot be sustained with a pH much below 7.0.

When I got to the hospital, Daphne and her son, whose heart the ER team was able to get started again, had already been taken by ambulance to the local children's hospital. The ER doctor's report read,

> The patient is a 1-month-old male with the chief com-
> plaint, according to the mother, of having been put in the
> car seat, some blankets put over his head and face while
> he was being transported to the car for travel. Then the
> mother put the child in the car, removed the blankets,
> noted the child looked as if something was wrong. He had
> some blood in his mouth, he was unresponsive, and he
> was then rushed immediately by car here to the emer-
> gency room. On arrival, he was pulseless, without any
> spontaneous breathing.

I never saw Daphne's infant again. Remarkably he survived, but
he suffered anoxic encephalopathy and is now severely develop-
mentally delayed and has a seizure disorder. He is being followed by several pediatric specialists. Children's brains are
remarkable at healing, but only time and intense physical therapy will determine how well he will develop.

Daphne's infant's near death was investigated by the social
worker at the children's hospital where he was transferred, and it
was determined that he had not suffered trauma or abuse prior to
his cardiopulmonary arrest. Her child, in their determination, was
a near Sudden Infant Death Syndrome (SIDS) case. SIDS, as the
name declares, is the sudden, unexplained death of a child
before one year of age. To date, there is no clear cause of SIDS.
There are, however, several risk factors associated with this devastating syndrome. Risk factors that increase the chance of SIDS
are poor health of the fetus during the pregnancy, as well as the
sleeping position on the stomach as an infant.[11] From my knowledge of Daphne's prenatal care and the ER report, her infant had
neither of these risk factors. The maternal risk factors that
increase the odds of SIDS include smoking during pregnancy,
maternal age less than twenty years, poor prenatal care, anemia,
use of illegal drugs, and a history of sexually transmitted diseases
or urinary tract infections. Daphne had at least three of these
maternal risk factors. In retrospect, I should have been more vigi-
lant in my assessment of them. But after the delivery, Daphne's
and my patient-doctor interactions had eroded to the point that I
am not sure if any amount of counseling on this subject would

have made a difference. The thought still plagues me whether I could have done more.

The next time I saw Daphne was at the end of my intern year. She came to the clinic for her postpartum check-up and had regressed back into the withdrawn teenage girl whom I had met ten months earlier. The eye contact was absent, and she only answered my questions with a minimum of effort. I inquired as to how her baby was doing, and she declined to answer. I told her that I was worried about her, and that I wanted her to see our social worker. She told me that she would, but never did. In fact, she never came back to our clinic again.

When I try to piece together the parts of this tragedy and make sense of it, I feel that I am obliged to reflect on the patient-doctor relationship that Daphne and I experienced. There are two psychoanalytic concepts that all doctors are taught in medical school. The first, transference, is the projection of the patient's feelings, thoughts, and wishes onto the doctor, who represents some person from the patient's past.[12] Transference can be harmful to the patient-doctor relationship if the doctor represents someone in the patient's life who conjures negative memories. This may inhibit the patient from allowing the patient-doctor relationship to be as open and honest as it should be. Transference can also be beneficial, however, especially if the patient feels that the doctor represents someone from her life whom she respects. This, for example, can help motivate the patient to be compliant with the doctor's advice. During the initial period that I cared for Daphne, she gradually developed an increasing amount of trust in our relationship. Perhaps, during this period, I became a figure in her life that she needed, such as the father she always wanted but never met. This trust continued until she gave birth. At this point, I surmise, my failure to make her delivery may have triggered in her feelings of betrayal and a subsequent loss of trust in our relationship. This would help explain her initial pulling away from my care after the delivery, and then her final decision to stop receiving care from me altogether.

Psychoanalysis, like any form of analysis, is instructive to a point, but using it as a tool to understand relationships, to the exclusion of other explanations, can lead one to a less than complete conclusion. Perhaps Daphne was also suffering from post-partum depression; this would clearly have colored the way she interacted with me and the world. The social workers and I suspected depression and even addressed it to the extent that Daphne allowed us. Finally, the strains of motherhood on a teenager are immense. Daphne's withdrawal from the world was most likely her way of coping with this stress. Regardless of what the true explanation is, anytime there is a bad outcome there are always many questions that the caregivers will ask themselves. And when there are few definitive answers, such as with Daphne, there inevitably will be lingering disquiet.

As professional and objective as I have been trained to be, I did have feelings of remorse when Daphne stopped getting her care from me, especially after her infant's near SIDS episode. I particularly regreted that she did not trust me enough to help her get through some of her most difficult times. These feelings, however, need to be recognized by all doctors, and this is where the second psychoanalytic concept, countertransference, arises. In countertransference the doctor transfers (many times subconsciously) his emotional needs and feelings onto the patient, who undoubtedly represents some person from the doctor's past.[13] Daphne, a patient who I went out of my way to help—some would say save—may have represented a person in my life who I had felt a strong need to care for. The feelings I had around Daphne leaving my care were similar to the frustration and hurt that I had during medical school when I was unable to offer the one closest to me in my personal life the care she needed.

Her name was Katarina. I met her three years prior to entering medical school when I was a graduate student in education. She was from the Czech Republic and had taken a one-year leave from her job as a college instructor to come to my graduate school to take classes. We met in one of the university's computer labs as a result of my dog—a moderately neurotic, high-strung Standard Poodle in constant need of attention—sitting down next to her and placing her snout on Katarina's lap, my dog's none-to-subtle way of asking to be petted. Most people found my dog's forthrightness to be charming and rewarded her with a kind word and a stroke of her head, thus encouraging her to continue this behavior. Katarina, like most people, complied with my dog's wishes and over this awkward moment we started our first conversation.

Katarina was half Russian, half Czech, stunningly attractive, and mysteriously intriguing. She had grown up in Prague, which, like the rest of her country, had been under the control of the Soviet Union until a few years before we met. Prague's citizens enjoyed a fairly uncensored literary and artistic culture because of the city's close proximity to Western Europe. The people of Prague, due to comparatively lenient government control (by Kremlin standards), were very knowledgeable about—and influenced by—western politics and democratic ideals. The "Velvet Revolution" in 1989, when a dissolving Soviet Union peacefully withdrew its troops from Prague and the Czech Republic after six weeks of massive citizen demonstrations, was a natural transition of power from the Soviet Union to the Czech leaders and citizens. But growing up and working under the Soviet rule, where one was unsure of who was a friend or a possible government informant, forced Katarina to maintain an air of secrecy about her work. Subsequently, and ultimately unfortunately for us, she maintained this secretiveness about her life as well. To this day I am not sure of all of the facts of what transpired during the later months of our relationship.

Our year together at graduate school was one of excitement and joy. She, having lived under a repressive regime and in a land-locked country, displayed the wonderment of a wide-eyed child during each of our explorations to many of the natural wonders of California. I remember taking her to the beach for the first time and experiencing how exquisitely happy she was; she tore off her shoes and socks and ran back and forth between the surf and me, squealing with delight the whole time. Everywhere we went and everything we did that year she enjoyed, and her positive energy was infectious. Katarina's excitement for me and for our relationship was gratifying, but it also made me feel insecure. Until this point in my life, I had felt a certain amount of awkwardness and discomfort in social situations. And my relationships with my previous girlfriends had been a struggle. In a few of these relationships I knew at the time that my partner was not right for me, but mostly it was the other way around. With Katarina this was not the case; I felt perfectly compatible with her. Her attractiveness, wit, and charm, as well as her unique upbringing were all very enticing. At the time I believed, and thought that she did too, that we were a perfect match and would always be together.

As our year at graduate school came to an end, Katarina, eager to see the United States, proposed that we spend the summer driving across the country. However, during my graduate year of education, I had turned my sights toward medical school and, feeling the added pressure of my advancing age, proposed that we postpone this trip until after I had been accepted into medical school. Katarina gracefully acquiesced, and we spent the summer in California while I took several prerequisite classes for medical school. This is the first example in a series of many decisions when I let my professional aspirations come before my personal life. At the time I did not feel guilty about this decision on account of the strong edict instilled in me that "work comes before play." In addition, I told myself that there would always be a chance to take this trip in the future. I did not realize at the time that I had started down a path of behavior that would become increasingly frustrating and ultimately prove to be detrimental to Katarina's and my happiness and our relationship.

In the fall, Katarina, eager to work again, returned to Prague. Over the next two years I stayed on in California and continued to teach middle school while finishing my premedical requirements. My vacations, however, half a dozen over this time period, were spent with Katarina touring Prague and many fascinating eastern European countries. During these enchanting vacations we would find renewed strength in our relationship and talk about our future together. However, at the end of each vacation, we would inevitably part, with Katarina reluctantly staying on at her job and I returning to the states to continue teaching and preparing for medical school.

This practice of delaying one's personal life in pursuit of one's professional goals is not unique to me or my profession; it is true of many people and professions these days. But the time commitment needed to learn the body of knowledge of medicine and the immense number of hours that medical students, residents,

and doctors are required to be in the hospital during their training and attending years makes this practice of delaying gratifica-
tion particularly common among people in the profession of
medicine. As I observed from Katarina's hectic professional life,
teaching and research also require an immense time commitment; however, Katarina's view of her personal and professional
life was more balanced and, in retrospect, healthier than mine.

Katarina did attempt to bring our lives together by moving to
Chicago during the beginning of my first year of medical school.
But the combination of several events complicated our time
together. Shortly after arriving she told me that she had recently
been diagnosed in Prague with cervical cancer. This news was
devastating. Hearing that one has cancer, even if it is as readily
curable as cervical cancer (if treated early enough), can be life
altering. Katarina's mood was understandably gloomy, and our
interactions were strained. Knowing that cervical cancer is at the
end of a long continuum that begins with treatable pre-cancerous
cells, I wanted to see Katarina's medical report with the hope that
she might have been misdiagnosed. Katarina did not have a copy
of the report and even though I pushed for her to be examined by
a gynecologist in Chicago, to my frustration, she refused. She said
she was too afraid of the cost, even though my medical school
advisor had offered to find a colleague to do the exam and any
needed procedure free of charge.

This was a seminal moment in my understanding of the
dilemma that people without healthcare insurance face in the
U.S. when they try to get much-needed care. At this point in my
medical school training, I had witnessed first hand, through my
volunteer work in a homeless healthcare clinic, a juvenile detention center, and a gang-tattoo removal program, my patients'
struggle to get affordable and adequate care and the detrimental
effects that the lack of access to healthcare meant for them. But
these patients were only professionally involved with me, and I
was somewhat removed from their plight. Now for the first time I
was forced to experience the ills of our healthcare system on a
personal level, and the anger I felt was intense. Given the choice
of receiving free healthcare in her own country or potentially
expensive healthcare in the U.S., Katarina, understandably,

chose to be treated in her own country. In addition, Katarina had stated that if she had received a "handout" of free medical care that was not available to everyone, she would have felt both "embarrassed" as well as "looked down upon." Interestingly, these potent feelings of self-consciousness and belittlement that Katarina feared are similar to the feelings that many of my patients have expressed to me through the years when they are forced to receive free healthcare in a system that is predominantly based on one's ability to pay. The toll that this sentiment of inferiority takes on a patient's spirit can only be injurious.

Katarina also wanted to get married. With all of this happening at once, and unfortunately being overwhelmed by my first year of medical school, I once again postponed our life together, promising that we would be together once I passed my first—and toughest, I thought at the time—national board exam. After this rejection and with Katarina's desire to have her cancer treated in Prague, she left Chicago. I distinctly remember watching Katarina get into my sister-in-law's car to be driven to the airport. I was unable to fulfill even this important responsibility because of an exam I had that day that I could not postpone; my studies had interfered with my personal life once again.

Over the next several months we communicated, but our conversations were notably distant and distracted. The most difficult thing for me, however, was that I was unable to receive any information regarding Katarina's medical condition. Her reserve in sending me her gynecologist's reports and her unwillingness to update me on her condition—almost with a fatalistic attitude— were very frustrating. Wanting to help her but not having any information and fearing the worst, all of this was incredibly trying. The only information that I did receive regarding her medical condition was that her gynecologist was "watching the situation." The aggravation of being uninformed about her condition and powerless to help combined with the distance between us, contributed to our drifting apart over the remainder of my first year in medical school.

However, our strong feelings for each other brought us back together during the summer between my first and second year of medical school when we agreed to meet in South Africa where I was to do a volunteer medical rotation. At this time Katarina's gynecologist was still following her cervical cancer with periodic pap smears and had not yet decided to perform any type of corrective surgery. Our summer was enjoyable, but there was an element of melancholy about Katarina because she was preoccupied about her condition. The summer ended, and I knew that it would be hard for Katarina and me to see each other during this year because of my intense upcoming preparations for the national boards.

This was the first time I started to recognize the quandary I had put myself in. I was stuck in a relationship pattern that I could not extract myself from. I had originally delayed our coming together back in California when I was preparing to apply to medical school, with the idea that once I was over this hurdle my personal life would fall into place. But once I was accepted and enrolled in medical school, I soon had another obstacle to overcome: getting through my first year. Once I accomplished this, it was the challenge of studying for and passing the national boards that loomed before me. After that I would be faced with the long and grueling time requirements of a third and fourth year medical student on the floors of the hospital. I felt powerless in the face of all of this; I was continually being forced to let my personal life suffer on account of my studies and professional obligations.

During this consuming second year of medical school, I had an intense desire to make sure that Katarina made it through her cervical cancer. Staying in touch with her, however, was the most frustrating part of the year. Months would go by and she would not return any calls. She was not sharing any information with me, either about her life or her medical condition. Then one day she called and said that her condition had advanced and the gynecologist told her that he needed to perform a cone biopsy. This surgical procedure entails removing, with a sharp instrument that resembles a cone, the tissue that is on the surface of the cervix. This tissue is then examined by a pathologist to ensure that it contains both the layer of cancerous cells as well as a good margin of healthy cells, thus ensuring a complete treatment.

I did not hear from her until a number of weeks after the procedure and all she said at the time was that everything was "OK."

This time period was incredibly hard for me, and part of my frustration was inevitable. Being in the medical profession and having knowledge of these diseases can be trying, especially when you are intimately involved with a person afflicted with one of them. I wanted to know all of the information, especially about Katarina's care, but the lack of medical information that her doctors had given her—not uncommon, I was told at the time, of eastern block physicians—was maddening. Because of my feelings for her, I was desperate to help her, but the lack of communication in the relationship and the physical distance stood in my way.

The next time Katarina and I saw each other was when we met in New York City during my third year of medical school. She had come to NYC for a conference and had asked me to fly in from Chicago. With the two most stressful years of medical school behind me and her cancer now treated, the strain of our last two years had faded and our relationship over that weekend was as it had been when we first met. We were in love again.

I flew to Prague over the Christmas holiday of my third year of medical school, and, unknown to us at the time, we conceived a child. Katarina told me the news in early February, and she and I were overjoyed. We started planning the time that she would come to this country, and this news of her pregnancy made her arrival even more exciting. We were finally putting our personal lives first! I pushed for her to come to the States immediately, but she preferred to have me join her in Prague for the delivery in October. She said that we would then get married at the U.S. consulate and all three of us would return to the States. At the time, our many months away from each other and our independence made this suggestion seem natural to me. However, over the next several months, I noticed retrospectively, that Katarina was harder and harder to get in touch with on the phone. Days would go by and she would not return my phone calls. However, when we did talk, she would always reassure me that everything was fine with our relationship and that her tardiness in returning my phone calls was due to her demanding teaching schedule. Our conversations during these times would always be warm and loving, and we would reiterate our plan to be together in October.

Then during one phone call in June she said that she was moving into an old apartment in the center of Prague that did not have a telephone, and that I would only be able to call her at work. When I asked her why an apartment in Prague would not have a phone, she said matter-of-factly that some of the older apartments in the city did not have phone lines. Having walked the narrow and meandering streets of Prague many times and having seen the city's wonderful—yet old and often decaying architecture—I assumed that she was telling me the truth. When one is in love and trusts someone in a relationship, one has a way of believing anything, and this was true for me at the time. I took her at her word and only called her at work. Not long after this, there came a time when her doctor informed her that she needed to have a suture placed in her cervix (cerclage) to help it remain closed through the remaining months of the pregnancy. Being in a relatively less time-consuming part of medical school and wanting more than anything to visit Katarina in Prague—as well having a sense that I needed to make up for the many times I knew that I had not been there for her during her ordeal with cancer—I bought an airline ticket, and I told her that I was flying out to be with her for this procedure. To this she emphatically said that she would prefer to have me save the ticket for the time I came for the delivery. Besides, she added, her mother and sister were there and they would be of help to her. Although I objected to this, I told her that I would do what she thought was best. The procedure went well.

A week later, during the sixth month of her pregnancy, the bottom dropped out. Katarina called me to say that she was not coming to America. As I listened to her in stunned silence, she told me that she was not sure if the baby was mine. She gave me few details except to tell me that she was no longer involved with the other possible father, but she still did not want to come to the United States. She asked me to call her at a specific time in three days at a phone booth in Prague and then hung up.

I did not sleep for the next two days and hardly moved from the couch I was sitting on when I heard the news. I lay there for long periods holding my dog and watching the daylight shift across the room's walls. During this time my thoughts wandered between many feelings. First there was shock, a complete numbness in my mind and body. This feeling slowly gave way to disbelief; I felt that this could not possibly be happening to me. These feelings then gave way to what I realized in retrospect was a protective intellectualization. I reasoned with myself that of course it was understandable that Katarina had seen other people. We had been apart for so much of our relationship it was inevitable that we would see other people. I regretted the possibility that I was not the father of her baby. During these two days of introspection I was also keenly aware of wanting to make the relationship work out. I kept telling myself—and hoping I believed it under the present extraordinary circumstances—that I had it in me to take care of another man's child. I went over and over in my mind what this would entail and the many mixed feelings that I am sure I would have for her and the baby. I also knew that if Katarina and I did stay together our relationship would be forever changed. The child, rightly so, would always come first. During the morning of the second day of waiting, Katarina's sister called me and told me that Katarina had again not been honest with me, and that she actually had been living with and recently married the other man.

The next day I called a pay phone in Prague and had a tearful conversation with Katarina. She told me she was not married; she had asked her sister to tell me this lie with the hope that I would not call her and forget all about her. (The fact that she was waiting at the phone if she did not want me to call her gave me a glimpse into the mixed messages that Katarina was to send me over the next several months.) Although she went on to tell me that she was no longer romantically involved anymore with the other potential father, they were still sharing an apartment. In a desperate outpouring of hope for our relationship, I told her that I was going to fly to Prague the next day and see her. She begged me not to, saying that she needed time to think things over and was so distraught she might lose the baby if I were to visit her now. In addition, the father of the other man was dying of cancer, and it would be too hard on him to learn about me at that time. She gave me a specific date two weeks in the future when I could see her. What I suspected was that Katarina was trying to keep the whole event secret from him, and she was going to have me come into Prague when he was out of the city.

Having a life crisis during medical training is particularly trying. One has to deal with not only the emergency, but also with the added pressure of knowing that one is going to fall behind in the grueling rotation schedule. Taking enough time away from my rotation to be in Prague to try to put the pieces of my personal life back together was almost impossible, but getting a few days off I hoped would be manageable. As I prepared myself to talk with my advisor and rotation attending, I thought back to a moment during my surgery rotation a year before when, during our early morning rounds, one of the other medical students and I, gazing out the window, had commented on what a nice sunrise it was. To this, the senior resident within earshot gave us a disapproving look and said, "It is irrelevant!" Her comment—that what was happening outside of the hospital, whether it was the weather or something more personal, was unimportant to becoming a doctor—was a sobering and unfortunately accurate statement about medical training. I imagine that most of what was happening outside of the hospital was irrelevant to her at the time; she was in the middle of a very stressful residency. However, this event, even though it was indeed outside of the hospital, was very relevant to me, and subsequently, on account of my emotional state, could affect my ability to adequately care for my patients. Fortunately, at the time I was in the middle of my family medicine rotation and was on good collegial terms with my advisor and attending. I remember starting to tell my advisor the sordid details of this trauma. Before I spoke more than a few words she stopped me. Recognizing how tough it was for me to talk about this event, she told me that I did not need to go on, and that I could have the time off I needed. Her only request was for me to make up this time by working at a camp she ran for physically challenged adults for one week upon my return. (This experience started to help me put this troubled time in my life into perspective. I think that my advisor knew that this would be the case, and I appreciate her wisdom to this day.) My advisor also needed to have my rotation attending agree with the leave, so I went to him next. He did not cut me off and listened to the whole sad tale. When I finished there was a moment of silence, and then he said, "You know, you are not going to believe this, but just last year I had a resident tell me the exact same story. You are not alone." I doubt this was true; I doubt anyone has ever gone though such a uniquely painful event, but I appreciated his trying to make me feel better during the worst time in my life.

In the intervening two weeks, while I waited to travel to Prague, I wrote many desperate letters to Katarina, and we talked often on the phone when she was at her office. Surprisingly, during this time, it felt as if we were closer than we had been in years, and eerily it was almost as if we were coming back together. I still did not have many answers about all that had transpired in her life, especially the other possible father, their relationship at present, and her thinking about where she wanted to be after the delivery. I figured I would get these answers when I flew to Prague.

When I did get to Prague we had, surprisingly, an enjoyable and stress-free two days together. We did talk about the options that were available to us. Before I left for the airport I told her that regardless of whose child it was, I would be the father, if she wanted. She did not expect to hear this, but I had been thinking about it for the last two weeks and had come to the conclusion that I would accept this responsibility, regardless of who the real father was.

However, during the final two months of Katarina's pregnancy, she and I communicated less and less, mainly because she would not take my calls at her office. When we did talk, our conversations were distant and, like those of a couple going through a divorce, increasingly focused on the details of breaking up. I stressed to her my need to know if I was the father. This she resoundingly objected to. Her fear, I am sure, was that if the child were mine, I would have a reason for us to continue to be together as well as a legal right to visit our child. How I would accomplish this was another matter. Seeing a child in another country on a sporadic basis would have surely been difficult for me to manage, not to mention disruptive to the child's life. During our last conversation before she gave birth, Katarina agreed to let me come to Prague after the delivery to test the paternity of the child. Two weeks later I heard from Katarina's sister that she had given birth to a healthy girl.

I flew back to Prague a month after the delivery and met Katarina at a small hotel a few miles from the airport. It was a gray and windy November day. The hotel, a classic soviet-era, utilitarian, cement structure, emanated no warmth. I was waiting in the lobby when Katarina arrived carrying her baby in a detachable car seat. Before greeting me or letting me see her baby she handed me a large piece of folded paper. As I started to unfold it, I noticed that there were many small round holes in it. As I opened it further I saw a silhouette of a man's head and upper torso with increasing concentric circles centered on the man's chest; it was a target from a shooting range. Although none of the holes were actually through the heart—giving me small solace that Katarina probably had terrible aim—the message was clear; she had bought a gun and would do anything to keep me away from her and her baby. There was an uneasy silence, and then I told her that I had no interest in being here for any reason other than to find out the paternity of the child. To this she told me that she was not ready for me to test the child yet, and that she would meet me at her friend's apartment in Prague later that day. After a few more uncomfortable moments she left.

At this time I honestly did not know what I would do if the child were mine. Living in Prague was not an option. I was near the end of medical school and needed to start my residency. In addition, the government, through the National Health Service Corps, had put me through medical school and I would owe a four-year payback commitment after residency in an underserved area in the United States. This would preclude me from living in Prague for at least seven years. If the child were mine, it would have indeed put added pressure on Katarina to come and live with me in America, but with her increasing resolve to stay in Prague, this was remote. In addition, if I were the father of the child, it would have complicated further whatever relationship she was having with the other presumed father. I had come to the conclusion over the last three months that, if I were the father of the baby, I would encourage Katarina to come to the States. If she refused, I would offer child support, and I would try to see the child as much as I could, if she wanted me to.

A paternity test is an easy test to do. During medical school, I had given several mothers—and even a couple of dads—instructions on where to obtain the test and how to collect the genetic material. I remember thinking to myself at the time how sorry I felt for them that they had gotten themselves into a situation that required this test. Now it was I who was in the same situation. My hands shook as I took the long, yellow-colored Q-tip out of the package. I gently swabbed the inside cheek of the baby and put the swab back in the proper envelope. I then gave Katarina the white-colored Q-tip to swab her own mouth—a check that would ensure that she had actually brought her own child to the test. I then swabbed my own mouth and placed this blue-colored Q-tip in the envelope marked "Paternal Swab."

Although there were similarities between my patients and me at this moment, there was also one glaring difference. For all of my patients who took this test, it was either the mom using the test to prove paternity for child support reasons or the putative father trying to prove that the baby was not his. Never had I seen the situation that I was in: the mother not wanting the possible father to take the test for fear that he might actually be the father, or the potential father instigating the test to learn the identity of the child with the hope that it was his. This apparent difference between my patients' and my experience did not make me feel any better; in fact it made me feel worse, for it clearly showed Katarina's desire, regardless of whether or not I was the father, to deny me any part in her child's life. Never have I felt so alone in my life. However, as painful as this whole process was for me, I did gain an understanding of a not uncommon, but sad, situation that affects many, my patients included.

After the test Katarina drove me back to the hotel. We said little along the way as the dreary, gray city of Prague floated by. As I was getting out of the car, I told her that I wanted her and her baby to be happy, and that I would honor whatever decision she made.

The next morning as my plane lifted up from the runway and banked east on its way toward London, I looked back at a snow-dusted and mist-covered Prague, sensing that I would not be returning to this city again. It may sound inconceivable to the reader, but I don't harbor any animosity toward Katarina. A failed relationship is never one person's fault. As I had often regretted, there were many times during the relationship when I was unable to be with her when she needed me most. I had let my professional life and career aspirations overshadow my personal life, and this lesson was a tough one!

When I try to put the pieces together and make sense of the last year of our relationship, I believe that after her cervical surgery and her doctor informing her that it would be close to impossible for her to get pregnant, Katarina changed. Perhaps out of desperation, loneliness, or a desire to try to get pregnant, or any number of other reasons, Katarina became involved with someone else. I do not know the exact answer to this, for she never told me. And when she did get pregnant, she was forced, out of desperation, to begin the charade that was our life for the first six months of her pregnancy. Her family, the other alleged father, and I were all kept in the dark about her double identity during this time. It was not until she progressed far enough into the pregnancy that she realized that she could not keep living two lives and that she would have to be honest with me.

Two weeks after I returned to Chicago with the paternity test, Katarina called and told me that regardless of the results of the test that she would not come and be with me in America. I thanked her for finally being truthful with me. A month later I received the results of the paternity test from an American lab, but hid the envelope away before reading the contents. Although Katarina had said that she did not want to be with me, she continued to call me several times a week, and our conversations were again warm. She even started to suggest that we should think about trying to be together in the future. At this time, regardless of all that we had been through, I still held out hope that we would be together, even though repairing our relationship would have been close to impossible. I think that what held me back from opening the envelope was the truth. If Katarina's daughter were mine and I were unable to see her on a regular basis, it would tear me apart. Similarly, if she were not my daughter, I would lose Katarina forever. Still, I knew that living with the unknown—in this case an unopened envelope— would ultimately be more difficult. After several weeks of reflection, I understood what I had to do. It was time for me to start pulling away from Katarina, and the only way I was going to do that was to open the envelope.

As I sat on the plane heading to the West Coast to start one of my final rotations in medical school, I pulled from my breast pocket the sealed business-sized envelope. It was cream colored, slightly worn on the edges, and thin, perhaps containing only one piece of folded paper. The postmark indicated that it had been in my possession for over a month. The return address on the back of the envelope was in dark, simple font. The actual name of the lab, Beta Genetics Research Institute, was not spelled out, only the initials BGRI, giving a level of anonymity to its contents. As I had done many times during the past month, I traced my index finger along the top and side edges of the envelope, contemplating if I should open it. I hesitated once again, and then I took a slow, deep breath; I poked my index finger into the seam of the top flap and then sliced an even tear across the top of the envelope. I pulled out a sheet of white paper and unfolded it. In bold lettering centered at the top of the sheet was written, "DNA Test Report." Below this on the left-hand side was a case number followed by a reference number. On the next three lines were written "Mother," "Child," and "Alleged Father," respectively, and across from each of these appeared our names. I looked at our three names, one on top of the other, and wondered sentimentally for a moment what it would be like to bring up this child with Katarina. Two lines below my name, "Interpretation of DNA Test Results," appeared. And three lines under this was the three-sentence paragraph that I had traveled twelve thousand miles to learn and waited five months to read, disclosing the truth of the child's paternity: "The alleged father is excluded as the biological father of the child. The alleged father lacks the genetic markers that must be contributed to the child by the biological father. Based on testing results obtained from DNA analysis, the probability of paternity is 0%."

That was all there was written on the letter. No condolences or congratulatory remarks, just an emotionless, scientific report. For the remainder of the flight I absorbed the fact that I was not the father of Katarina's baby.

The preceding months had been an ordeal. Although I had prepared myself for either result, and I now had the information that I needed in order to move forward with my life, relief was not forthcoming. In actuality, a sense of sadness overcame me, and it would be many months before I would accept that this result was for the best.

This story of my fractured personal life during medical school may be unusual, but the feelings I experienced are not uncommon among healthcare providers. The profession can consume so much of one's time, as well as physical and emotional resources, that little energy is left over for families and personal relationships.

As I reflect now, I realize that I poured myself into Daphne partly to make up for missed opportunities with Katarina. Daphne's situation and her vulnerability moved me, as did her gradual acceptance of my help. During those months when she checked-in with me regularly, I could feel the suffering that surrounded the drama of Katarina's pregnancy lessening. Although my relationship with Daphne was strictly professional, I felt immense satisfaction when her trust in me deepened. Here I could make a difference, I thought. Here I was needed.

But relationships are changeable and can be impacted by all sorts of events unforeseen and beyond one's control. Indeed, life is seldom a straight line. It follows, more often, an irregular and unpredictable path. We may try to do our best in our professional and personal lives, but there are times when we still meet disappointment and heartache. In the end, Daphne was as unreachable as Katarina. Although she did not live thousands of miles away, her personal history, coupled with deleterious social conditions, led her to make choices that perpetu-ated a destructive cycle.

So, I am left now fearing for Daphne's son's future. Will her infant, if he is ever cognizant enough to realize his start in this world, make similar choices when he is a young man? Will the abuse that his grandmother showed his mother and his mother's disinterest in him show up in his relationships? Will he neglect his children like his mother neglected him? I hope not, but I have seen enough cases like this to fear that this cycle will remain unbroken.

SIX

Evelyn Howe

October 5

One of my first patients during my inpatient family medicine month was Evelyn Howe. I first met Evelyn when I walked into her room to introduce myself as her doctor for the duration of her recovery in our hospital. The room was dark except for a streak of soft sunlight that gently illuminated Evelyn's face. She lay in bed sleeping peacefully with the edge of the sheet pulled to her shoulders. A bright-colored scarf hid her thinning hair; her face was pale and there was a fullness to her neck. The contours of her ribs could be seen through the white sheet that had been tucked tight against her body by the night nurse.

Not wanting to wake her by placing my cold metal stethoscope against her bare chest, and admittedly feeling a little awkward about exposing a sleeping woman's chest for a cardiovascular exam, I took the safer, yet less precise, route and placed my stethoscope on top of the sheet directly above her heart. I listened to her muffled heart sounds, insulated from my stethoscope by her nightgown and sheet, when I heard her chest resonate with her voice. I glanced up and saw that she was looking at me with a faint and tired smile. I slipped the stethoscope out of my ears and caught the remaining part of her sentence, "…you can hear better if you place it on my skin."

And so I met Evelyn, a quiet and dignified middle-aged African-American woman who could have exposed my unsophisticated cardiovascular exam, but rather had the kindness to bridge my inelegance with her humor.

I loosened her sheet, pulling it only down to her waist—my attempt to give her some sense of privacy. I then undid her hospital gown, exposing her chest and abdomen, and noted the contour and symmetry of her chest wall. I watched her respirations, somewhat labored, but with equal inspiratory and expiratory effort. Her abdomen was thin, sunken, and drawn firmly against the lower part of her rib cage. Her aortic pulse pushed upward rhythmically against the tight skin of her belly. Her ribs stood out sharply under her ebony skin, each one like a furrow of upturned earth. Halfway up each side of her chest, with flawless symmetry her conscientious surgeon must have taken pride in, were her scars. Each one started at the mid-line and then extended laterally toward the outside of each chest wall, continuing up and into each armpit. Where her breasts once were, her skin, drawn tight against her rib cage, now lay.

I placed my hand on her chest to palpate her heart; her skin was firm and leathery to the touch. I searched with my fingers for the spot her heartbeat felt the strongest. Her heart surged against my hand on the whole left side of her chest, but it was in the midline where I could make out a subtle increase in pulsation. Her heart appeared normal in size.

I next placed my cold stethoscope on her chest and heard what I had already been able to palpate. I listened as I moved the stethoscope down her sternum and across where her left breast had once been; I apologized for the coolness of my stethoscope, but she said she no longer had feeling where the scars were. I then moved the stethoscope down to her thin belly and could hear her rhythmic aortic pulse, each one rising and announcing to my stethoscope that she was very much alive. Her bowel sounds were absent, which was ominous.

Finally, I placed my hand on her abdomen. Her skin was dry and warm and there was a hardness to her belly that was foreign to me. I could not make out the normal landmarks of her internal organs. The edge of her liver on the right, her soft and pliable stomach on the left, and the hard pelvic bones on the inferior aspect of her abdomen were all obstructed by a firmness.

I fastened her gown, pulled her sheet back up to her neck, and thanked her for being such a pleasant patient. Evelyn, unfortunately, is one of the one-in-nine women in this country who, at some time during their lifetime, will become breast cancer victims.[1]

Breast cancer, like all other cancers, starts off as a single normal cell gone awry. What triggers a normal cell to become cancerous is not entirely clear. Environmental insults on the cell's DNA or genetic or chance mutation within the cell's DNA blueprint can cause normal cells to become cancerous. There are theories, for example, that cancer cells, unlike healthy cells, have had their normal living and dying cycle altered and subsequently lost their ability to turn-off or die. These cancer cells, once ordained with "immortality," will continue to multiply, and if unchecked, will consume the body's healthy tissues and resources, hastening its demise.

When cancerous breast cells migrate throughout the body in search of hospitable tissue and organs to infiltrate, they often first travel, via the lymphatic system, to the lymph nodes in the chest region. Once there, the cancerous cells, by way of the body's vascular system, can find their way to any number of organs including the brain, lungs, liver, bones, and other breast. Once breast cancer has metastasized, the prognosis for survival plummets.

A little over a year ago Evelyn, with no health insurance but a mounting health concern, had visited a primary care doctor to inquire why an ulcer she had on her breast would not heal. By the time she had decided to scale the financial barrier of seeing a doctor, the ulcerating sore, which was pathologically shown to be infiltrating ductal carcinoma, had long before migrated from her breast and seeded itself in the soft tissue of her abdomen and neck. Evelyn had metastatic breast cancer.

Evelyn's treatment at that time, due to the extensive involvement of each breast, was a double mastectomy, radiation, and chemotherapy. The chemotherapy had made her hair fall out, and the radiation had turned the skin on her chest hard and leathery. Evelyn's surgery was for palliative reasons, to give her comfort, and to decrease the risk of infection from an open wound. The chemotherapy and radiation were to help slow the inevitable.

In the year following her diagnosis and treatment, Evelyn, a once vibrant and lively person, began to notice a gradually increasing fullness to her neck and abdomen. Not long afterwards her appetite waned, her weight dropped, and her thinking slowed. Evelyn's family brought her to the hospital this morning because she was not able to defecate and had stopped eating.

Her weight and energy had dropped to the point where she wanted only to lie in bed and rest.

The surgeon and attending assigned to her case came to the conclusion that Evelyn had a bowel obstruction, almost certainly from the cancerous growth that had overtaken her abdomen. The choice now was to operate or not to operate. An operation, which eager doctors in training and more aggressive surgeons prefer, could possibly reverse the obstruction, thus giving her some palliative relief and additional time. The other choice was to do nothing—just to sit, watch, and wait for the inevitable. The inevitable outcome for Evelyn would be her bowel strangulating, then perforating, resulting in her quietly succumbing to the ensuing infection.

Surgery in a case like this is questionable; the extent of her cancer made her a poor surgery candidate. The surgeon, attending, Evelyn, and her family knew this, but, after discussing the options with them, it was decided that she would go to surgery. What this family, like many families of cancer patients undergoing exploratory surgery, also knew was that a long surgery is more hopeful than a short one. A long surgery, to the family's reasoning at least, can indicate that the surgeon is taking the time to correct the problem.

Thirty minutes after the surgeon had left the family in the waiting room to scrub in for the surgery, he walked back into the waiting room to give them the bad news. Evelyn had what the surgeons call carcinomatosis, cancer everywhere. There were no heroic measures to be performed to extend her life.

Evelyn now became one of the 35 percent of women with breast cancer who would not be able to say, "I am a survivor."[2]

The use of the term "breast cancer survivor" is an interesting study in patient psychology. Some patients call themselves "breast cancer survivors" if they are beyond the median time of survival for the stage of breast cancer they have. Other patients call themselves "breast cancer survivors" if they are five years out and recurrence-free, while still other patients wait until they are ten years out and recurrence-free. It is one of the high points in medicine to hear a patient proclaim she is a "breast cancer survivor." But with this statement there flows a mighty undercurrent. Because of the very nature of cancer, can anyone truly be declared cancer-free? Statistics show that even if there is no evidence of breast cancer metastases to the axillary lymph nodes at the time of diagnosis, one third of these women will develop distant metastases somewhere else in the body within ten years.[3] These distant metastases can wait silently for many years. And therein lies the terror of cancer. You never truly know if you are a survivor until the day you die of another cause, a paradox in its cruelest form. A "cancer survivor" will always wonder if she is cancer-free, with every lump in a soft tissue or ache in a muscle or bone becoming a source of concern. Many "breast cancer survivors" talk about this fear. The psychology is the rub; trying to get one's mind off the thought that a cancer waits silently in one's body must be close to impossible.

But the psychology of someone with a disease and how that person feels about the disease are very important components of the healing process and do have an effect on survival. Studies of breast cancer support groups at Stanford University show that women who utilized support mechanisms increased their mean survival significantly over women who did not.[4]

Evelyn never had to wonder if she would ever be cancer-free. Her metastases were so extensive at the time of her diagnosis that I am sure she was told that her chance of living longer than twenty-four months was small. And after the exploratory surgery, Evelyn and her family were told that she had less than one week to live.

I wonder what goes through a person's mind when she is told that she has less than one week to live. Evelyn's cognition was too clouded to understand, but the family, which consisted of two daughters from her first marriage and her present husband, all registered this news differently. The husband, with bowed head, stood in silence. The two daughters went to their mother's side and cried. There was a long silence and then, in a matter-of-fact manner, the attending said goodbye and left the room. I hesitated, hoping that some inspirational words of healing would find their way to my tongue, but none did. I put my hand on Evelyn's shoulder, said goodbye and left the room.

An interesting aspect of Evelyn's care was the family's interactions. The husband, from the onset of the disease, had been resigned to the inevitable outcome. The daughters, however, wanted everything that was humanly possible to be done to save their mother. Adding to these differing opinions on what Evelyn's care should be was some obvious longstanding friction between the stepfather and one of Evelyn's daughters. The stepfather had agreed to allow this daughter to visit her mom, but would not allow her to move back into their house and care for her during her final days, a decision that the daughter openly criticized. From my vantage point, I felt this decision was indeed cruel and would create lasting conflict amongst the family members once Evelyn had made her final transition.

I was left in a bit of a quandary. How do I step in and try to help heal this family's wounds of many years in the few remaining moments of Evelyn's life? How do I help the stepfather see the importance of his stepdaughter's wish to be at home with her mother? And how do I get these two family members, who did not share eye contact with each other once during the entire week I spent with them, to start the process of healing and acceptance? I had counseled several dysfunctional families in my past as a teacher, some with mild success and the majority without any success. And all of these past interventions took longer than the week Evelyn's family had. After much contemplation I decided to leave the family's healing to fate and faith in family. There are times since then that I have wondered about the choice I made, but I have started to appreciate that there are times in patients' lives when doctors can only do so much. I believe that this was one of those times.

Evelyn's family decided on using hospice to help with her care during her remaining days. I discharged her home with enough morphine to keep her comfortable. As the family gathered her belongings, I tried to convey my good wishes for them as a family, but having been in only a few end-of-life situations, I felt my words were inadequate. I left feeling self-conscious.

I heard a week later that Evelyn had died at home, peacefully, with her whole family around her. I was Evelyn's doctor for only seven days before she went home, and as with many of my patients I was left with the very real sense that she had given me far more than I was able to reciprocate. She had shown me a grace that certain people have even during the most trying time in their lives. But mostly, through being her doctor, I had the privilege of caring for her during one of the most important times in her life, that being the process of dying.

With this privilege, however, came the inevitable feeling of powerlessness that doctors feel when all we can do is watch nature take its final course. Once again, as with the mother who left three young daughters when she was murdered, I had ended up at the end of the line in another patient's life. Although the circumstances of Evelyn's end were different from those of the patient who was murdered, my feeling of helplessness was the same. But just as my resolve to be an interventionist and provide primary care medicine was awakened by this murder, so was my determination aroused to try to right the wrongs of our healthcare system, a system that unfortunately had contributed to Evelyn's demise.

SEVEN

Sheri

November 1

It was not until Evelyn Howe became sick enough to be admitted to the hospital that she finally secured healthcare. Her lack of health insurance had deterred her from getting the care she needed for a year after she had first noticed a lump in her breast. Unfortunately, many Americans without medical insurance are forced to use our healthcare system in a similar manner: foregoing routine preventive healthcare checkups at outpatient clinics and then being admitted to the hospital at a later time with a greater degree of illness. In fact, hospital emergency rooms, the gatekeepers to hospital beds, cannot deny care to patients as outpatient clinics can. Anyone who arrives at an emergency room and is sick enough to be admitted will be admitted, regardless of whether the patient has health insurance or not.

Like many doctors, I care for patients who are uninsured and underinsured. These underinsured individuals often have insurance that is inadequate to cover all of their healthcare needs. The economically impoverished who qualify for public aid and Medicaid are an example. Although Medicaid is accepted by hospitals, there are many outpatient clinics that will not accept this type of insurance. Regrettably, this forces many of these people to use our healthcare system in the same costly, inefficient, and ineffective way the uninsured do. This is how I met and came to care for Sheri.

Sharice Miller, or "Sheri" as her mother liked to call her, was born one week after I was in 1963. I knew this because it was one of the only two pieces of information that we had about her when she arrived semi-comatose at our Intensive Care Unit. The other piece of information was that Sheri was HIV positive.

The on-call resident had done the best she could at getting this minimum information from her. The resident's sign-out to me was as brief as Sheri's moments of consciousness: "In room 5437 is a thirty-six-year-old African-American female with an unknown medical history except for possible HIV. She presented to the ER early this morning with a temperature of one hundred and five. She has been in and out of an obtunded state since. I think she also had some type of seizure about an hour ago."

I walked towards room 5437 not knowing what to expect. A history on a semicomatose patient is either going to be unobtainable or highly suspect of being erroneous. Thus, one's whole clinical judgment must rely on the physical exam and lab work. I was halfway through my intern year and had seen and learned an enormous amount, but I had not yet treated a critically ill, semiconscious patient.

Occasionally, with a patient like Sheri we will "luck out"; a staff member in the ER or ICU will recognize the patient from past visits and will be able to give you the information you need. (A patient familiar enough to be recognized by the medical staff is usually given the distinctive title of "frequent flyer.") Unfortunately for me, Sheri was not earning "frequent flyer" miles at our hospital. I was left on my own to determine what ailed her.

I entered her room wondering what I was going to do with my new mystery patient, or more accurately, what my new mystery patient was going to do to me. Sheri lay in bed with her eyes half closed. Her hair was matted, her skin was oily, and her head was cocked up and to the left as if straining to see what she had left behind. Her lips were cracked from dryness. Her thin arms, covered in sores, lay upon the clean white sheets. She did not look alive.

The ER nurse had already placed two IV's, one in each hand. The monitor on the wall that continually records her heart rate, blood pressure, and rectal temperature beeped at what seemed a rather fast pace. The rectal probe recorded a temperature of 105 degrees, and her heart rate of 120 beats per minute was like that of a newborn trying to catch up with the world. I spoke her name and there was no response.

In medicine, as in male adolescent playfulness, it is acceptable to get a response out of someone by rubbing your knuckles quite firmly into their sternum. As kids we called this, "giving a nuggie," and as kids we considered it great fun. In medicine we call this firm knuckle rub, "eliciting the deep pain response" and consider it an important part of the neurological exam. Regardless of what you call it or how old you are when you do it, rubbing your knuckles into someone's chest is a very effective way of getting even the most obtunded person to respond. Some doctors think it is a cruel test. One of our neurologists in medical school chastised us whenever we tested the "deep pain response" in this way. When we prodded him as to how he measures the "deep pain response," he stated that he sticks long, cotton Q-Tips deep into the patient's nose, eliciting a grimace. *Clearly more humane*, I sarcastically thought to myself at the time.

The purpose of subjecting patients to this test is to determine if you can arouse them out of their neurologically impaired state. If you are successful, it is a favorable sign; it shows that the patient has at least some higher neurological, or cortical, brain functions intact. If this test elicits no response, then one is left with the very real possibility that the patient, if not on sedatives or seizing at the time, has sustained significant higher brain injury. These patients are often left with major neurological deficits, if they are to awaken from their obtunded state at all.

Sheri did respond to the knuckle rub. She woke up long enough to tell me through a strained whisper that she had a cough and had been feeling run down for two weeks. I started to ask her about her diagnosis of HIV when she nodded off mumbling something about being exposed to TB.

Mentioning TB (tuberculosis) to a doctor or nurse in an ICU gets even the most laid back and disinterested medical staff member moving. Once Sheri mumbled the phase, "I was exposed to TB," she put into motion a series of mandatory precautions. She was put on "Airborne Precaution" and quickly moved to a negative air-flow room. These rooms, as their name implies, are at an air pressure slightly below that of the adjacent hallway. This ensures that when you enter the room none of the room's potentially contaminated air can flow back into the hospital. These rooms also have their own ventilation systems, usually exchanging air directly to the outside of the building. My only experience in working in these rooms was during my medical school training at Cook County Hospital, or County as it is called. At County these rooms were real relics; they looked as though they had not been updated since the hospital's construction during WWI. Each one of these rooms at County had a giant fan haphazardly cemented into the outside wall. The "negative pressure"—which technically was not negative pressure—was created by swiftly drawing the room air directly to the outside of the building. These giant fans were so windy and loud that I often had the sensation that I was a medic on the battlefield under the whir of a hovering helicopter. Speaking in a normal voice in these rooms was essentially useless, and one often resorted to shouting. Luckily, the negative air-flow rooms at my residency training hospital, like the hospital itself, are fairly modern and no shouting was needed. The final precaution that one takes with TB is to wear a respiratory mask officially approved by the Occupational Safety and Health Administration (OSHA). These disposable masks, in the shape of a duck's bill, fit around the nose and mouth so tightly that many users have had the feeling that they are suffocating—proof positive for OSHA, several of the other residents and I mused, that the masks work. I donned my OSHA mask and entered Sheri's new room.

Sheri was burning up with a dangerously high temperature which multiple doses of Tylenol had not brought it down. We started a cooling blanket, a thin inflatable rubber mat infused with cool water, and turned our attention to her other vitals. Her heart was racing, her blood pressure was low, her respiration rate was alarmingly high, and she was pale and sweaty. She looked like she was in shock. We drew blood from her radial artery and analyzed her blood gases. Normal arterial blood has a pH of 7.4, a bicarbonate of 24 (milli-equivalents per liter), and a partial pressure of carbon dioxide of 40 and oxygen between 85 and 100 (millimeters of mercury). Sheri's blood pH was 7.2, her bicarbonate was low at 18, her partial pressure of carbon dioxide was low at 32, and her partial pressure of oxygen was dangerously low at 60. Medically speaking, she was in metabolic acidosis: her body's positively charged ions (protons) and negatively charged ions (electrons) were not balancing. A body can survive for short periods with a minute imbalance between these ions, but, if this imbalance is not corrected, the body's fundamental metabolic pathways start to shut down.

The likely cause of Sheri's acidic state was an infection. And her low blood pressure was an ominous sign that the infection—its source yet unknown to us—had already infiltrated her circulatory system. Her heart, in an instinctual effort to compensate for her low blood pressure, raced, attempting to push blood rapidly to all her vital organs. In addition, she was hypoxic; the blood that her heart was pushing did not have enough oxygen in it to keep her tissues and organs alive. Her body's natural attempt to increase the oxygen level in her blood was to raise her respiration rate, now close to fifty breaths per minute.

Unfortunately, the body is not able to breathe at this rate for very long. The muscles of breathing, the intracostal muscles of the chest wall, the muscles of the neck, and the diaphragm, all exhaust themselves. When respiratory muscles fatigue, a predictable cyclical pathway ensues. Specifically, respiratory muscle fatigue leads to reduced oxygen intake into the lungs, which in turn leads to decreased oxygen diffusion into the blood, and diminished oxygen availability to all the cells of the body. And when these cells are deprived of oxygen, they are inhibited from performing their most important life-sustaining task: the production of energy.

This energy is in the form of adenosine-tri-phosphate (ATP), a three-ringed molecule made up of carbon, nitrogen, oxygen, phosphorus, and hydrogen atoms. And here we get a chance to gaze at the beauty of nature. This molecule, which is no more than a total of five different atoms, is the fundamental energy source for all of our body's molecular processes. The energy is stored, like a compressed spring, in the molecular bonds of the phosphorus atoms. When one of the phosphate bonds is broken, the "spring" expands, releasing its energy. This energy is used to fuel many cellular and molecular processes, from cellular intake of nutrition, to metabolic waste removal, to the life-perpetuating process of cell replication, to the movement of muscle fibers; all these life-sustaining processes require ATP. And ATP could not exist as a molecule without oxygen being both its main building block, as well as an integral part of all of the biochemical reactions that produce ATP. Just as a light bulb will start to flicker and fade when its energy source is low, so too will the muscles of breathing start to fatigue when there is not enough oxygen to produce ATP.[1]

We have now come full circle, back to the beginning of the cyclical pathway of muscle fatigue. But now, with each new breath the body is in a more compromised state: more muscle fatigue leading to less oxygen intake, leading to less energy production, leading to additional muscle fatigue—each breath bringing the body one step down a "spiral staircase" of respiratory failure.

When patients exhaust their respiratory muscles to the point they do not have the energy to breathe, the medical team has to intubate them. Intubation is nothing more than passing a flexible rubber tube into the mouth, through the vocal cords, and into the trachea. The other end of the tube is then attached to the respirator, which in its most basic form is nothing more than a machine that pumps air into the patient's lungs. The ultimate goal of intubating a patient is to control the amount of oxygen that is delivered to the lungs, which in turn diffuses into the blood. This is respiration in its simplest form.

Sheri was using all of her respiratory muscles to breathe at this time, and still her oxygen saturation was dropping; she was nearing the bottom of the "spiral staircase" and needed to be intubated.

Intubating a patient is not a particularly complicated procedure. The doctor first sedates the patient enough to relax him, but not enough to depress his respiratory drive. Next, with the patient lying flat on his back, his neck is extended and a long, thin metal blade is inserted into the mouth, compressing the tongue, thereby allowing a view of the vocal cords. When the patient exhales, the vocal cords will briefly open, giving a momentary opportunity to slip the tube into the trachea. In theory this is easy to do, but in practice it is far more difficult. Intubation can be complicated by many factors, such as inadequate sedation of the patient, using the wrong size tube, anatomic anomalies in the patients' throats, as well as difficulty in visualizing the vocal cords through the copious amounts of mucous in the back of the throat. In addition, the patient is not being ventilated during the procedure; this limits the amount of time one has to insert the tube before the patient can become severely hypoxic.

The whole act of intubating, viewed from the outside, can look very frantic. And in actuality, for the doctors, nurses, and respiratory therapists involved, it is a high tension situation. The tension comes from "the window of opportunity" that you have to intubate a patient. Critically ill patients cannot be without oxygen for even short periods before they can start to develop cardiac arrhythmias or, worse yet, brain injury. An interesting aspect of the tension is that in teaching hospitals, interns get first attempt at any procedures done on their patients. Out of all of the procedures that are done on patients, such as drawing blood, placing intravenous lines or draining ascites fluid from a belly, intubating a patient is a procedure that most interns value very highly. When it was obvious that Sheri needed to be intubated and the pulmonologist asked me to do it, I eagerly agreed to my first attempt at intubation.

Inherent to mastering any task is a learning curve. In addition, learning is best accomplished by doing. In medicine there is no substitute for learning on patients. Some patients do not like the fact that medical students, interns, and residents are learning medicine on them, but it is one of the necessities of medical education. In fact, a teaching hospital is a better place to be treated than a nonteaching hospital—albeit maybe not the most enjoyable because of all the extra needle sticks and finger probes. The mortality rate at teaching hospitals has been shown to be lower than at nonteaching hospitals, in part because the patients have so many more doctors and students thinking about their case.[2]

We started the intubation by first having the nurse sedate Sheri, and as she slipped off into unconsciousness, the respiratory therapist supported her breathing with 100% oxygen delivered through a manual respiratory bag. He oxygenated her until her blood saturation was 98%. I then pulled the mask off her face. She was barely breathing; I needed to work quickly. I opened her mouth and inserted the long thin blade down along her tongue towards the back of her throat. *Easy*, I thought. Just then she started to gag, buck, and thrash around with such force that I had the feeling that I was on a bull that had just been let out into the ring. My left hand that would have been tied to the bull's back was holding onto the blade that was now clenched with a vice grip between her teeth. My right hand that would have been circling wildly for balance with each buck of the bull, was trying to steady her and hold my balance. With each buck I tried to move with her, all the while attempting to pry her mouth back open and insert the tube. In professional rodeo, one tries to stay on the bull for the full eight seconds and any time after that, with good style points, will usually get the win. After forty-five seconds of her thrashing around, her oxygen saturation had dropped to 88%. The attending yelled at me to bail and start bagging her again. I pulled the blade out of her mouth, and she relaxed. The bull had won this time. I picked myself up from the dust and wiped her saliva off my mask and gown. The nurse gave her more sedation while the respiratory therapist manually oxygenated her back to a saturation of 98%. With my second attempt she gagged and bucked again, but with less force. I attempted to see her vocal cords but the blade was positioned wrong; a blind insertion of the tube would have been foolish. I repositioned the blade but she bucked again and her oxygen saturation had again dropped to 88%. I pulled the blade out and the nurse gave her more sedation while the respiratory therapist again used the respiratory bag to oxygenate her to 98%.

Sheri's complication was sedation. We gave her a generous amount of sedative and morphine for her body size, but each time we inserted the blade and attempted to intubate her, she, like any non-sedated person having the back of her throat prodded, started to gag and thrash around. Interestingly, the amount of sedation that is needed for each patient varies immensely. The size of a person has some bearing on it, but more important is the person's drug history. Drug users consistently require many more times the amount of medication for sedation than non–drug users. The fact that Sheri needed more and more sedation with each attempt at intubation gave us a little more information about her history—she most likely was a heroin or cocaine user.

My initial attempts at intubating were inadvertently becoming a study in my attending's patience. With each attempt, I could sense he was becoming increasingly nervous. No attending would allow a patient's oxygen saturation to fall much below 88% before stopping the procedure and starting to oxygenate again by hand. Her oxygen saturation had now twice been at this level. In addition, she had been given enough sedation to suppress her own drive to breathe. Intubating her became a critical matter. When an intubation is successful, which it is most of the time, calm comes over the doctors and nurses in the room. When I started to intubate Sheri on my third and last attempt, the attending, who would take over if I failed, nervously shifted his weight back and forth between his feet while he rubbed his temples as if he was having a terrible headache. But any bull with enough sedation can be ridden. I intubated Sheri, and a collective sigh of relief came over the room.

With Sheri intubated and now breathing safely under our control, I had time to think and plan. To learn more about her medical history, I contacted the hospital where she was probably receiving her HIV care—County.

I have always been in awe of County, a massive public hospital in Chicago that fills a complete city block and where wards stretch for what seems like infinity. Its dedication to the underserved and its historically highly coveted residency positions, have endowed it with legendary status. But, I also knew about the disorganization of the hospital. I had spent many hours during my medical school training in the hospital's deep interior, helping frustrated file clerks look for a patient's misplaced medical records. I knew of lost X-rays, mislabeled specimens, empty supply cabinets, and even forgotten patients. The last happened during my medical school training. A homeless gentleman, who the internal medicine team thought had been discharged, was still there days later. Forgotten, he lay in his room and ate the meals that were brought to him by the uninformed nursing staff. Unseen, he sat there for days as dozens of doctors and medical students passed by his room unaware that he had not left the hospital. It was not until our team was assigned a patient sharing this gentleman's room that we realized our error. The senior resident—to my amazement—quickly wrote several days of back notes to cover up our oversight and save himself from being reprimanded. The patient, much to his chagrin and disappointment that our hospitality had come to an end, was discharged home, this time for real.

I was skeptical that I would get information about Sheri over the phone from County. But, like a cub reporter trying to get a hot tip to clinch a story and look good in his editor's eyes, I sought information that would help us understand her condition better, making myself look good to the attending, since only the most dedicated interns are motivated enough to get through to County on the phone.

I called County, and after being disconnected and indefinitely put on hold several times, finally talked to a live clerk. He told me over a line filled with static that they had no record of Sheri. I assumed that the hospital had just misplaced or lost her records. The thought of calling every hospital in the city, with the slim hope that she had by chance received care somewhere, seemed too overwhelming. Besides, I was not that eager to impress my attending. I now had to wait until she was taken off the ventilator and able to talk, or be fortunate enough to have a family member take enough interest in her to come to the hospital. This last option was doubtful, for she had been dropped off at the ER in her present state by a family member who left without saying a word.

Ward clerks in a hospital have a difficult job to do. ICU ward clerks have an almost impossible job to do. They have to be able to answer several phones at once, read and enter into a computer barely legible physician's orders, and juggle the needs of distraught family members, tired and edgy residents, underappreciated nurses, and curt attendings. The clerk's area in the ICU is a whirl of movement, chatter, energy, and noise. As a resident you quickly learn to tune it out. It becomes the white noise in the background of your busy day. I started to slumber to the constancy of this static while attempting to write a progress note about the new patient whom I knew little about when I heard the clerk yell, "Doctor, you working with patient Sharice Miller?"

"Yes," I mumbled as I struggled to come out of my half sleep.

"There's a family member on the phone."

I picked up the phone and heard a soft and measured voice on the other end.

"She's going to be all right, right, doctor?"

It was Sheri's mother. There was a long silence.

"She's going to be all right, right?" she said again.

"Well," I paused. I had no idea where to begin. I had a strong feeling that her daughter was not going to be all right, but I did not have the heart or words to say it.

I covered myself with medical speak: "Ms. Miller, presently Sheri is intubated, we are assisting her breathing with a respirator. She is on seizure precaution, and we have started to use a cooling blanket to help with her fever. We are monitoring her cardiac status and are awaiting her chest X-ray, white blood cell count as well as her basic metabolic panel...."

She cut me off and with a touching gentleness said, "But, she's going to be all right, right. doctor?"

I paused and exhaled, "Yeah, she's going to be all right."

A feeling of inadequacy took hold of me. I had just lied to a patient's family member to spare her some grief.

■ ■ ■

Lying to a patient or her family is one of the biggest mistakes a doctor can make. Following close behind this is a lesson that was taught in my medical school's Medical Ethics and the Law class.

Of the countless classes that I took during my first two years of medical school, this class was particularly memorable. Just the idea that a medical school would teach medical ethics as a course combined with medical law was a none too subtle way to instruct aspiring doctors that they need to be ever mindful of the legal ramifications of any and all decisions they make. This course used the "stick" of the "stick and carrot" approach to teach ethics, instructing doctors that, if they failed to act ethically, they and the hospital could be sued. The course, not surprisingly, was taught predominantly by our hospital's legal counselors, a sizable team of full-time lawyers who, when not defending the hospital's doctors in malpractice suits, were instilling the fear into naïve medical students that every patient could potentially be a plaintiff. One of the first class discussions we had with an instructor-lawyer concerned the following pragmatic question: As medical professionals, what do we do when we make a mistake? His answer, one reiterated many times during subsequent classes with other lawyer-instructors, was that the doctor should not admit to any error and that any statement to the patient should be handled by a lawyer. We were given a pager number to call if we made a mistake in the middle of the night.

Imagine that you are a patient and your doctor, whom I assume you have trusted enough to be your caregiver, makes a mistake and then, before he talks to you about the mistake, pages the hospital lawyer. Now, at this point two potential harms have been done: the honest, open and communicative relationship that you had enjoyed with your doctor has been taken away. You have also been forced to enter a confrontational legal environment. Either is enough to incense you or other patients, and it is no wonder that revenge and litigation result.

Of particular interest here is that doctors who communicate openly and effectively with their patients before, during, and after a medical mishap are far less likely to be sued than doctors who do not communicate with their patients. Studies of patients injured by medical errors have clearly demonstrated that the predominant interest of the injured patient is not in monetary compensation. Rather, the patient desires assurances that the mistake will not be repeated, and that an apology will be made to them by the doctor and hospital.[3]

The challenge of satisfying the patient's desires, while keeping the important doctor-patient relationship intact, and in addition, avoiding a legally binding situation (which no doctor or hospital would want) is a difficult one. But, with honest and open communication between the doctor and patient, mutual satisfaction can result in the majority of cases. When communication does break down, solving the problem and still avoiding a confrontational litigious environment could be attempted through mediation.

A mediator, as an impartial third party, would allow the doctor and hospital to take a route which would have the doctor apologize in person to the patient for the mistake, thus leaving the honest and open doctor-patient relationship intact. Second, a mediator could facilitate interchange between the patient, doctor, and hospital on changes or safeguards that would insure that the same mistake is not repeated. This type of dispute resolution can be easily implemented and can be effective, as a pilot program in Massachusetts has demonstrated.[4]

A mediated solution can also involve a financial agreement between the parties. Interestingly enough, in cases where mediation has been in place, only a small minority of patients demanded payment of money. But most important, the real power of these suggestions is that in each case the patient's concerns are validated, the doctor-patient relationship is left undiminished, and the doctor and hospital have been accountable in an open and forthright fashion. If only the lawyers from our medical school had taught us that. We would not have to wake them up in the middle of the night with pages!

There is no doubt that mistakes are made by medical professionals each year that cause injury and harm. And it is important to say that even one mistake that leads to any amount of harm in a patient is unfortunate. But the fact is that medicine is practiced by humans and by their very nature humans err. And when we do, we need to be as honest and forthright as we can.

■ ■ ■

As I finished my phone conversation with Sheri's mom, I found out as much as I could about Sheri's medical history. In addition, I made a mental note to set the record straight when I saw her.

It turned out that Sheri was getting her HIV care at one of the large private hospitals in the city where she was able to receive free care, compliments of the Ryan White Care Act. The infectious disease clinic at this hospital did know Sheri. They knew her from her sporadic visits for blood work and medication refills. She was, in their eyes, a "noncompliant patient" who would not take her medication either at the prescribed times or dosages. Sometimes she would not take her medication at all. The enormous number and complicated dosing regimens of HIV drugs, not to mention the many side effects of these medications, make the behavior of "noncompliance" easy to empathize with. The infectious disease clinic also knew her four-year-old daughter; they had been treating her for HIV since her birth.

Human immune-deficiency virus (HIV) interacts with the body on the molecular and cellular level in a complex way. On the microscopic level the virus looks like a hexagonal lunar space module with multiple protruding legs. Once the virus has entered the body, through blood, semen or vaginal fluids, it will travel throughout the circulatory system at the whim of the body's blood flow. If the virus is not first detected and destroyed by our immune system, it can find a safe "landing pad" on the cell wall of one of the most important cells in our intricate immune system, the CD-4 cell (also called the T-Helper). Once touchdown has been accomplished, the virus will inject its "cargo" of genetic material into the CD-4 cell. And now the virus's genetic code, in one of its more diabolical acts, copies its own viral genetic code into the CD-4 cell's genome, the equivalent of the cell's genetic library. The damage has been done.[5]

The CD-4 cell, now with a copy of the virus's genetic code as its working blueprint, will cease carrying out all of its normal biological functions and instead start to produce, with assembly line efficiency, virus after virus. The CD-4 cell, its genome now held hostage, becomes an HIV factory, producing and releasing a logarithmic number of viruses to infect a logarithmic number of healthy cells, each virus a near replica of the initial virus that infected the cell in the dawn of its demise.[6]

The way that HIV interacts with our immune system is more easily understood if we use a military analogy. Just as our armed forces, with their many branches and levels of command, defend our country against invaders, so too does our body's immune system, which is no more than an intricate interplay of several different cells. The body's "invaders" can be bacteria, parasites, viruses, toxins, and any substance that the body recognizes as being foreign. The CD-4 cell, arguably the most important part of our immune system, would be equivalent to a commanding officer in the military. HIV is a unique virus in that it attacks the commanding officer of our immune system. Staying with the military analogy, imagine an invading force entering this country and first silencing our military's commanding officers, the very personnel that give the orders to destroy the invaders. If this were to happen, any subsequent invader would be able to enter this country without resistance. This is analogous with HIV. The virus first attacks our CD-4 cells, incapacitating them from performing their most crucial role: the signaling of our immune system to protect our body from pathogens. The repercussions of this are immense. Our body is left immune-compromised, unable to protect itself against any invading bacteria, parasite, or virus.[7]

One safety measure built into our immune system is its ability to detect and destroy its own wayward cells in a number of ways. The first is through the cell's "self-recognition" that its behavior is maladaptive. Here the cell will perform apoptosis, the equivalent of cell suicide. The HIV-infected CD-4 cell can also be destroyed by other cells in our immune system, once it is recognized as functioning improperly. Finally, through the sheer act of producing and releasing exponential number of viruses, the infected cell can swell and burst. But regardless of its end, the CD-4 cell, once a noble and integral part of the body's intricate and beautiful immune system, is now in the dusk of its demise.[8]

A healthy person who is not infected with HIV has a CD-4 count between 600 and 1,200 (cells per micro-liter of blood). Sheri's CD-4 cell count (probably because she was not taking her medications) was four. For all intents and purposes, she had no immune system. She was susceptible to every pathogen that could infect a healthy person. In addition, she was susceptible to infections from the infinite number of benign bacteria and fungi that harmlessly colonize a healthy person's skin and mucosal membranes.

More immediate than Sheri's HIV status was her present state of shock, a condition in which the vital organs are not receiving enough oxygen-rich blood. The cause of shock is low blood pressure, and Sheri's low blood pressure was due to her infection releasing vasodilators into her blood stream.

Fluid mechanics tells us that the pressure of fluid in any given pipe is a function of three components: the volume of fluid entering the pipe, the speed at which the fluid enters the pipe and, most important, the diameter of the pipe. As the diameter of the pipe increases, the pressure of the fluid in the pipe falls precipitously. The same is true, to a reasonable extent, for the body's blood vessels; that is, as the body's arteries and veins dilate, the blood pressure decreases. An analogy to this is when you are taking a shower, enjoying a warm, high pressure flow of water, when suddenly the pressure drops, triggering you to yell a series of expletives while fumbling to turn the faucets all the way on to increase the flow of water. The heart, when presented with the same problem of low fluid pressure, reacts the same way, save for the expletives. It attempts to increase the flow of blood by increasing the rate at which the heart beats. And this is why Sheri's heart raced. It was a natural compensation for her low blood pressure, a desperate attempt to push her blood to her vital organs.

Sheri was young and had a strong heart, but even her heart could not beat for long at the present rate of 120 beats per minute. The problem before us now was to support her blood pressure and correct her underlying infection. Curing her would entail killing this infection. But treating infections in immune-compromised patients is always difficult and close to impossible when the patient is so critically ill.

I sat in the ICU writing up orders for the blood work and radiological tests we would need to help determine where her infection was when the clerk told me that Sheri's mother had arrived. I left the nursing station, walked down the hall, and found Ms. Miller standing in front of Sheri's room, peering uncertainly around the closed curtain as if contemplating if she wanted to go in. She was a petite, pleasant woman with a soft voice. I took her small, warm hand in mine and greeted her. We entered the room, and she was silent for quite some time. The hiss of the respirator and the constant beat of the cardiac monitor ticked away the seconds. She shifted nervously and glanced at the monitor and then back at the respirator. She started and then stopped. She tried again.

"What's this?" she said in a quiet voice pointing at the tube coming from Sheri's mouth.

"It's a tube that is helping her breathe," I said.

Her voice rose slightly with concern, "A tube is helping her breathe?"

I stammered, "Yeah…it's a…it's a tube in her throat, a small tube, and it helps her breathe."

"She's breathing on her own, right, doctor?"

"The respirator is helping her breathe," I said nodding in the direction of the ventilator that was next to the head of the bed.

"But, she is taking breaths on her own, right, doctor?"

I tried to sound reassuring, "She is taking some breaths on her own, but the machine is helping her breathe."

"How many is she taking on her own?" she asked, looking at the respirator with unease.

"About four or five a minute, I think; the machine takes the rest."

"She's going to be all right, right, doctor?"

Trying now to be completely honest I started slowly, "She is very ill…."

She interrupted, "But she is going to be all right?"

I continued, "I hope, but you need to know that she is very sick."

She paused, shifted nervously, and then asked, "How many breaths did you say she took on her own?"

"Only a few," I said trying to put the graveness of her condition into my voice.

"But, she is going to be all right?" she asked again.

Nothing I was saying was getting through. Her same question, continually asked over and over, like a child hoping for a different answer, was tempting me again to appease her and say that her daughter was going to be "all right," when I really did not believe this. I told her she could call anytime, and we would keep her updated about any changes in Sheri's condition. I excused myself and went back to the nursing station.

At admission to our ICU, Sheri, due to her immune-compromised state, was started on several very broad antibiotics. She needed to be covered for many bacteria and several parasites and fungi, any and all of which could be causing her infection. In addition, from the moment that she entered the ICU, we aggressively supported her blood pressure by repeatedly giving her 500 cc's of IV fluid. The nurse called me each hour with her blood pressure, and with each reading under 90/50 I gave her another 500 cc's of fluid. The infection, in addition to causing her blood vessels to dilate, had also made them very porous. For every liter of fluid we gave her, over three-quarters of it leaked out of her blood vessels and into the surrounding tissue. By the end of forty-eight hours, we had pumped twelve liters of fluid into her to help maintain her blood pressure. Sheri, like many critically ill patients in sepsis, swelled. The additional twenty-five pounds of water in her made her unrecognizable.

When a patient receives this much IV fluid, even someone with as strong a heart as Sheri's, there is a risk of congestive heart failure, a condition in which fluid backs up into the lungs, filling the lungs' air sacs, and decreasing the ability to oxygenate the blood. There is a fine line between giving patients enough fluid to support their blood pressure and giving them so much as to cause them to be fluid-overloaded. It is not bad medicine to put someone into congestive heart failure, since it is rather easy to step over this fine line, but it is bad medicine not to recognize when someone is in congestive heart failure. To this end, we diligently listened to her lungs every hour and took daily chest X-rays. Three days into her care, we started to hear "rales" on her lung exam. "Rales," which sounds amazingly similar to the "snap, crackle and pop" of your morning Rice Crispies, is the sound that the lungs' air sacs make when they struggle to open when filled with fluid. We had stepped over the line and put her into congestive heart failure.

At this point, we decreased the amount of IV fluid she was receiving and started to support her blood pressure with a strong synthetic catecholamine hormone called dopamine. This hormone is structurally very similar to epinephrine, the same hormone that your body secretes when you are confronted with a life-threatening situation. It increases the heart rate and constricts the body's blood vessels, thereby increasing blood pressure.

Critically ill patients like Sheri usually have more than one organ system that is not functioning properly. Even though we had pumped over five gallons of IV fluids into her, she had not urinated in three days, a sign that she was still intravascularly dehydrated. If she continued down this path, she would end up in acute renal failure, possibly requiring lifelong dialysis, if she survived at all. Fortunately, dopamine, in addition to increasing blood pressure, also increases blood flow to the kidneys and the likelihood of the patient urinating. On the fourth day of her care she began to produce urine for the first time, not a lot, but enough to reassure us that her kidneys were still functioning.

This, however, was the only good news about Sheri. Her hourly lung exams and daily chest X-rays were worsening. Her X-ray on the first day showed a small white area in the lower left lung suspiciously like pneumonia. Over the course of the next five days, we watched helplessly as her lung infection spread up into the apex of her left lung, crossed down into the base of her right lung, and then finally engulfed her remaining right lung tissue. As each day passed and a greater portion of her lungs was compromised, she took fewer and fewer breaths on her own. The ventilator was doing almost all of the work for her now.

Most people when confronted with an infection will mount a response to the infection by increasing the number of white blood cells (WBC) in their body. This increase in WBC is a sign that one's immune system is functioning properly. Healthy people with an intact immune system can fight an infection on their own, only occasionally needing an antibiotic. The combination of a healthy immune system and an antibiotic working in concert can effectively treat most infections. Sheri's infectious agent, streptococcus pneumoniae, was one of these, infinitely curable in a healthy person with a simple antibiotic.

The problem with Sheri was that she was not healthy. Her immune system did not work, and her WBC count remained low to nonexistent in the face of her infection. Curing her would not be a combined effort of her immune system and our medications; it would rely solely on the latter. We gave her the strongest and broadest antibiotics available, and we even tried to jump-start her immune system with powerful immunological stimulating medications, but days five, six, and seven passed and her temperature still remained high, her WBC count low, and her hourly lung exams and daily X-rays showed no improvement. She was not getting better, but there was an even more ominous picture starting to develop.

Sheri was starting to go into adult respiratory distress syndrome (ARDS), a condition in which the lungs' air sacs become porous and start to fill up with fluid, drastically reducing their ability to oxygenate the blood. This condition occasionally happens with critically ill patients who have an underlying infection, and the fatality rate can be high. The treatment is to support the patient with oxygen, fight the infection with antibiotics, and wait. We were already doing two out of the three, so we were forced to wait and watch. Day seven passed, and we entered day eight. With each day Sheri was taking fewer breaths for herself. It was becoming clear that she might never be able to come off the ventilator, if she lived at all. At the end of day eight her condition worsened when she started to show signs of disseminated intravascular coagulation (DIC).

DIC is a condition in which the body's coagulation pathway starts to malfunction, subjecting the patient to the risk of simultaneously forming life-threatening blood clots and bleeding spontaneously. The difficulty in treating DIC is inherent in the fact that it is two disorders occurring at the same time, too much clotting and too much bleeding. Treating one of the disorders can exacerbate the other. With our hands tied, we were again forced to sit and watch and wait.

If Sheri started to form blood clots, we would try to thin her blood, knowing that this could cause her to bleed. Conversely, if she started to bleed, we would give her blood products that would help her clot, knowing that this would increase her chance of forming blood clots elsewhere in her body, possibly with devastating effects.

Days nine and ten passed, and we kept a very close eye on her. She had not yet started to bleed, but her condition had deteriorated. The ventilator was now completely breathing for her.

On day eleven, the pulmonologist who had been working closely with me on Sheri's care said, "You know, when you've done all you can do, you can't do anymore."

I paused and looked at him. The statement was trite, yet it confused me. "What do you mean?" I inquired with uncertainty.

He continued, "Sheri is dying. You have done everything you can. You should help the family understand the gravity of the situation and talk to them about their wishes for relieving her suffering."

I did not know what to say. I questioned him with caution, "Do you mean I need to talk to them about withdrawing care?"

He nodded.

The three most important things that support life are nutrition, water, and air. Without nutrition, people have been known to live upwards of three to four months; without water, people can live about five to seven days; but without air, people cannot live longer than five to seven minutes. When a layperson hears that someone's "life support" is being pulled, it can be very confusing. There are many "life supporting" measures, such as IV fluids, tube feeds, and ventilators that support a patient's life in the hospital. Turning off any one of these will at some point hasten a patient's death, some more rapidly than others. In the medical profession "pulling one's life support" means turning off the patient's ventilator, removing the breathing tube and allowing the patient to expire through asphyxiation. This is the talk that I had to have with Sheri's mom.

How do you tell a patient's family that you have done everything that you can do but that it is still not enough? How do you tell a mother that her daughter is going to die? How do you tell a four-year-old that her mother is going to die? In medical school and residency doctors are not trained to lose, we are trained to fight death with everything we have. And when it is clear that the medical team is losing the battle and our collective armament of knowledge, medications, and multiple remedies is inadequate against the resilient forces of a disease, we are taught to pause, collect ourselves, and then like Shakespeare's King Henry V's valiant and outnumbered soldiers, we charge head first into the final battle, even if defeat is foretold.

I called Sheri's mom and asked her to come to the hospital to see her daughter. My voice must have conveyed a sense of urgency, for she said only, "Yes."

Sheri's Mom arrived with her son and niece. I took some comfort seeing that she had brought her family for emotional support. I asked them to come into Sheri's room to talk. I wanted them to be around her when we spoke so that her lifeless form would help convey what I was about to say.

I started slowly, "Ms. Miller..." I stopped. I was at a loss for words. I started again. "Sheri, as you know...has AIDS...."

I was cut off by her son, "You know doc, she looks a little better than she did yesterday, doesn't she?"

I was caught off guard and stammered, "Well, I...I don't...."

Sheri's Mom now cut me off, "How many breaths is she taking on her own?"

I regrouped. "None," I said assuredly.

Her brother countered optimistically, "We saw her move her hand yesterday."

I started again, "Sometimes people in this condition will have some movement...."

Her Mom continued, "She's going to be all right, right, doctor?"

I paused and tried again, "Ms. Miller, I know I said that I thought that she was going to be all right, but she is not getting any better and her condition has worsened...."

Sheri's Mom stopped me again, "She is taking breaths on her own, right?"

I answered trying not to show my frustration, "The machine is taking all her breaths for her now."

"But she is taking some breaths on her own, right?"

I shook my head.

I had tried, but I knew that this conversation with Sheri's mom was going to be futile. I finished with, "Ms. Miller, I think it's important for you and your family to spend as much time with her now as you can. I'm hoping for the best, but it is important for you to be ready if things get worse and she...." My voice trailed off. There was silence in the room. I looked at the floor for several seconds and then up at Sheri's Mom. I caught her sad, dark eyes; there was a longing for hope. I tried to smile, but the lump in my throat would not let me; I swallowed hard, turned and left.

Signing out my patients at the end of the day to the on-call resident is always a time of mixed emotions for me. On the one hand I am happy and relieved to be able to go home after a long and stressful day, but I also carry an inevitable sense of unease knowing that any one of my patients might not make it to the morning. There have been many mornings that I have entered my patient's ICU room only to be greeted by an empty bed. It is an unsettling feeling knowing that your patient was not healthy enough to be transferred down to a less critical floor, but rather has made her transition up.

I signed out Sheri's care to the on-call team for the last time that evening. It was Friday. I had a rare weekend off and would not be back in the hospital until Monday morning. On my way out of the ICU, I walked into Sheri's room, squeezed her swollen hand and hoped she understood. I walked out of the hospital into the cold, wintry evening knowing that Sheri would die over the weekend.

I have never been a very religious person, but I have occasionally found myself on Sunday mornings frequenting a church on the South Side of Chicago. The service, with its hundred-member gospel choir and ten-piece band, can be very inspiring and uplifting. This Sunday was no exception—the choir sang for nearly three hours. On past occasions I have sheepishly slipped out the back door halfway through the service, often using my busy schedule as a justification, but for some reason this Sunday I stayed for the whole service. While I was struggling to exit the church with the masses of real worshipers, someone grabbed my hand from behind. Startled, I turned around. Before me stood a thin, petite, middle-aged African-American woman in a long colorful dress. Her brown eyes were slightly covered by her large brimmed hat, which held a row of woven flowers. She looked vaguely familiar and wonderfully at peace. She took my hand and smiled knowingly. There was an awkward pause and I smiled, nervously hoping this woman could not tell that I did not recognize her.

She spoke in a soft, measured voice, "I want to thank you for all you did. She's going to be all right."

I was stunned, it was Sheri's Mom.

I attempted to nod and say something, but my mouth was as frozen as the rest of my body. I mumbled several incoherent words. She understood.

She smiled warmly, let go of my hand, and continued out.

My mind raced as I slowly meandered my way home through the snow dusted South Side neighborhoods. Too many questions. What was the chance of my randomly visiting the same church that Sheri's Mom attends? How could she be so peaceful during this painful time? And her comment, "She's going to be all right," was a statement, and not her usual question, *right?* I turned this statement over in my mind trying to make sense of it. I dismissed it as her unwavering faith and belief in the hereafter, a place where I knew Sheri was now. I admired her for her strength during this painful time.

On Monday morning when I returned to the hospital, I was expecting to see Sheri's room either empty or occupied by a new ICU patient, but to my surprise Sheri was still there. I entered her room and noticed that the respiratory therapist had switched her ventilator from assist mode to pressure support. Sheri had started taking breaths on her own. Her color looked better and she was less swollen. I looked at her daily chest X-ray, and for the first time in over two weeks I could see clearing in areas that had been clouded with infection. I logged on at the computer, and her morning blood work showed that her WBC count had increased. Sheri's body was starting to fight her infection.

Over the next several days her white count continued to rise, her high fever subsided, and her lungs sounded clearer. The infection was now being turned back by the combination of our strong antibiotics and her awakened immune system—awakened by powerful immunological stimulating medications and, perhaps, also by her own will to survive. With the infection now coming under control, her body's vessels were able to constrict, and the massive amount of fluid that she had needed to support her blood pressure was filtered through her kidneys and out of her body. And with each liter of urine that flowed from Sheri, a little more life seeped back into her. Later that week we removed the breathing tube and after a fit of coughing she composed herself and said her first words, "I'm really hungry! Can I have something to eat?"

It is a surreal experience when you enter your patients' ICU rooms and see them for the first time, without a tube in their mouth, not sedated, sitting up in bed, and talking. The first time I saw it, I did not believe it. I did a double take at the patient and then stepped back to recheck the room number. In the ICU you get so used to caring for lifeless patients day in and day out that you lose perspective on what life is. The patient becomes a manikin, lifeless in spirit and personality. The hiss of the respirator and the constant beat of the cardiac monitor are all that the patient speaks. For days on end you poke and prod the still and silent body trying to give it life again. You measure clear fluid going in and yellow and brown fluids coming out. You look at many numbers and compare these to yesterday's many numbers and these again to the many numbers from the day before that. You poke and prod some more trying to make tomorrow's many numbers better than today's many numbers. You listen to the lungs by looking at the ventilator's computer display. You evaluate the heart by studying the cardiac monitor. You study the body's chemistry by looking at a computer screen. You are removed, work in isolation, feel only sensory depravation. You are numb to life. And just when you think that the still and lifeless body that you have prodded and poked for days will forever be still, something happens. Life enters. Slowly at first and then with more confidence. It awakens your patient, and then it awakens you.

Sometimes it is from something you did, but most of the time it is from nothing you did.

I sit and think about Sheri often. I think about all that we did. I think about all the medications we gave, blood draws we analyzed, specialists we consulted, and hours we pondered. I think about our ultimate acceptance that she was going to die. I also think about Sheri's mom. I think about her simple and constant drumbeat of positive thinking. A drumbeat of constant questions about every aspect of her care, all ending with her proverbial drumbeat question, "She's going to be all right, right, doctor?" There were many times that I mistook her unwavering faith in her daughter's recovery, and her endless denial of the gravity of her daughter's condition, as naïveté. But in the end, it was Sheri's mom who was as much of the healing process as we were, and maybe more, for she understood the healing powers of nature.

And so, it is a good lesson: nature heals people, some completely and some not. Doctors and nurses can facilitate nature, but it is nature that does the healing.

Twenty days after Sheri entered the hospital in a semicomatose state, she was going home to be with her daughter and mom for Thanksgiving. She had walked to the precipice of death and stepped back. Sheri was going to be "all right."

EIGHT

Harold Brown

December 24

Christmas Eve marked the halfway point of my intern year. I chose to schedule my ICU months as late as possible during the year, affording me time to practice my clinical skills. Up until November, my first month in the ICU, I had had four months of inpatient rotations, consisting of maternal child health (obstetrics and pediatrics), family medicine, and one month of night call in the ICU. Although each day I walked into the ICU with moist palms and unease in my belly, I was slowly gaining faith in my ability to treat critically ill patients, and Sheri was one of the more memorable.

Our residency program was unique in that the interns rotated for two months and took night call for four months in the ICU. Very few residency programs give their first-year residents this much critical-care experience and responsibility. And in the sleep-deprived and agitated state we existed in as interns, we regularly questioned what the benefit was to have us spend one-third of our year's call nights in the ICU. Our empathetic senior residents would nod their heads, smile, and quickly add, "In the end you are better doctors because of it." *Better doctors because of it?* I thought. Small solace for us who did not yet have the whole year's perspective.

Harold Brown, a fifty-three-year-old African-American gentleman, was one of our few patients on the floor this Christmas Eve. He had arrived at the ICU four days earlier, after having been found unresponsive in his bathroom by his seven-year-old daughter. Harold suffered from a disproportionate number of medical problems. He had high blood pressure that had gone untreated for many years. His blood sugar was constantly elevated from diabetes. The combination of his hypertension and diabetes over the years had narrowed his peripheral arteries to such an extent that the blood stopped flowing to his feet and legs which necessitated the amputation of his left leg below the knee several years ago. Harold had also been an alcoholic for many years. The constant alcohol in his bloodstream had dilated his heart to its present weak and inefficient state. In addition, years of smoking along with the alcohol use had contributed to a mouth cancer that had been successfully removed along with half his tongue. Finally, Harold had contracted HIV through his past drug use. Due to the misguided policies of our healthcare system, it was only after Harold acquired HIV that he was able for the first time in his life to get health insurance (Medicaid).

Harold had collapsed in his bathroom after suffering a stroke. This stroke had affected the left side of his brain, leaving him unable to speak as well as paralyzing the right side of his body. The MRI of his brain showed that the infarct was most likely ischemic and not hemorrhagic. Although these two types of strokes occur in different manners, both have the same effect— the cessation of blood flow to vital brain tissue beyond the stroke area. An ischemic stroke occurs when a blood vessel in the brain either becomes clogged from a blood clot or has a spasm and closes off. A hemorrhagic stroke, as the name implies, is the result of a blood vessel in the brain rupturing. The cause of Harold's ischemic stroke was unknown but could have been from a number of sources. For one, a blood clot, formed in his dilated and inefficient heart or dislodged from his atherosclerotic carotid arteries, might have flowed up into his cerebral vasculature until it became wedged in a narrowing vessel. Second, there was the possibility that Harold's cancer had recurred; this in itself could have enhanced the formation of a blood clot. Finally, Harold's cerebral blood vessels, like the vessels in his legs after years of narrowing, may have occluded. It is hard to know what exactly caused Harold's stroke; the ICU team searched diligently, but nothing was definitive. What was definitive, however, was that Harold, although stable, was in critical condition and had a long recovery ahead of him.

Working in the ICU, obviously, gives one an opportunity to care for critically ill patients and, from this, to learn medicine in a highly charged environment. However, it also does something less obvious. It forces the doctor to interact with the patients' families. In most healthcare settings the doctor communicates primarily with the patients and, secondarily, with the patients' families. In the ICU this pattern is often reversed. Because of the critical condition of most patients, the family members are often the doctors' contact, and these interactions, because of the intensity of the situation, can provoke many emotions for family and caregivers. What I have seen through these interactions with family members, when the life of their loved one is most tenuous, is an openness and honesty that is heartening. It has helped me to have a deeper understanding of the patients and those who love them. Harold's wife exemplified such openness.

Hope Brown, Harold's wife of nine years, was a tall, thin woman in her mid-forties. She would visit Harold each evening after a long day of work at a drug rehabilitation center. Even during this trying time in her life, she had a warm smile, and optimism flowed from her. Each evening she would sit at Harold's bedside, hold his hand, and tell stories about his life.

They had met ten years ago at a drug rehabilitation clinic on the South Side of Chicago, he the addict, she the counselor. Through many hours of counseling and behavior modifications, she had accomplished the very difficult task of weaning Harold off all his vices. And in those long hours of therapy and self-remaking, Hope had also done something more important for Harold—she had injected him with the idea of becoming a rehabilitation counselor himself. On his one-year anniversary of sobriety and staying clean, Harold, now craving his new addiction of rehabbing others, was hired as a counselor at the clinic where he had been helped. Not long after, Harold and Hope started dating.

Hope's eyes would widen and her language quicken when she spoke of Harold and his ability to get people to believe in themselves. "Harold has a way," she said, "he connects to people." She paused mid-thought and then continued with a smile, "He'd love to go to the neighborhood, into some of his old [crack] houses, and come back with one of the young users. He had belief that there's something in everyone…" She paused again, her eyes searched the room in an attempt to hold back her emotions, and then she continued, "worth saving. He helped lots [of addicts], more than he lost. You don't see a whole lot of folks who can stay clean...all the way...off the drugs. It didn't get him down, either; he would always come back again with someone new."

Hope's optimism was apparent. From my several short interactions with her, it was easy to understand the positive impact that one person may have on another: Harold on the many addicts that he had helped through the years, and now Hope on Harold.

But, despite how spirited and effective a counselor Harold was four days ago, at present he lay in bed unable to speak or move half his body. He communicated with me by squeezing my index and middle fingers which I had placed in the palm of his left hand. One squeeze meant yes, two squeezes meant no.

"Do you know where you are, Harold?" I asked.

One squeeze.

"Do you know who this woman is?" I looked in Hope's direction.

One squeeze.

"Are you in pain, Harold?"

Two squeezes.

"Do you know what happened?"

Two squeezes.

"You had a stroke."

A pause and then one weak squeeze as his eyes drifted to Hope.

And so began what we expected would be a long recovery for Harold. The most important aspect of this care, though, was clearly Hope, his wife. She had been his inspiration to get clean ten years ago, and her optimism and dedication were now going to get Harold through this crisis.

As I checked on Harold this Christmas Eve, I noticed Hope was in a particularly good mood.

"He seems like he is getting better; he smiled at me today," she beamed.

"I think he has improved a bit," I responded with a cautious tone.

"He has Hope," she said with a grin.

I caught her eye, and she giggled.

Hope and I talked till visiting hours were over, and then she kissed Harold goodbye, wished me a Merry Christmas, and said she would be back in the morning.

At a few minutes past midnight, the ICU nurses put out a remarkable cornucopia of food to celebrate Christmas. Fresh-cut vegetables, spinach dip in a bread bowl, lasagna, several salads, and the proverbial bucket of Kentucky Fried Chicken were all neatly arranged on a festive tablecloth in the nurses' break room. The ICU, save for Harold Brown and two other patients, was completely empty and uncommonly quiet. (It always strikes me as a curious phenomenon that patients who are sick enough to be in the ICU during the year are miraculously better and eager to be discharged home by their willing doctor around the holidays. I guess it speaks to the healing powers of the anticipation of family and home—if not to the desire of the overworked physician to have the holiday off.) Either way, the peacefulness of the ICU was welcome, and it allowed the nurses, my senior resident, and me to have an uninterrupted early Christmas dinner.

After celebrating, several nurses, my senior, and I lazily sat talking in the nurses' station. On quiet nights like this, one usually heads off to bed to catch up on needed sleep. Tonight, however, perhaps on account of the festiveness of the holiday, we stayed up and talked into the early morning. But as the hours passed and the soft, monotonous voices of the others droned on, my eyelids grew heavy and I fell asleep.

I was in the middle of a dream when I was awakened by my senior's sharp voice. As I struggled out of my grogginess I could see that she was looking at me with concern. I focused more closely and realized that she was actually looking past me at the nursing station's cardiac monitor. As I swiveled my chair around, she yelled, "He's bradying down!" As my senior raced past me I could see Harold Brown's heart rate had dropped to thirty beats per minute.

I followed my senior, along with several nurses converging from all directions, into Harold's room. The cardiac monitor above Harold's head showed the same agonal rhythm.

"Do you want to run this code?" my senior asked looking at me.

"Yeah," I said, my voice conveying my apprehension.

"Call the code," I said to the nurse at the head of the bed. She hit the "Code Blue" button below the monitor as another nurse pulled opened Harold's nightgown, exposing his thin chest and the three monitoring wires.

"We need someone to bag," I said.

The nurse at the head of the bed, who had already assembled the resuscitation bag and mask, rotated the knob on the oxygen regulator producing a loud hiss. In a fluid motion she clamped the mask tight against his face, muffling the sound. Her right hand squeezed the large, green, oxygen-filled bag and the flutter valve belched out its reassuring sound. Harold's chest rose.

"What is his heart rate?" I asked.

"Twenty-seven," one of the nurses responded nervously.

"Is that the monitor or his pulse?" I asked looking at the nurse checking his femoral pulse.

"They're the same," she said.

"Give him one milligram of atropine," I said.

The nurse popped open the vial, attached the syringe, and pushed the clear fluid into his arm. "One of atropine in," she said.

We all watched the monitor hoping the powerful cardiac medication would stimulate his heart. The thin, green line which is the tracing of his heartbeat showed the same occasional wave, and then went flat.

"Asystole," the recording nurse yelled.

"Start chest compressions!" I responded.

The nurse taking his pulse stepped up, intertwined her fingers, placing the heal of her hand between his nipples. Her first several compressions were the audible snaps of his ribs breaking off his sternum. Her nervousness at being at her first code showed, she was compressing his chest at a rate of over one hundred and fifty times a minute.

"Slow down a bit," I coached. "Someone check the strength of his pulse."

"It's good," the nurse at his pulse said.

"Let's give him one milligram of epinephrine."

"One of 'Epi' going in," she said.

"OK, let's keep doing what we're doing," I said trying to buy myself some time to think. In my head I was frantically trying to go over all of the many algorithms we use in cardiac arrests, but my mind was too tired.

"Let's go over this so we're not missing anything," I said more for myself than anyone else in the room. "We got an airway, but he's not intubated," I said checking with the nurse at the head of the bed.

My senior interrupted, "We can intubate him later."

"How are the chest compressions?" I asked turning to the nurse on his pulse.

"They're good," she responded.

"And we have good IV access," I said to calm myself. "Let's stop the compressions and see what we've got."

The nurse at his chest paused. The monitor showed a heart tracing that looked like the haphazard waves children send down a jump rope, the electrical equivalent of a heart quivering ineffectively in place.

"Ventricular fibrillation," my senior said.

"Let's shock him," I responded nervously, "Two hundred joules."

The nurse who had stopped compressing his chest took the paddles from the defibrillator and placed one on his sternum and one under his left breast. We waited for what seemed eternity for the defibrillator to charge.

"Charged," the nurse yelled in time with the defibrillator's beep.

"Everyone clear," another nurse shouted.

Everyone moved away from the bed and a chorus of, "Clear," was heard.

The nurse simultaneously squeezed the red buttons on the end of each paddle sending a current of electricity through Harold's heart. His body flinched. The heart rate tracing on the monitor momentarily went chaotic from the overload of electricity. We watched it clear and the same haphazard wave pattern came across the screen.

"What do we have?" I asked looking at the monitor.

"Looks like V-fib still," someone said.

"Give him one of 'Epi' and shock him at three hundred and sixty joules," I said while resuming the chest compressions myself.

The nurse with the paddles dialed three-hundred and sixty joules into the defibrillator and we waited for it to charge. The nurse at the head of the bed continued ventilating while another nurse pushed the epinephrine into his arm.

"Ready," the nurse said.

"Everybody clear!" my senior intoned.

We all stepped back, and the nurse discharged the paddles into Mr. Brown's chest. His upper torso jumped from the jolt of electricity. The screen cleared and someone yelled, "V-fib again!"

"Let's give him one of atropine and then shock him at three hundred and sixty joules again," I countered with rising apprehension.

We continued CPR while the defibrillator charged. I looked at my senior for support. She looked at the screen.

"Ready," the nurse said.

"Clear," I shouted.

Everyone in a choreographed move cleared the bed, and the nurse shocked Mr. Brown again. His spine arched as if he was having a seizure, and then settled back on the bed. I looked at the monitor.

"Asystole," I uttered. "Come on Harold, nobody dies on Christmas." A queasy feeling had entered my stomach. I looked at the nurse at his IV site, "Give him another epinephrine." I resumed chest compressions and looked again at my senior. This time all I got was a blank stare. After a couple of minutes I stopped the chest compressions and looked at the screen.

"It looks like V-fib again," I said with mounting frustration. "Give him one more of 'Epi' and another shock."

The nurse stepped up and shocked him again. He arched off the bed again and then settled back. The smell of burning skin was starting to fill the room.

A nurse then yelled, "V-Tach!"

Harold's heart, in response to the powerful stimulants, had gone from quivering to now beating at such a high rate that it could not effectively pump blood to the rest of his body. We were going to have to try to control the rate with medication, as well as defibrillating it back into a normal rhythm.

"Give him one hundred milligrams of lidocaine and shock him again with three hundred and sixty joules," I yelled.

The nurse stepped up again, placed the paddles on what now were two well demarcated burn marks on his chest and defibrillated him. He jumped once again and settled back, and then his heart stopped all together.

"Asystole," the nurse said with resignation.

I looked at my senior to see how much longer we should let this go on; she gave me no answer.

"Continue CPR and give him another 'Epi' and one of 'Bi-carb,'" I said forcefully.

I continued chest compressions while the nurse pushed the medicines into his arm. Two minutes later I stopped compressions and looked at the monitor.

"Hey!" I exclaimed with hope. "That looks like a normal rhythm—slow, but normal."

The tension in the room eased.

The nurse at his abdomen quickly went between his two femoral pulses. "There is no pulse," she said nervously.

I reached down to his groin and searched for his pulse, there was none. He was in pulseless electrical activity, a condition where the heart is putting out electrical signals but not contracting.

"Damn it! Give him one of 'Epi' and one of atropine," I said urgently as I resumed chest compressions. After another two minutes, I again stopped and looked at the monitor. The sawtooth pattern of ventricular tachycardia moved across the screen.

"He is in 'V-Tach' again," my senior said.

"All right, give him another 'Epi' and shock him again," I exclaimed with rising desperation.

The nurse shocked him again, and we looked at the monitor.

"Still in 'V-Tach,'" my senior said.

"One more 'Epi' and one more shock," I countered quickly.

The nurse shocked him again and we all looked at the monitor.

"Asystole," the nurse said with resolve.

I continued chest compression. My arms and back ached, and my body was wet with perspiration.

The recording nurse cleared her throat, paused, and then said timidly, "Doctor, are you going to call the code?"

I ignored her and continued compressing Harold's chest.

After a few more minutes the recording nurse said more assuredly, "Doctor, are you going to call the code?"

"How long has it been?" I asked wearily.

"Twenty-five minutes."

I stopped the chest compressions and looked up. The heart monitor displayed a flat green line and whined a constant tone. I looked at the line several moments, hoping that even one faint wave of life would ripple across its flatness, but none came. I looked at Harold's face, it was pale and his lips had a tinge of blue. His eyelids were slightly open; his pupils were dilated and fixed. His gaze was upward and beyond us, to a place he already was.

The nurse at his pulse shifted and then spoke with consolation, "There's no pulse, are you going to call the code?"

I nodded.

"Code called at 04:47," the recording nurse said.

Someone behind me exhaled slowly, and several nurses quietly left the room. The nurse at the head of the bed gently passed her hand across Harold's face closing his eyes. Another nurse pulled a clean white sheet up to his chin. The recording nurse wrote in her chart. The room was quiet except for the monitor's constant dull tone.

I reached up and turned the monitor off. The monitor's tone disappeared instantly, but the thin green line—the line of Mr. Brown's life that ended at 4:47 but stretched back into the past, back through his work as a drug and alcohol counselor, back through his daughter's seven years of life, back further still, through his troubled days as a drug and alcohol user, still further back through his childhood growing up in a housing project on the West Side, all the way back to his beginning and the thin line of life that was the connection between him and his mother some fifty-three years ago—the green line glowed defiantly on the screen, perhaps as an affirmation of life, and then slowly faded.

I pronounced Mr. Brown dead.

I walked out of the room, and the charge nurse informed me that Harold Brown's family was in the waiting room. They had been called at home when we started CPR on Harold. They now sat anxiously waiting for some good news.

The best part of being a family doctor is in the victories, those moments when you have made positive influences on someone's life, whether they are as momentous as delivering a healthy baby to an emotional mom and dad, or those occasions when you sit in your clinic examining room, for what seems to be an infinite amount of time, trying to make a connection with a suicidal teenager who believes only that he has a finite amount of time to live, or those mundane moments helping elderly patients make sense of their many medications. Those are the types of victories that make being a family doctor so enjoyable. What I had to do now was the worst part of the job.

I walked to the family waiting room with a dry mouth, quickened pulse, and an unsettled feeling in my stomach. I am struck by the similarity in feelings I have at these moments with the ones that I used to have before walking out on stage. The moment before each is the same. The audience is in their place, I enter the still and darkened stage, find my mark, the spotlight slowly brightens, everyone is completely still, all eyes on me, I am standing alone, with only the words I have learned so well. I start to speak, and here the similarities end. Where I was once trained to "live truthfully under imaginary circumstances," I am now forced to live truthfully under real circumstances; where I once had the security of the actor's "fourth wall," I now have only insecurities; where I once had a well rehearsed monologue, I now have an improvised dialogue.

I looked at Ms. Brown and started slowly, "Ms. Brown, I'm sorry..." I didn't get a chance to finish.

"NO!" she screamed. "Tell me my baby's OK!"

I shook my head, "I'm sorry...."

The room exploded, people running everywhere, bodies slamming down to the ground, wails of anguish, cries that come only from deep within. The senior went to a family member who lay motionless on the floor, overcome with emotion. The chaplain took another family member in her arms.

Ms. Brown slid down onto the floor from her chair, looked at me, and screamed, "No, you told me he was getting better; you said he was going to be all right!"

I went to her, "Ms. Brown, we tried, but his heart was so weak."

She rolled into the fetal position and moaned, "This is not happening, this is not happening to me!" I rubbed her back in an awkward attempt to comfort her.

A moment later she sat straight up, started to pinch herself, and repeated over and over again, "I'm not here, I'm in a dream, I'm dreaming right now, I'm not here."

I tried to soothe her with words, but I had forgotten my lines and chose only silence. Ms. Brown was now mumbling an incoherent monologue; I was now the audience.

After several minutes Ms. Brown jumped to a standing position, looked above, and screamed, "God, why on Christmas? Why did you take my Harold on Christmas, God? I loved you! How could you do this to me, God?" At the end of her breath she broke down and sobbed.

One of her friends came over and helped me sit Ms. Brown in a chair. She wrapped her arms around her and softly repeated, "It's going to be all right."

"How am I going to tell my baby?" Ms. Brown moaned.

"It's going to be all right."

"I can't tell her he died on Christmas."

"It's going to be all right."

"Why, God?"

"It's going to be all right."

After a few moments the chaplain came over to console; she looked at me and nodded, allowing me to take my leave.

I walked away from the anguish, back towards the emotional safety of the nursing station. Overhead the smooth voice of Nat King Cole singing "Silent Night" was joined in an unlikely duet with the heart wrenching moans of Ms. Brown. I walked until Ms. Brown's cry was distant and faded, and all I could hear was the serenity of "Silent Night."

I entered the nursing station and let my body sag into a chair. I laid my head down on the table but knew that I would not sleep. My mind was racing, and my stomach was in a knot. A moment later the knot tightened, a wave of nausea overcame me and my mouth filled with saliva. I ran to the bathroom and threw up—and then the tears.

After some time I collected myself. I left the bathroom and walked down to the first floor, slipping out an emergency exit. The frigid December air felt good on my wet skin. I leaned up against the cold, steel door and let myself down to the frozen ground. My warm breath, white with frost, danced in the first slivers of morning light that had slipped through the trees to the east. A distant church bell announced that it was Christmas. I closed my eyes, took a long exhale, and then breathed in the new day.

■ ■ ■

My encounter with Hope Brown over the death of Harold was emotionally draining. Several months earlier I had felt a degree of frustration from having missed a meaningful social interaction with Baby X's mother. However, having just experienced a very dramatic family interaction, I could now begin to appreciate why some attendings portray a cool professional manner and choose to avoid emotionally loaded doctor-patient and doctor-family interactions.

To help my fellow family medicine interns and me process these draining encounters, our training program had two monthly support groups, a Balint group and a group lunch with one of our social workers. Our Balint group was modeled on the Balint Society in England, which endeavors to help general practitioners understand more fully the emotional makeup of the doctor-patient relationship. These faculty-facilitated discussions were case-based and centered on the patients and care that the interns had found to be particularly trying, emotionally and otherwise. The two attendings tried their best to give each intern a chance to work through difficult experiences, but with a class of twelve interns, we were like an oversized litter trying to get some nourishment. The less forceful interns, like the runts of the litter, were pushed out of the way and never debriefed. Two months into these sessions, many of us were so busy on the floors we never went back.

The intern group lunch meetings, however, were more successful, partly because our seniors took our pagers for an hour, thus shielding us from their constant tonal announcement of more work. These lunches were relaxing and a time to decompress. The social worker, often silent, allowed the discussion to go where it might, and this lunch hour often became our time to support each other. But one hour of support each month is woefully inadequate. And at the end of each support group the stress of our internship came crashing back upon us, often in the form of our beepers being handed back to us with pages needing to be answered.

This inescapable and unrelenting stress interns are subjected to is compounded when they have to attend to personal or family matters during that demanding first year of training. I remember joking at graduation with a fellow fourth year medical student about how it seemed we were joining the Peace Corps and were being assigned to some remote area of the world! We determined to get all our personal needs (including eye, dental, and medical exams) completed before the internship commenced, knowing full well that our future schedules would afford little time for such matters. I specifically recall hoping that my immediate family members would stay healthy so I could avoid any additional pressures.

And added to these time constraints was the self-imposed pressure that nags beginning interns. We wanted to avoid any emergency time off, knowing that already overworked fellow interns would be called upon to fill a sudden gap in the schedule. We could only imagine what the added stress of the exacting internships in surgery or obstetrics and gynecology was like, where the resident has even less time to debrief or reflect on professional and personal traumas.

Clearly, there is room in medical education and residency training to improve the way we monitor and debrief our doctors-in-training, who at times can be under enormous stress. Giving these individuals an adequate amount of time and space—as well as support—to process their challenging experiences will benefit them and their future patients.

NINE

Dr. Martin Milioni

December 31

Being in a profession like medicine, in which the hierarchy of the system is paramount, an intern is subjected to excruciating hours, innumerable nights on call, as well as being at the bottom of the pecking order for having holidays off. This year I had to work both Christmas Eve and New Year's Eve. Although I was not excited about taking call on two consecutive holidays, I was somewhat intrigued to be working in the ICU as our nation entered the new millennium.

For over a year, the nation's newspapers and media had run stories about the potential detrimental effect entering the new millennium would have on all of our computers. These speculative, and sometimes spectacular, news stories painted scenarios of traffic lights not working, computers freezing up, and even planes falling out of the sky at the stroke of midnight. As hospital employees, short of one of those falling planes hitting our hospital, we were more concerned with our life-support equipment failing.

To this end, to make everything year 2000 (Y2K) compliant, our hospital's electricians worked overtime for months on end to ensure that every piece of our hospital's electrical equipment would glide smoothly into the new millennium. Each piece of equipment that passed the electricians' rigorous tests was anointed with an orange sticker embossed in bold, black letters with Y2K.

In an amazing show of overkill, every piece of electrical equipment, right down to the toasters in our hospital's cafeteria, had a Y2K sticker placed on it before the New Year. Now, why we needed to make sure that the toasters worked the morning of New Year's Day is anybody's guess. Perhaps it had once been shown that a patient had an early demise after eating untoasted hospital bread. Keeping with the spirit of safety, and in my continual effort to portray an image of confidence, I placed a Y2K sticker on my name tag next to my photo to allay any of my patients' fears that I would crash come the midnight hour.

Regardless of the thousands of orange stickers that were placed in our hospital and the reassurance they brought, it still did not stop our ICU staff from planning what emergency actions we would take if the life-support equipment stopped working. After a few worst-case-scenario drills, several of us gathered in front of a TV and watched Peter Jennings on ABC as he attempted to ring in the new millennium for all twenty-four time zones around the globe. He was eighteen time zones into this act of brazen bravado, and he looked terrible. His speech was slurred and his eyes, heavy with sleep, were half closed. He even joked about his inability to drive a car home after work. He looked like us at the end of one of our thirty-six-hour shifts. And I do not think that he would care to be on the roads when we drove ourselves home.

As it had been during the Christmas holiday, the ICU was empty that night, save for a lone gentleman in room 5438. We were thankful for the low census count, if not for the minimum amount of work we would have to do, then for the available personnel we would have if indeed there was a crisis at midnight. In this unusually quiet period, I took the opportunity to meet our only ICU patient. His name was Martin Milioni, an impressive eighty-eight-year-old, thin, white gentleman, who, interestingly enough, was a family physician. He had worked a good portion of this century, and now, near the end of his life and in the waning hours of our aged century, it seemed only fitting for him to be cared for by a family physician who was at the beginning of his career.

Four years ago he had all but diagnosed himself—one of the curses of being a doctor—with cancer. He was well aware of the initial thin, bloody stools, and then the fatigue and weight loss: his demon unmasking itself. After surgery, radiation, and multiple chemotherapy treatments, his body was still not rid of the colon cancer. Knowing well this cancer from the other side, and now having to suffer its onslaught, he decided to retire a few years ago, as he put it, "to make the most out of what I have left."

Quite optimistic, I thought. Optimism, however, was not what I, or any of the other interns, felt in this the sixth month of our intern year. Both physically and emotionally we were overworked, tired, and now often wondering aloud why we had gone into this grueling and often unforgiving profession. In this emotional state, I sat down on the chair next to the head of his bed and asked, with obvious sarcasm in my voice, if he liked being a family doctor.

To my surprise, this tired, pale, and emaciated gentleman talked for over an hour about how much he loved his job, enchanting me with several stories of his more memorable patients, each a telling confirmation of his career choice. More compelling than the content of each story, was the enthusiasm with which he spoke, and even now, after sixty years of work and close to death, he still longed to practice medicine. His passion for the profession from the first labored words he spoke was straight and true. And as his words gathered momentum and flowed into sentences, a small eddy of hope began to flow in me, gathering by hour's end into a current of optimism.

Dr. Milioni was a tonic at just the right time. Our ICU months were unusually tough, and the lack of sleep had taken its toll on our bodies and spirits. Interns traditionally have little time to rest, and even less time to regroup after intense and draining experiences. We are forced to keep going, long after the body has started to shut down and the mind has numbed. Never fully able to relax while on call because there is always the patient in the next room who needs our attention and our beepers are just a few seconds away from announcing more work, we long for our time away from the hospital. But those short periods when we are not on call or tethered to our pagers are not refreshing either, because of the exhaustion and stress built up from the many on-call shifts. Like Harold Brown's failing heart, I, too, felt that I was failing both physically and emotionally, the inhumane hours and many sad outcomes having taken their toll. However, Dr. Milioni's fervor for his vocation, even after all these years, was uplifting and his spirit inspiring. He had been through rough times just like those I had experienced, perhaps even rougher, and had even mentioned his own struggle to finish his intern year. But he did finish. And now, more than sixty years later, nearing the final finish, he lay in bed radiating love of this tough profession.

And in some subtle way, which I did not realize until later, Dr. Milioni had, either consciously or not, flipped our roles, assuming his proverbial place as the comforter; he was once again the doctor, and I now the patient, my sputtering soul boosted by his sage advice and reassuring presence. Dr. Milioni, as I was coming to realize about many of my patients, had given me more than I could return.

■ ■ ■

During residency, our long work hours and frequency on call were a constant conversation piece for all residents, but especially interns, since we were the residents subjected to the toughest schedule. But more than just a subject about which we vented our frustrations to each other, our inhumane work environment was a topic of concern that several of my fellow interns and I continually voiced to our administration. On a hospital level our small band of outspoken interns was just a mirror of what had already begun on the national level fifteen years earlier. And on July 1, 2003, the Accreditation Council for Graduate Medical Education's (ACGME) new work-hour rules took effect.

These rules state that a resident must not work more than 80 hours a week (averaged over a four-week period), must have one day off for every seven days worked (again averaged over a four-week period), and must have ten hours off between shifts. In addition, a resident cannot be on call more often than every third night (again averaged over a four-week period) nor be continuously on duty for more than 30 hours.[1]

To a casual observer, these new work hours probably still seem extreme. Indeed, do these limitations go far enough? With the flexibility to average over a four-week period a resident's hours and frequency on call, there is ample latitude for residents to be overworked in any given week; for example, residents still can be on call every second night and end up working over 100 hours. In addition, the ACGME allows residency programs to apply for exemptions to the new work rules, enabling training programs to increase residents work hours an additional 10 percent.

What these rules have done, however, is to inhibit residency programs from working interns and residents over 100 hours for months on end, a common practice in the past and one, thankfully, that has been precluded by the new guidelines. In addition, a marked redistribution of the workload can be discerned. Traditionally, in teaching hospitals interns disproportionately worked longer hours and were on call more frequently than senior residents. Every intern, as did I, looked forward to the end of the intern year, not only for the added prestige of being a senior resident but also for a more humane schedule. However, with these changes, which benefit first-year interns, many residency programs have been forced to redistribute the workload, increasing the number of hours and nights on call allocated to senior residents (and sometimes attendings). Not surprisingly, this change has generated considerable irritation, since more than a few feel that they have already paid their dues.

From my perspective, the work hour changes are beneficial. Interns, who staff the front lines in the hospital, will now be more rested, increasing the quality of their lives and enabling them to learn more effectively and to offer safer care.[2] Another more subtle reason is that the new rules will force interns, residents, and attendings to share the workload more equitably, hopefully eroding some of the entrenched hierarchy and entitlements that have characterized the delivery of medical care in teaching hospitals.

Having served on several committees that studied work hours during my residency and having closely followed the issue nationally, I applaud these work-hour changes—long in the making and not easily won. The first rumblings of change could be discerned in 1984. Amy Braverman wrote about the problems of resident work hours in the October 2002 edition of the University of Chicago Magazine:

> In March 1984, 18-year-old Libby Zion was admitted to Cornell Medical Center's New York Hospital emergency room with a high fever, chills, and dehydration. A few hours later, under the care of residents, she died. Her father, a New York Times columnist and former federal prosecutor, called for a grand jury investigation. In its 1986 report, the grand jury found neither hospital nor physicians at fault. It did cite the residency and physician-

training systems as potential dangers: New York Hospital residents routinely worked more than 100 hours a week; second-and third-year residents supervised entire wards and services, with attending physicians available only by phone; and residents provided patient care for 30 or 40 hours at a stretch.

In 1987 New York's health commissioner appointed a committee to study the grand jury's findings. Calling for 24-hour supervision of residents in acute-inpatient units, the committee also recommended limits on resident duty hours—including 80-hour workweeks, 24-hour shifts, and at least one day off per week. When the recommendations became state law in 1989, the state provided $200 million for hospitals to hire additional aides and board-certified physicians to maintain service.

Adding to the reform movement's ammunition was a barrage of sleep deprivation research. In a 1991 *Journal of the American Medical Association* survey of 145 residents, 41 percent cited fatigue as a cause of their most serious mistake. A July-August 1997 *Nature* report found that staying awake for 24 hours impairs thought processes as much as does a blood-alcohol level of 0.1 percent—higher than many states' legal driving limits. A study in the March 2002 *Annals of Internal Medicine* showed that three-fourths of residents at the University of Washington suffered from burnout, emotional exhaustion or detachment from patients. Other studies linked resident schedules to increased car accidents, mental health problems, and pregnancy complications.

The clincher came in 1999 when the Institute of Medicine, associated with the National Academy of Sciences, reported that medical errors might play a role in 44,000 to 98,000 deaths a year. In the public outcry that followed, the American Medical Student Association (AMSA) approached Rep. John Conyers, D-Mich., about proposing legislation based on the New York regulations. The bill now has more than 70 cosponsors in the House and a companion bill in the Senate.

Public scrutiny mounted last year when the medical students' association, along with the Committee of Interns and Residents (a union created in 1999) and Ralph Nader's group Public Citizen, submitted a petition to the Occupational Safety and Health Administration calling for duty-hour limits.

Because many in the medical community are loath to submit to government guidelines, the legislative threat was a major catalyst for the ACGME's proposals, says the group's executive director, David Leach.[3]

The ACGME did not engage the issue until faced with the threat of federal legislation drafted to deal with the problem of intolerable work schedules, and it was frustrating to see how long it took the ACGME to address this issue properly. Subsequently, the Occupational Safety and Health Administration (OSHA) turned down the residents' petition to regulate work hours, stating that ACGME is the appropriate governing body to oversee residents' work hours. In passing it should be noted that the federal legislation for resident work hours sponsored by Representative Conyers is now in a House subcommittee on health, and the companion bill in the Senate is in a subcommittee on finance. Neither bill has made it to the floor of Congress for debate or vote.

My hospital did not take our residents' proposals for fewer work hours seriously until an effort to unionize was initiated. As a result of our campaign, the hospital implemented the ACGME's new work-hour regulations nine months before its official start date.

During my involvement with these work-hour issues, I continued to reflect on the level of resistance shown by our hospital administration. Given salaries of approximately $30,000 to $40,000 per year, residents provide a low cost labor force and any restructuring of hours would put pressure on the bottom line. Moreover, the profession of medicine is deeply rooted in tradition, and overworking and undercompensating residents have been normal practices for over a century, which is why changing them has not been easy.

But resistance has also come from attendings who firmly believe that the work-hour changes will be detrimental to residents and their professional development, as well as more generally to the field of medicine. Many of the attendings I spoke with gave thoughtful answers based on their concern for the resident's educational experience, believing that residents need to train under difficult and exhausting conditions to enable them to respond appropriately to extraordinary situations or crises. They argue that being awakened in the middle of the night and having to perform in a groggy state is good training, teaching the resident to cope effectively with such emergencies in the future. But no research supports this theory. In fact, a significant body of evidence shows that sleep deprivation decreases one's cognitive ability, and a growing body of literature demonstrates that sleep deprivation also impairs one's motor ability.[4]

Another concern voiced by attendings is that the resident work-hour changes will be disruptive to the continuity of care that the patient receives. The attending doctors fear that resident doctors working fewer continuous hours, and subsequently transferring the care of their patients to other doctors more often, could possibly increase the chance that an error in the care of the patient could occur. Having only eight hour shifts instead of twenty-four or thirty-six hour shifts will indeed increase the number of different providers working with a patient. But I have seen no literature that suggests that patients having more frequently changed providers—and rested ones at that—has ever been detrimental to care.

Other concerns of the attendings I queried related to whether reduced work hours would allow residents the time needed to see a disease process through to its completion, and whether shortened hours would allow residents to master the vast amount of material that must be assimilated during their training. To the first concern, my answer is that there is no disease process that I know which progresses to completion within a predictable time frame. A resident who works under the present ACGME work-hour rules—still an immense number of hours—will indeed see and learn the pathology of disease processes. To the second concern, during my residency there came a time, roughly near the end of my second year, when I felt comfortable managing the majority of the disease processes that I encountered. Repetition certainly improves the ability to perform at a higher level, but how much repetition is required to master a skill is unknown. Future study may be needed on the subject, but I do feel that future doctors graduating from our country's residency programs will be as skilled and competent as the doctors who were trained before them.

Now that I am an attending, I understand more fully the thought process of attendings who want to maximize the learning experience of interns and residents. However, we must not forget how difficult our schedules were, and we need to question the value of such exhausting work hours. I believe it is imperative that we continually press for more humane working conditions for our residents. It will demonstrate that we, their supervising doctors, respect and care for them as people as well as interns and residents. This powerful and compassionate role modeling, I believe, will in turn make them more empathic and concerned doctors.

■   ■   ■

A few minutes before midnight, buoyed with hopefulness, I left Dr. Milioni's bedside and the old millennium and walked to the roof of our hospital. I met the other residents on call, and we toasted the new millennium, drinking grape juice from plastic champagne glasses as we watched the panorama of fireworks dot the midnight sky, and listened to the residents of the West Side of Chicago fire off their guns in celebration. The turn of the clock to year 2000 had come with nary a hint of a plane falling out of the sky or any equipment failure in our hospital.

I went to my call room and had a rare uninterrupted night of sleep. The next morning I went back to the ICU to check on Dr. Milioni. The nurse had placed an oxygen mask on him during the night and he looked peaceful. With a bright smile that belied his exhaustion, he wished me a Happy New Year, and I the same to him. I took his thin, bony hand in mine, and I thanked him for being who he was. And in an awkwardness that I have come to expect in end-of-life moments, I told him I hoped I would see him again. I signed out to the oncoming intern and went home refreshed for the first time in months.

I never knew what came to pass with Dr. Milioni. In all honesty, I could have inquired about him, but I did not; I did not want to hear what I already suspected. But I cannot help thinking that on that last night of the century, I met my guardian angel.

■ ■ ■

Dr. Milioni was one of the few patients that I took care of during my intern year who had healthcare insurance. Even though this insurance would not save him from dying of colon cancer, it did allow him to receive timely medical treatments when he was first diagnosed, and enabled him to live the remaining years of his life to the most satisfying and fullest extent possible, without the worry of large medical bills. I have seen too many patients and their families forced to spend the precious last moments of their loved one's life agonizing about how the medical bills will be paid. Dr. Milioni and his family were not so burdened.

TEN

Cutting through Stereotypes

February 5, 2000

Rotating on a surgical service involves a number of responsibilities ranging from the much-coveted "first assist," giving you the privilege to cut and suture in the operating room, to the less desirable (and non-educational) "scut," or gopher, work of finding lost X-rays and pulling surgical drains on patients waiting to be discharged. Of all the rotations in medical training, surgery is the most hierarchical, with the chief resident being at the top, the remaining residents next in decreasing order of seniority, and the medical students at the bottom. They also have been notorious for having the longest hours, the greatest amount of work, and least welcoming attendings and residents.

My surgery rotation during my intern year, however, was far less "malignant" than my surgery rotations during my third year of medical school. To this day I distinctly remember stepping onto the floors of my teaching hospital for the first time as a very green and nervous third-year medical student. Three other third-year students and I had chosen surgery as our first rotation because we had heard, "beginning third year medical students are not expected to know anything," an accurate reflection of my knowledge level at that time. In addition, none of us were interested in pursuing a surgical residency; we would wait to do the rotation of our calling, family, pediatric, and internal medicine, until later in the year when our increasing knowledge level would impress the attending who would write our much-needed letters of recommendation for residency placement.

Our medical school was a rarity in that our dean was a family physician. Most medical colleges reserve this important position for medical doctors who are specialists or internal medicine physicians. It is a highly coveted appointment and carries an enormous amount of influence, not only within the academic section of the hospital, but also within the larger medical center itself. From this position of authority, our dean had been able to influence the medical school's first-and second-year curriculum to include a substantial amount of information about, and thus emphasis on, primary care, a subject that many medical colleges do not stress. The course took the form of a mentorship with a primary care doctor during the first two years of training. Each medical student was paired with a family physician, pediatrician, or internal medicine physician on a regular basis at an outpatient office. The goal was to ground each medical student in the importance of primary care, with the hope that it would entice more medical students into primary care training, specifically family medicine.

In addition, our medical school, at the urging of a few of our very outspoken faculty members who were concerned not only with our medical school's curriculum but also with the lack of availability of healthcare for the underserved, had created an extensive volunteer outreach program through which the medical students were able to work in a variety of healthcare settings, such as homeless and women's shelters, pediatric HIV and asthma programs, halfway houses, and prisons. I took full advantage of several of these volunteer opportunities. The first was at a medical clinic in a homeless shelter in Pilsen village, a predominantly Spanish-speaking community just southwest of downtown Chicago. Right from the start, under the attending's watchful eye, we were able to examine, diagnose, and treat patients. We were medical students forced to think and act like residents, and the residents were forced to think and act like attendings. We saw and treated the full gamut of physical and mental diseases and observed firsthand the detrimental effects that substandard living conditions and lack of social services have on health. And, through our attending's modeling, we also gained valuable knowledge about ways to assure our inequitable healthcare system would work more effectively for some of our patients. The experience was an invaluable part of my medical training. In fact, no other experience, until I was well into my third year of medical school and on the floors of the hospital, furthered my understanding of clinical medicine and the art of healing more than the work that I did at this homeless shelter.

Another instructive and meaningful primary care experience I had during medical school involved my work in the Cook County Temporary Juvenile Detention Center (TJDC) through an Albert Schweitzer Urban Fellowship. The yearlong fellowship, modeled upon this great doctor's commitment to the underserved, gave students in the healthcare fields an opportunity to create and implement projects in urban settings that would provide for the healthcare needs of the disenfranchised. The TJDC, the oldest and largest juvenile detention center in the United States, with its inadequate number of activities and programs for inmates—many of whom would sit idle for days in their cell blocks—was a perfect place for me to do my fellowship. My project, which combined my interests in theatre and preventive medicine, was working with the Music Theatre Workshop, a nonprofit performing arts organization that encourages young people to create original theatrical and musical performances about their own experiences and lives. Specifically, I helped direct "Temporary Lockdown," a play which was inmate-generated and focused on issues of social interaction. A truly remarkable piece of theatre, the play was performed for parole officers, judges, and the inmates' family members.

What I learned through working on this theatrical piece was twofold. The first was the power that art holds in the rehabilitation process for inmates; namely, through the process of completing their own work of art about their own lives, the inmates gained an immense amount of self-confidence and self-esteem as they struggled to put their feelings on paper and the stage. Moreover, important communication and teamwork skills were honed, all of which are important in helping prevent these youths from falling back into their past behaviors, with the resultant unhappy and unhealthy futures.

Anthony R., at the time an inmate in TJDC and actor in "Temporary Lockdown," wrote about his experience:

"By participating in this play, I discovered that anything is possible if you put your mind to it. Putting this play together was fun, but not easy; it took lots of hard work to accomplish it. At first I thought I couldn't do it, but not only was it done, the play was successful. Knowing that I achieved what I thought I couldn't is now motivating for me to achieve anything I want in life. So, to those who will read this, always remember that nothing's impossible if you put your mind to it."

These are powerfully optimistic words coming from a young man who has not been given much to be optimistic about. Anthony R's words are a hopeful and reassuring sign that if given the opportunity, individuals can turn their lives around. Remarkably, Anthony R., and the majority of inmates who have participated in Music Theatre Workshop's theatrical pieces, have worked for and earned their GEDs. Some, while incarcerated or after release, have even continued their education and earned associate's and bachelor's degrees, and several have steady jobs and are raising families.

The second lesson my Schweitzer Fellowship taught me was that the process of healing, when done effectively, is accomplished not only in the sterile rooms of our clinics and hospitals but, in fact, in the many homeless shelters, safe houses for battered women, school-based programs, and even prisons.

My final volunteer experience was with a gang tattoo removal program on the West Side of Chicago. A patient's story illustrates the work of the program.

Julio was a short, muscular twenty-year-old with bright eyes, a nice smile, and a pleasant demeanor, which belied some of the experiences that he had had for a fair portion of his life as a "gang banger" on the streets of Chicago. I met Julio at Fresh Start, an innovative tattoo removal program initiated in Chicago by Dr. John May and funded by a number of charities and foundations.

Dr. May, who has worked as a physician in the prison system for most of his professional life, noticed that people with tattoos were twice as likely to have been shot as people without tattoos. A sociologist would want to tease out what exactly the relationship is between tattoos and getting shot. Is it the lifestyle of people with gang tattoos that places them in a situation to be shot? Can you say that people with gang tattoos—especially ones who are not gang bangers anymore but still have gang tattoos and live in gang-infested neighborhoods—still continue to lead certain types of lifestyles? How much is the environment (neighborhood) contributing to these shootings? Or is it the gang tattoo itself that is the reason? Regardless, Dr. May, a practitioner at heart, cuts to the point and says that he does not care what the relationship is, "The fact of the matter is that the program is saving lives and allowing people to have a fresh start."

Julio's reason for having the four gang letters removed from the knuckles of his right hand was to help him get promoted to a "front job" at the store where he was employed. He had been working in the storeroom and wanted to be promoted to working with customers, but his supervisor informed him that he must have the tattoos removed before he could work with customers. Julio also had a woman's name removed from his chest.

Others in the program had similar job-related reasons for removing tattoos, and many, like Julio, wanted to have old girl-friends' or boyfriends' names removed. Still others had more compelling reasons—they wanted to be able to walk down the street in their neighborhoods and not be shot.

Julio also worked the graveyard shift at American Airlines in food preparation. I asked him why he was working two jobs, and he told me that he was expecting two babies, one in November and one in January. Having had a little bit of embryology by this time and being able to count nine months on a calendar, I determined he was having two babies with two different women. He added he was only seeing one at present, hence the reason he had a woman's name removed from his chest! However, he was committed to supporting both of his children, and in a world where child support is not a given, his intent was commendable.

Fresh Start charges twenty-five dollars per session to remove any and all of one's tattoos. The procedure is straightforward and encompasses simply tracing the tattoo with a laser which burns the skin and breaks up the dye in the underlying skin. Usually four sessions, evenly scheduled over a two-month period, are needed to remove a tattoo completely. The procedure can be painful, but the results are excellent. After four sessions most tattoos are completely removed without a trace of dye, and the skin is healed and indistinguishable from the surrounding skin. A few tattoo removals are only 90 percent successful, but for these tattoos the remaining dye resembles more of a minor skin blemish than a tattoo.

Incidentally, if one were to have a tattoo removed by a dermatologist, who would typically charge two hundred dollars for a one-time-only treatment of a 1 square centimeter area of tattoo, the cost would be in the thousands of dollars for the same results that Fresh Start achieves. By charging one hundred dollars, Fresh Start has made this important cosmetic procedure accessible, and, most important, it has enabled many people to move forward in life as well as helping them stay out of harm's way. This program is one of the many where primary care doctors regularly participate.

These types of volunteer opportunities were instrumental not only in attracting medical students into the field of primary care, but also in helping cultivate a healthy and respectful environment among fellow medical students for the work of primary care physicians. I felt particularly fortunate to have attended a medical school which offered such broad and diverse opportunities.

However, many of my medical school's attendings who were specialists, particularly those trained in surgery, discouraged entering a primary care field, in particular family medicine. My budding fellow family physicians and I often heard comments such as, "You're too smart to be a family physician," or, "You'll be bored after the first day in family medicine." Luckily, we medical students have healthy egos that do not bruise easily, and also strong wills. The idea that primary care, and family medicine, in particular, are "boring" is an inaccurate portrayal of the profession. Throughout medical school, residency and now my career as an attending, I have never been bored by the work that I do as a family doctor. In fact, it is quite the contrary. Every patient that I see poses unique problems which are often intellectually challenging.

■ ■ ■

Whatever the feelings that specialists may have about primary care and family medicine in particular, the fact is that too few U.S. medical school seniors are selecting these specialties (especially family medicine), and a national shortage is developing.

In the last seven years the United States has seen a steady decrease in the number of first-year family physician residency training positions offered through the National Residency Matching Program (NRMP) or the "Match." The "Match" is the selection process by which the vast majority of all first-year residency training positions are filled each year. When examining this NRMP data, an alarming trend can be seen between the years 1998 and 2005: 511 first-year family physician training positions have been eliminated (a drop of 16%).[1]

The decrease of family physician internships can be attributed in part to the Federal Balanced Budget Act of 1997, which reduced the federal funds available for medical education; the drop in states' Medicaid reimbursement to hospitals; the increasing cost of malpractice insurance; and the low priority given to training family doctors by teaching hospitals.

Also contributing to the diminished number of family doctors, is the decreasing interest in the specialty among U.S. medical school graduates, who in the 2005 "Match," filled only 41 percent of the first-year training positions in family medicine residency programs, down from a high of 73 percent nine years ago.[2] There are reasons for decreased interest in family medicine: a negative medical school culture towards the profession, the feeling that the specialty is low in prestige, an apprehension about the extent of knowledge a family physician must master, and the high cost of medical school education combined with the comparatively low salaries for family physicians (1/3 to 1/2 of other specialists).[3] Further, an increased desire among medical students for a flexible lifestyle and more control over their schedule have increased interest in specialties like radiology and anesthesiology.[4] Fortunately, foreign medical school graduates, eager to train in our excellent residency programs, fill these primary care vacancies. Even this healthcare "life raft," however, is taking on water with changes implemented by the government that make it more difficult, especially since September 11, 2001, for foreign medical graduates to obtain visas to train in this country.[5] The long-term effects of the loss of these future family physicians should concern all of us.

Primary care physicians (family medicine, internal medicine, pediatrics, and obstetrics/gynecology) treat every sector of society (especially the uninsured) and serve the health needs of more than 58 percent of Americans.[6] Family physicians handle the highest percentage (23%) of office visits in the United States, higher than any other specialty, while representing a much smaller fraction (11%) of the total number of physicians.[7] As noted by the American Academy of Family Physicians, in rural areas the dependency on family physicians is even greater; in fact, in these areas, family physicians outnumber general internists and pediatricians by 3 to 1.[8] Family physicians also see a higher percentage of racial minorities (except Native Americans) than any other specialty and disproportionately treat the underserved.[9] A study conducted by the Robert Graham Policy Center determined that if one were to remove all of the family doctors now in practice, 60 percent of the counties in the United States would instantly become M.D. deprived, or, in government terms, Primary Care Health Personnel Shortage Areas.[10]

Furthermore, given the fact that 15 percent of our citizens lack health insurance, combined with the public's increasing reliance on government insurance (Medicare and Medicaid), it is clear that our health care system cannot afford to decrease the training of the very doctors who disproportionately treat our people.[11] If we fail to correct these medical education issues, we risk developing, in the words of the American Academy of Family Physicians, "a health care delivery system that is severely compromised...limit[ing] our capacity to meet the needs of our nation's most vulnerable populations."[12]

But while there are many reasons for the decreasing number of family physician training positions, there are solutions that might correct this troublesome trend. On the very basic level, the monies that have been cut from medical education due to the Balanced Budget Act of 1997 need to be completely restored, and states, even during these tight fiscal times, need to continue to fund primary care training.

Moreover, medical school graduates should be encouraged to enter the field of family medicine by increasing federal and state scholarship money available to those who commit to the specialty. The federal government should increase more generously the number of National Health Service Corps' scholarships, which have been shown to channel medical students into primary care training and subsequently into underserved areas. Although the budget for this federal program has increased in three of the last five years, at present it can fill only 1 in 4 underserved healthcare vacancies.[13]

Foreign medical school graduates take the same medical board exams that U.S. medical school graduates do, as well as serving the underserved and minority populations in this country to a greater degree than their U.S. counterparts, so a strong case can be made for the U.S. government to simplify the visa requirements for those qualified physicians who seek training in this country.

On an institutional level, medical schools, just as my medical school has done, need to make family medicine an integral part of the curriculum; residency training programs need to continue to train as many family physicians as possible, and specialists need to realize that encouraging medical students to enter the fields of primary care, and family medicine, in particular, is vitally important for the future health of our nation.

■ ■ ■

My interest in a specialty other than surgery, which was shared by the three other medical students, was not lost on the surgery attendings and residents with whom we rotated during our first month as third-year medical students.

On our very first day we were greeted by the surgical intern, our superior for the month. It was his first day as well, and he was as green as we were. Whereas we were nervous and anxious, he was overconfident. Pacing back and forth in front of us with the demeanor of a military officer, he recited his rules to the new draftees, the most important one being, "It is the medical student's job to always make the interns and residents look good in front of the attendings." With fear etched across our faces, we nodded in unison, affirming our place in the chain of command, at the absolute bottom. His commands in the following days and weeks included all types of "scut" work, his favorite being the coffee runs that he would send us on "for the team." Quietly, we hoped our superior officer would be captured by the enemy.

Our supervisor's attitude, unfortunately, was not unusual among doctors, especially surgeons. On several occasions in the operating rooms during medical school, I have observed an irate surgeon verbally insult a resident or medical student for not answering a question correctly. But there are exceptions to any rule; the surgeons at the small community hospital where I was a resident were far more approachable and welcoming. So, too, were surgeons I worked with internationally (Africa, Cuba, and Nepal). However, operating room "humor" can be the same anywhere.

One of my first surgical patients as an intern was Ms. Jackson. I first saw her when she was already under anesthesia in the operating room having an abscess on her bottom incised and drained. I would officially meet her face to face several hours later when she awoke in her hospital room.

But, as the surgeon cut deeper and deeper into her backside to drain the pockets of pus, it seemed that the discussion in the operating room cut deeper and deeper into our own pockets of intolerance. Partway into the procedure, with the patient asleep, the surgeon, nurse, and even anesthesiologist all started to muse aloud why Ms. Jackson, who had no medical insurance, but who had a son who was a popular rap recording artist, could not pay her medical bills. One of the nurses even wryly suggested that they get the son to sell some of his many gold necklaces to pay for the operation. It was apparent from this conversation that this surgery, being done at the hospital's expense and surgical staff's time, annoyed all of them. It was also apparent to me that the dark humor or language of the surgical trade spoken behind the closed doors of the operating rooms I have been in was routine.

Regrettably, as with Sarah's public embarrassment during our surgery rotation in medical school, I choose to be silent during these less than professional moments in the OR. Why I choose silence is not absolutely clear to me yet. Perhaps once again, it was in order not to ruffle any feathers, lest the wrath of the surgeon be turned on me. Also, I figured that what I would say would not do any good; I did not feel that I would be able to change anyone's viewpoint. But, most important, I felt that I could not speak up because I was at the absolute bottom of the hierarchy of medicine and did not have a right to speak up. On reflection, I can see this is inaccurate, for one always has a right, even an obligation, to speak up. It is learning how to phrase your objection so that it does not come across as moralizing, but as informative.

Ms. Jackson, a charming African-American woman in her early fifties, had for several months prior to this surgery developed an increasing number of yeast infections. Most recently she had noticed a series of low grade fevers and a sharp pain in her bottom. A visit to the ER diagnosed a perirectal abscess, which was drained by the ER attending, and she was sent home on a week's supply of antibiotics. After another week of fevers and discomfort, realizing that her abscess was not improving, she came to our surgery service to have the infection drained properly under anesthesia.

So Ms. Jackson became one of the 3 in 1,000 Americans who each year develop type II (non-insulin dependent) diabetes. She joins the 16 million (or 5% of total Americans) that already have this chronic and devastating disease.[14] Fortunately, she came to us in the beginning stages of her disease, before she had started to develop any long-term complications. She "declared" herself a diabetic, as many others do, with her increasing number of infections. With this early detection and her own good compliance with diet and medication, she should be able to lead a normal and healthy life. To help her maximize her own good health, she needs to learn about her disease. She will be taught the signs and symptoms of hyperglycemia (high blood glucose level) as well as hypoglycemia (low blood glucose level); she will be instructed on how to check her blood sugar level twice a day and shown the importance of good nutrition and taking her medications as prescribed. In addition, she will need to have her eyes and feet checked once a year and have her blood pressure monitored closely. And even with the strictest adherence to diet and medications, there is always the very real possibility, because of the complexity of the disease, that Ms. Jackson's blood sugar level at some point will become too high or dangerously low, posing a high risk of morbidity or mortality and requiring an admission to the hospital. With all these dangers, one can begin to understand the enormous challenges that face diabetics and the physicians who care for them.

Several hours after her surgery, Ms. Jackson, despite being in some obvious pain, was awake and sitting up in bed. She looked young for her fifty-three years. Her skin was as smooth as polished marble and dark as a forest floor. Her tightly woven rows of black hair, all beginning at her forehead, arched backward along the perfect contour of her head. Her dark eyes cast warmth from her thin face. After a series of pleasantries, I told her that I needed to change her dressing; she slowly shifted her weight to help, but paused, the discomfort showing in her eyes. I told her not to worry and had the nurse administer some morphine. After a few moments, Ms. Jackson's eyelids slowly closed and she mouthed silently that she was ready.

I gently pulled the tape from her skin and then slowly peeled the dressing, thick with necrotic skin, from her backside. This revealed a one centimeter open incision that the surgeon had cut to help release the pockets of infection. Running into this incision was a thin rubber tube that reemerged from another incision cut several centimeters above the first. The two ends of the rubber tube had been tied, forming a loop that tracked under the skin, to help her abscess drain and prevent the epidermis from closing before the underlying tissue healed. I took two long Q-tips and with a stream of hydrogen peroxide reamed her wound clean of stagnant pus and dried blood. The stench was thick in the air and my eyes watered behind my mask. I turned my face, took a breath of fresh air, and then rinsed her wound with sterile saline. I finished by placing a large, clean dressing on her back, taping it snugly.

Three times a day for the next four days Ms. Jackson and I went through this same ritual. And each day our idle chat lasted a little longer before she would ease into a morphine-induced pain-free state, my signal to change her dressing. During these brief snippets of conversation, she mentioned with pride her son's successful recording career. Even though I do not listen to rap music and would be hard pressed to name even one rap star, I must admit that my interest heightened each time she talked about her son. The day before her discharge, overflowing with excitement, she told me that her son was taking time off from his busy recording schedule and returning to Chicago to care for her. In fact, he was coming to the hospital the following day to have me teach him how to care for her wounds. My interest piqued at this point. After the initial thrill I felt about the prospect of meeting this popular musician subsided, I reminded myself that I needed to keep my professionalism intact and not be swayed into giving Ms. Jackson or her son any special treatment just because he was a VIP.

That evening, as I thought about my upcoming encounter with this rap artist, I started to have stereotypes form in my mind, just as our surgical team had three days prior. I imagined a long limousine pulling up to the hospital's entrance and a jewelry-laden, tattooed, young man stepping out to be quickly whisked up the back elevators by his entourage to his mother's room. I even thought about putting the wound care instructions into a rap, if not to jump-start my recording career, then at least to amuse him.

Imagination has a way of taking over reality, and I checked mine before it was too late. I did meet her son the next day. He came to his mother's room, alone, and through the main elevators. He was not wearing any jewelry, funky hat, or baggy pants. He did not even wear sunglasses to hide from the row of gazing nurses that had been waiting for him all day; he was just a tall, broad-shouldered, well groomed young man with a soft voice and warm smile.

Admittedly being a little nervous, I stumbled on a few of my first words. (I did not attempt a rap.) I explained to him the proper way to clean and dress a wound. He listened intently, thanked me with a businesslike handshake, and told me he would do a good job. Kissing his smiling mother on the forehead, he left quickly after his lesson.

It is a humbling experience for anyone to clean a person's perirectal abscess. I imagine that it is even more humbling for a son to do it for his mother. And I assume that Ms. Jackson's son, being a successful rap star, could have easily paid a chorus of homecare nurses to care for his mother. But, instead, he chose to take time from his busy and lucrative recording career to care for his mother himself.

After being discharged from the hospital, Ms. Jackson visited me at my clinic every week for the next two months for inspection of her abscess and blood sugar checks. At each visit she would show me her exquisitely detailed food diary and blood sugar readings, diligently taken three times a day. She so impressed me with her dedication that I entrusted her with my pager number, allowing her to contact me anytime with questions about her blood glucose level. In the beginning she paged me on a regular basis, and then less as she became more knowledgeable about her disease and medications. She never missed a clinic appointment and healed faster than any of my patients with similar diabetic wounds. She also made a point at each visit to mention the wonderful job her son was doing with her dressing changes. I joked with her that perhaps her son might consider a career change.

As a patient, Ms. Jackson affirmed for me why I had become a doctor. She is the quintessential patient who allows me to use my interests in healthcare and education in a profession where I am able to see fairly immediate results of my work. She is motivated, which makes my job infinitely easier, and she is of a diverse and underserved population, which gives my work added meaning. In addition, she and her rap star son dispelled all of the stereotypes that had been spoken—or even surmised.

*Life flight coming into the Sertung village to transport
our Tamang woman to Kathmandu.*

Tullu Rong Tamang (on right) and the Himalayan HealthCare medical staff carrying the critically ill Tamang woman to the helicopter.

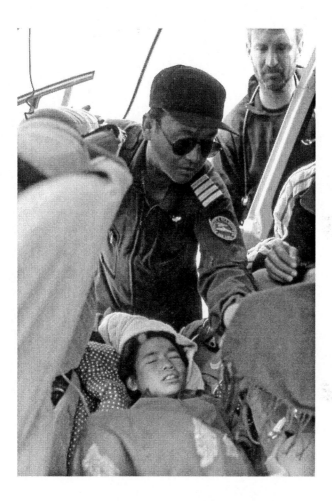

Our patient being secured for her flight as the pilot and Dr. John Rockwell, a family physician from New Mexico, look on.

The village of Sertung watches the evacuation.

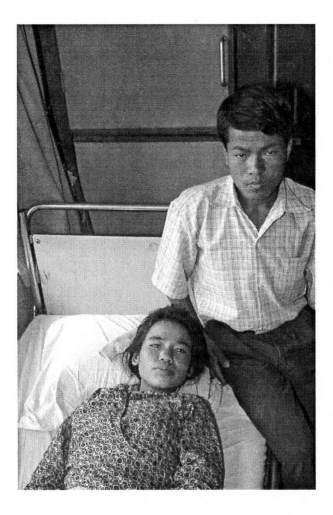

The Tamang woman with her husband recuperating in the Patan Hospital in Kathmandu.

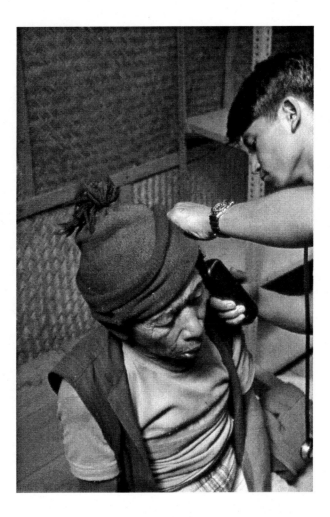

*Kamal Lama, Himalayan HealthCare
medical assistant and one of the heroes of
the mountain rescue, examines a patient
at Tipling medical camp.*

A *woman being carried in a porter's basket to Sertung medical camp.*

Ms. Kan Diki Sherpa, Himalayan HealthCare medical assistant, breaks camp at Deurali. (October 2002 medical trek in northeastern Nepal)

The porters sing to us at Kalpokhari. (October 2002)

Looking back at the trail on our way up to Sandakphu.
(October 2002)

Dal Bahadur Kumal and Babu Ram Pokhrel,
Himalayan HealthCare medical assistants, and Dr.
Jon Roberts, family physician from Missouri, at
Sandakphu peak (11,800 feet). (October 2002)

Trail from Kalpokhari to Mabu medical camp.
(October 2002)

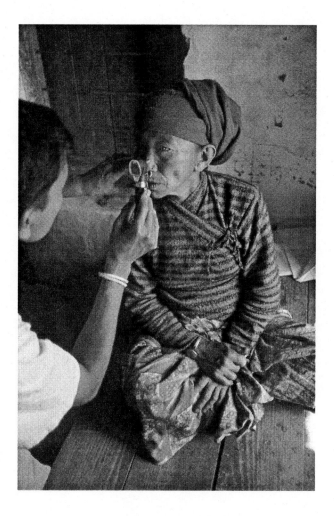

Babu Ram Pokhrel examines a patient at
Mabu medical camp. (October 2002)

Dal Bahadur Kumal and Dr. Jon Roberts review an X-ray at Sumbhek medical camp. (October 2002)

Drs. Maria Brown (left) and Vicki Samuels with a
patient at the Rush medical clinic in the El Centro De
La Causa homeless shelter in Pilsen village in Chicago.

Music Theatre Workshop (MTW) Director Meade
Palidofsky works with actor Deangelo Horton on one of
MTW's productions.

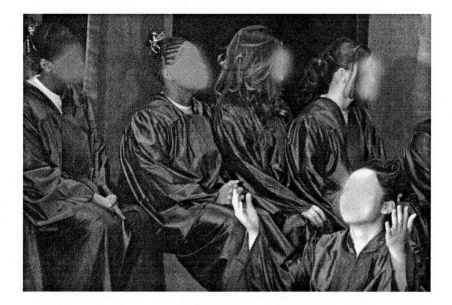

Incarcerated women at the Cook County Temporary
Juvenile Detention Center in Chicago perform one of
their Temporary Lockdown plays. (faces digitally
erased for anonymity)

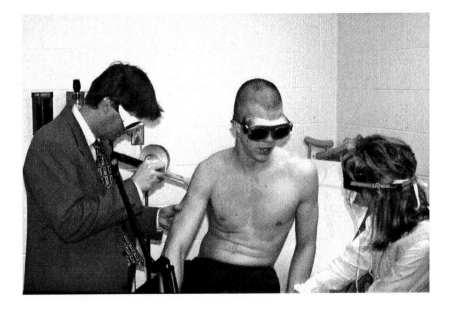

Dr. John May performing a laser treatment on a tattoo.

*Tattoos are commonly removed from hands and face
(see tear tattoo below right eye).*

James Freeman

March 26

"Cigarettes are killing my patient," I muttered angrily as I left James Freeman's room after examining him for the first time. The lone medical student sitting at the nursing station looked up, smiled with intent to please, and then went back to writing in a chart.

Cigarettes are killing not just James Freeman; they are killing enormous numbers of people in this country and worldwide. An estimated 440,000 Americans die each year from diseases caused by smoking, and 160,000 of these deaths are from lung cancer, now the leading type of cancer. Another 170,000 people are diagnosed each year with lung cancer. If you are "fortunate" enough to have lung cancer diagnosed at an early stage, you will have approximately a 50 percent chance of being alive in five years. If you are unfortunate enough to be diagnosed at a late stage, you will have a median survival time of five months.[1]

The cigarette industry spends $15 million dollars a day advertising and promoting cigarettes. "And much of that marketing directly reaches and influences kids." These are monies well spent by this industry since "a third of underage experimentation with smoking is attributable to tobacco advertising and promotion," and 90 percent of all smokers start when they are adolescents. The obvious aim of this advertising is to entice young people into an addiction that will, in more instances than not, last a lifetime. Sadly, this addiction will shorten their lives on average by more than thirteen years and, for one third of them, be the direct cause of their death.[2]

As noted by the American Lung Association, "Each day nearly 4,800 adolescents (age 11–17) smoke their first cigarette: of these, nearly 2,000 will become regular smokers, totaling to almost one million new adolescent smokers annually." From 1991 to 1999, the number of U.S. high school students who used tobacco increased from 28 percent to 35 percent, in part as a result of the massive and well aimed advertising campaigns of the cigarette companies. It is no secret that cigarette advertisements emphasize the themes that many teenagers struggle with: youthful vigor, sexual attraction, and independence. The good news is that the disturbing smoking trends of the 1990s have begun to level off and have even shown signs of declining, thanks to several successful educational campaigns, as well as the "sin tax," which has priced cigarettes out of the reach of many teenagers. Regardless of the trend, however, the fact that at least one in four of our youth is addicted to a deadly vice is quite sobering.[3]

I first met James when he was admitted to the ICU early one evening when I was on call. He was sitting on the edge of the bed, his upper torso was erect, his hands were on his knees, and his eyes were cast down and fixed on the floor. From the height of the bed, his feet were flat on the floor, making him easily over six feet six inches. The hospital gown had fallen around his waist, exposing his thin, long arms and barrel-shaped chest. With each inhalation, James's nostrils flared, the thin sheetlike muscles in his neck tightened, his abdomen dropped, and his chest slowly expanded. At the peak of his inspiration he would pause, purse his lips as if he were about to kiss someone, then squeeze his stomach muscles, forcing a long, slow exhalation. He ended the breath with a visible shake and weak wheeze that was barely audible over the loud hiss of the humidified oxygen that he was receiving through a mask. The process then started all over again, each breath consuming all of James's concentration and energy.

James started smoking as a teenager because of the "cool images of smoking in magazines and movies," and now at the age of sixty-seven, he had smoked two packs of cigarettes a day for fifty years, giving him what we call in medicine a "100 pack-year history," enough cigarettes to damage several sets of lungs. Sadly, his final passage would be a frighteningly long and slow suffocation from another cigarette-induced disease, emphysema.

Like many people with emphysema, James was much more prone to upper respiratory infections and pneumonia, and it was a simple cold that James had caught from his granddaughter that hospitalized him this time. He relayed his medical history to me in two- and three-word sentences, his speech a study in minimalism—no adjectives, adverbs or conjunctions. He spoke only in nouns and verbs, conserving as much energy as possible. The interview took forty minutes.

James, an African-American gentleman with graying hair and a gentle face, had worked all his life stocking shelves in a grocery store, retiring eight months ago to spend time with his wife of forty-five years and two daughters. James had been in and out of the hospital several times in the last two years, all for exacerbation of his asthma, caused each time by a simple cold. His hospital stays typically lasted a couple of days, and his treatment consisted of antibiotics, oxygen, steroids, and multiple albuterol treatments. In all of his hospitalizations, he had never been intubated, and he always walked out of the hospital under his own power.

Once overweight, James was now so emaciated that his ribs could be counted from across the room. His body, thin as a dancer's, was held motionless except for the rising and falling of his chest. Like a world-class athlete trained to focus all his energy on the event, James sat perfectly still, all muscles except the ones for breathing completely relaxed. From a distance, James looked meditative and appeared serene. But his eyes, cast downward and dark with apprehension, painted a different picture. There was a flicker of fear, a foreseeing of his fate, and a rising realization that he might not have the strength for another breath.

People who have come close to bleeding to death speak of its painlessness and peacefulness. You gradually become light-headed and then you slowly slip into sleep. People who have been in respiratory distress, on the other hand, describe it as the most terrifying experience of their lives. You are fully awake and completely aware that you are one breath away from suffocating. James was not yet in respiratory distress, but you could see in his eyes that he had spotted it on the horizon.

Treating someone who has emphysema for an upper respiratory infection has urgency to it. The underlying infection needs to be controlled and the bronchial airways must be dilated before the patient decompensates into respiratory distress. To this end, James was continued on oxygen, given two broad-spectrum IV antibiotics as well as both IV theophylline and continuous albuterol treatments to help dilate his constricted bronchial tubes. In addition, James was given IV prednisone to help decrease his bronchial inflammation. With James's medical care now maximized, we watched and waited to see if he would turn the tide or drift into respiratory distress.

For the next several days, breathing was all he did. Talking, eating, or even making small movements would have taken too much of his limited energy. James sat in his bed, day and night, his only motion, the rising and falling of his chest, his only purpose, to get the next breath in.

The act of breathing in a healthy individual with normal lungs consumes about 3 percent of the energy that the body expends in a given day. As one's lungs are damaged from emphysema, the efficiency at which the lungs can expel carbon dioxide and absorb oxygen dramatically decreases, forcing the lung muscles to work harder and use more energy to perform the same amount of work. With emphysema, the energy requirements for breathing, even at rest, can consume close to 30 percent of the total energy expended by the body in a day.[4] In addition, James was fighting an upper respiratory infection, which left his lungs in an even more tenuous condition. He had little energy for anything besides breathing.

High-altitude mountain climbers have a similar experience. As climbers ascend a mountain and the air thins, their respiratory rate must increase to compensate for the decreasing amount of available oxygen. Their increased respiratory rate, like James's, consumes a greater proportion of their body's energy. As climbers ascend higher and higher into even thinner air, the energy required for the act of breathing becomes even greater, and they ultimately reach a limiting factor, the point at which all of their available energy is being consumed by the act of breathing, leaving no energy to take the next step. At this point, they either decide to descend or risk dying.

James, however, was not at a high altitude. In fact, he was breathing oxygen at a concentration five times that found at sea level. But after four days of just breathing, James had climbed the equivalent of a dozen mountain peaks and needed to rest. His respirations were not keeping up with his oxygen demand, and his blood gas was worsening. James had ascended into respiratory distress. We were now going to have to bring him down from the mountain, or he was going to die.

The decision whether or not to intubate a patient is not easy for the patient or the family. For relatively healthy individuals who need to be temporarily intubated, the choice is simple. But for individuals like James, who have a chronic lung disease, the decision becomes more complex. The complexity arises from the very real possibility that the patient, once intubated, may not be able to come off of the ventilator. Ventilating chronically sick people is a balancing act between giving them enough time on the ventilator to rest their respiratory muscles, and not giving them so much time that their respiratory muscles decondition to the point that they are not able to take a breath on their own. Inherent also to all intubation is that patients are placed in the vulnerable position of having a machine breathe for them, and the medical staff at the control of the ventilator become the patients' guardians.

James agreed to be intubated by nodding his head. We gave him a combination of two powerful medications. The first was a medication that paralyzed his breathing muscles, allowing them to rest. The drug has no effect on a patient's cognition or ability to think. James, remaining fully aware that he was paralyzed and that a machine (with all of its possibilities of error and malfunction) was now breathing for him, could become quite anxious, so to prevent that we gave him the second medication, a benzodiazepine, and he surrendered to a peaceful, sedated state.

James's daughter arrived in his room soon after we had intubated him. When she saw her father on the respirator, she became angry with us for not calling her first. She knew well, from her work as a nurse, that she might not see her father off the ventilator again. I explained to her the urgent need for a quick intubation, leaving little time for notification, but my words did not seem to help. She was bending under the emotional pressure of her role as the main decision maker, not only for her father, but also now her mother, who, unfortunately, had just that morning suffered a heart attack. The strain of the situation was apparent, and I offered to listen. She was in the tough position of being the messenger between her father and mother. The mother knew of the father's hospitalization, but not of his intubation; the father knew nothing of the mother's hospitalization. Not wanting to aggravate either of their critical conditions, she decided to keep the knowledge of her parents' present medical conditions to herself.

And so James Freeman, once a tall, strong and independent gentleman, was now reduced to a silent being, lying motionless in bed, dependent on a machine for every breath. He was fed through a tube that entered his nose and followed his esophagus into his stomach. He was hydrated with two IV lines. We collected his urine with a tube that ran through his penis and into his bladder. He wore diapers. Over the next several days he would occasionally awake from his sedated state and gag violently on his breathing tube. The ventilator's alarm would sound, and a nurse would run to his bedside to push enough morphine and valium to ease him back into a euphoric and restful place.

James's daughter, always aware of her father's medication schedule, would visit when she knew his sedatives had worn off enough for him to be aware of her voice. During these brief moments, she would sit at his bedside, stroke his head, and tell him how much she loved him. His eyes would well with her words.

James was intubated for ten days. In that time we discontinued the paralytic medication and made several attempts to wean him from the ventilator. With each attempt, James, showing the eagerness of a little leaguer going up to bat for the first time, would take several enthusiastic breaths on this own. But as though worn down by an experienced pitcher, James would gradually decrease the rate and depth of his breath and then stop breathing altogether, his atrophied respiratory muscles succumbing to the laws of nature. After each failed attempt at weaning, we would resume supporting him with the ventilator, and like sympathetic coaches, we would offer him a few words of encouragement for his next time at bat. But his eyes and face would show the rejection of having been struck out.

Ten days is as long as one should leave a breathing tube in a patient; any longer and the patient runs the risk of developing an ulcer at the point of contact between the breathing tube and his trachea. An ulcer can lead to an infection and erosion of the tra-chea, a complication we wanted to avoid. James, having failed multiple attempts at weaning from the ventilator, now needed to have a tracheotomy performed.

The operation is a simple one, and it went well for James, but it marked an admission of failure for us that we were not able to wean James from his life support. After the operation, James spent another ten days in the hospital. In this time, he learned to sit up in a chair and had brief moments when he was able to breathe through the hole in his neck without the assistance of the ventilator. He would speak to his family in two-to three-word sen-tences. He had therapy to help him coordinate how to swallow liquids again, and when he failed this, he had another operation that inserted a feeding tube from the outside of his abdomen into his stomach. He would forever use this tube for milkshake-like feedings.

James went home by ambulance twenty-two days after being admitted. He will now spend the majority of his days attached to his ventilator. For brief moments he will be able to be off this life-line, but he will always have to carry oxygen with him. He will get out of breath simply by walking across the room. He will spend his remaining time sitting in a chair or lying in bed. He will con-tinue to communicate with his family in two- or three-word sen-tences. He will get sick again and he will be readmitted.

When James does come back to the hospital, there will come a time when he will forever be dependent on the ventilator. At that point, he and his family will have to make a decision about care. If he chooses to go on, his family will have the enormous task of car-ing for him, or he will be placed in a medical facility for ventilated patients. Either way, now permanently attached to his life-sup-port machine, he will be forced to be bed-bound. He will now be highly susceptible to bed sores and pneumonia. One of these infections will most likely be James's final battle.

James's life long addiction to cigarettes will have given him two things: a shortened life and a slow, horrific death.

After James left the hospital, I found myself reflecting on his care and the end of his life, which was near. Once again, as with the woman who was murdered and Evelyn Howe, who died of breast cancer, I had showed up at the end of the line in another patient's life, and once again I was left with a feeling of helplessness. This time, however, these feelings were not due to a hole in a heart that could not be closed or a breast cancer that would not be stopped. These current feelings came from the overwhelming powerlessness one has in the face of a multi-billion-dollar *legal* industry that peddles a product that is incredibly addictive and extremely deadly.

But again, with a feeling of powerlessness comes a resolve, and this time it was a determination to fight this industry the only way I can, through preventive medicine and education, patient by patient.

There is no doubt that getting a patient to stop smoking is one of the more difficult lifestyle changes to accomplish because nicotine, and many of the chemicals that are added to cigarettes are immensely addictive. But, with a motivated patient, some smoking cessation programs have an abstinence rate at one year close to 25 percent.[5] James, who lacked health insurance for the majority of his life, was never offered any preventive medicine, either in the form of education about the harmful effects of cigarettes when he was a teenager or smoking cessation treatments when he was an adult. Without these aids he was never given the opportunity to have a realistic chance of quitting. The irony here is that his many years of smoking caught up with him at age sixty-five, the year he became eligible for Medicare. A little inexpensive preventive medicine earlier in his life could possibly have saved the taxpayers his $120,000 medical bill, but more important, it could have saved his life.

TWELVE

Sammy Ellington

As an inner-city doctor, too often I see patients only momentarily during their lifelong trajectory of healthcare. These brief and far too few patient-doctor interactions are typically for a specific acute need, and once this need is addressed, the patient rarely returns. The concept of "follow-up" and "longevity of care" with a single caregiver is not realized to the extent it should be. The reasons are many and varied, but lack of affordable health insurance stands at the top of the list. With over 40 million Americans (15% of the population) without health insurance, and a disproportionate number of these uninsured being of low income, it is easy to understand why healthcare providers in low-income areas often have only temporary and fleeting relationships with some of their patients. What is needed is a constant force, a continual presence, to modify patients' health and to improve their quality of life.

Sammy Ellington, a middle-aged African-American male, could easily have been one of my passing patient-doctor encounters. I first met Sammy in the fall of my intern year when he was fifty-nine years old. His medical conditions precluded steady work, leaving him without employee health insurance or the means to pay for his healthcare needs. He was not deemed disabled enough by the government to qualify for Medicaid, and he was too young for Medicare. Sammy, like many Americans, was living in "insurance no-man's land."

Sammy could easily have followed the path those without health insurance take: multiple visits for acute illnesses to any of the many overcrowded Chicago emergency rooms—an inefficient solution because it uses the valuable resources intended for real emergencies, not the least being the overworked emergency room staffs.

The other healthcare option in Chicago available to the uninsured is Cook County Hospital. In front of this magnificent white brick Mecca for the marginalized is a small park, which besides being the summer home for a dozen homeless people, embraces a thirty-foot-high granite statue of Louis Pasteur, with head bowed in reverence to this great hospital. Etched in this stone monument are the words of the famous scientist and humanist,

> *One doesn't ask of one who suffers: What is your country and what is your religion? One merely says, you suffer, this is enough for me, you belong to me and I shall help you.*

On my many trips past this statue during my medical school days, I was often reminded of the Statue of Liberty and its awe-inspiring words, "Give me your tired, your poor, your huddled masses." The similarity of these two strong messages is apparent and timeless. If I had a chisel and the fortitude, I would have honored Pasteur and Cook Country Hospital by editing his words to reflect the twenty-first century, "One does not ask one who suffers: What is your ability to pay and what type of insurance do you have?" Uncarved, yet very much realized, these words are the brick and mortar of Cook County Hospital's foundation and philosophy.

The out-patient clinic at County is also wonderfully philanthropic. It offers affordable healthcare to the many uninsured Chicago residents, is the pride of public healthcare advocates who believe in the tenets of universal healthcare, and serves as an island of respite and care in the rough waters of unaffordable healthcare. A sizable number of inner-city Chicagoans will find themselves at County at some point in their lives even though it is not the most efficient medical facility. Patients frequently have to wait for hours to be seen by an attending physician or resident and often will not be seen by the same doctor on subsequent visits. This lack of continuity of care at County was the reason that Sammy and his wife came to my clinic in the autumn of my intern year.

Sammy shuffled into my examining room on that first day with the stiffness and unsteadiness of the unoiled tin man in *The Wizard of Oz*. His wife, much like the scarecrow, lion, and Dorothy all rolled into one, stood ready to straighten him on each stumble and sway. She was tall and thin, and whereas Sammy was perfectly groomed, his wife's presentation was slightly worn. Sammy wore his hair long and generously oiled; his wife kept her hair dry and cut close to her scalp. His skin was black as a moonless night; her's was lighter and the color of mahogany. Sammy, even taller and thinner than his wife, cut a striking figure in his immaculate shirt and pressed trousers. Both he and his wife had incredibly long, thin fingers with exquisite nails, but this is where she trumped Sammy. Where his fingernails were long, well trimmed, and clear-polished, her nails were immensely impressive, each with a different decorative design—some were of celestial scenes, others were delicate collages of geometric shapes and colors. Each nail was a marvelous display of her creativity. I surmised they spent most of their idle time at home attending to these manicures, and it was apparent from their discrepancy in dress that Sammy's wife—in selfless devotion to him—first dressed and readied Sammy for the day, leaving little time and energy for herself, except for the time she took for her nails.

During our clinic appointments, Sammy would sit quietly while his wife would animatedly and rhythmically cut the air with her decorative fingertips and lucid voice, detailing for me in sentences too long for one breath all that Sammy's body had been through since our last visit. Occasionally during these soliloquies she would pause, extend her longest fingernail like a baton, and with the gentleness of a conductor entering an adagio movement, signal Sammy to fill the emptiness. Preoccupied with his own thoughts, Sammy often missed his cue. And as the moments and stillness mounted, his wife would grow impatient, sigh, lower her finger, and tell me Sammy's thoughts.

Sammy's first visit with me was the morning after his visit to our hospital's emergency room for a neck strain. The emergency room doctor had wisely advised him upon discharge to find a primary care physician who would see him on a regular basis. Sammy inquired about the cheapest doctor available, and he was directed to our clinic, which offers medical care on a sliding scale to the residents of one of the poorest sections of the West Side of Chicago.

Sammy's medical history was varied and complex. His long-standing high blood pressure was diagnosed ten years previously when he suffered a stroke that paralyzed the right side of his body. After a year of intense physical and occupational therapy, he was able to walk with the support of a cane. Compounding Sammy's labored gait was the pain he felt from several degenerated vertebrae in his lower back. To control this pain, he repeatedly went to County for steroid injections, his equivalent to the tin man's oil. Sammy also had gout, a painful inflammatory condition that predominantly affects the feet and ankles. When he was young, Sammy's abdomen had been perforated by a bullet, which severed a portion of the nerves that innervate his intestines, leaving him with a lengthy abdominal scar and chronic diarrhea.

Sammy was on a number of medications, twelve in fact, all of which he had filled free at the Cook Country Hospital pharmacy. This widely known pharmaceutical loophole is where Sammy, as well as many other Chicago residents—in a Darwinian "survival of the fittest" fashion—learned to make our healthcare system work for their benefit. After our first meeting, Sammy's modus operandi became regular visits to our clinic for his healthcare needs, followed by a trip to County's pharmacy to have his prescription filled. In the event that he needed a medication that was not on County's formulary, we would apply for free samples from one of the pharmaceutical company's "indigent drug programs."

At first glance, these free medication programs might appear to be generous corporate philanthropy, but, on closer inspection, their true motivation is revealed. Rarely do these drug companies donate more than a few months' supply of any product, little help for a person who will need a lifetime of medication. This limit on free medication often forced me to change Sammy's medications or to seek out an unused "indigent drug program." In addition, many of these programs have such strict financial eligibility standards that only the most destitute of patients can apply. A further barrier is that these companies require an address and social security number, a requirement that effectively excludes the homeless and anyone in this country without citizenship, two populations that are most in need of free medication.

I sent Sammy home that first day with gentle stretching exercises and instruction to alternate hot and cold packs to his neck. I also referred him to physical therapy and gave him several free samples of Celebrex that we had in the office. I had the lab technician draw his blood for his basic metabolic panel, hemoglobin, and cholesterol level. These would help me determine if his long-standing hypertension had injured his kidneys. In addition, I wanted to see if he was anemic. I signed his chart, "No charge," and told him I would see him in a week. And so began Sammy's and my relationship, a mutual journey that would defy the typical inner-city doctor-patient relationship by being repeated over and over again and lasting three years. The following entries are taken directly from my daily journal.

September 27, 1999

Today is Sammy's second visit, and he informs me that his neck pain has improved. We discuss his renal function, which is of concern in light of last week's blood draw; his blood urea nitrogen and creatinine, both good markers for kidney function, are 57 and 4.3 (milligram per deciliter), respectively, substantially elevated over the normal values of 20 and 1. This is fairly clear evidence that Sammy has chronic renal disease, most likely from his long-standing hypertension. We talk about the importance of decreasing these markers by controlling his blood pressure, and I start him on an additional hypertensive medication today. To further quantify the amount of renal damage that he has suffered, I ask him to collect his urine for twenty-four hours in order to calculate the amount of protein and creatinine slipping through his kidneys. This request brings the expected response: Sammy's eyes widen further when I tell him that he has to keep the urine refrigerated while he is collecting it. Sammy, not surprisingly, is also slightly anemic, probably due to his chronic renal damage. The good news for the day is that his cholesterol is normal, one less risk factor for him developing coronary artery disease. His back pain is well controlled on Celebrex, and we apply to Pfizer

Pharmaceuticals for three free months of this medication. I tell him that I will see him in two weeks and send him home with a smiley face drawn on the large brown jug that he will use to collect his urine.

October 11

Sammy awkwardly ambles into the examining room today in good spirits. He returns with the large brown urine jug, empty, and in bold indelible ink a frown has been drawn over the smiley face. He tells me the jug is a present from his wife, given after she learned that he would keep the collection in her refrigerator. We spend some time musing about ways that he can conceal the jug from his wife, not one of the top reasons I went into medicine, but I imagine a part of the essence of comprehensive medical care. Sammy's back pain is well controlled, but his blood pressure is elevated, and his legs are swollen from his feet to his knees. When I question him about his diet, he confesses with a shy grin that he has been putting salt on his food. He modestly concedes that he will cut it out now that I am onto him. As Sammy leaves with his new brown jug and a few ideas on how to hide it in his refrigerator, I tell him that I will see him in two weeks.

October 25

Sammy's stiffness and pain is evident in his face and contorted posture as he shuffles into the clinic today. His main complaint is his chronic lower back pain, and it is apparent from his gait that he missed his last back injection at County. The encouraging news is that his blood pressure has improved, as a result of his not using salt and taking his blood pressure medicine. In a moment of rare spontaneity, Sammy relates to me, "I get so mad at times, I feel like I will explode." Not wanting to let this comment drop, I question him further. From our brief discussion it is clear that there are many triggers to Sammy's anger, but public settings when he feels that he is being disrespected and discriminated against provoke the strongest reaction. And, I imagine, his constant back pain adds to his frustration level and fuels his anger. We talk for some time about anger management, and I offer the concept of mental imagery as a tool to help him relax. By his initial response, the technique appears to be new to him, but he says that he is willing to try it. Sammy's twenty-four-hour urine collection has been analyzed and reveals a creatinine clearance equal to 23 (milliliters per minute) (normal is between 85 and 125), and a protein of 514 (milligrams) (normal is less than 150). These measurements, which are better markers of renal function than just blood urea nitrogen and creatinine, make it clear that Sammy is in chronic renal failure. He is not a candidate for dialysis at this point, but with time and a continued uncontrolled blood pressure, he inevitably will be. I refill his medications and refer him to our hospital's pain clinic for his back injections, with the hope that he can start to receive these treatments on a regular basis. We still await our free Celebrex sample from Pfizer.

November 22

Sammy's mood is somber today. He complains that his back is again giving him significant pain. He had diligently gone to County's pain clinic but was unable to receive his steroid injection because the X-ray machine, used to image the needle as it enters his spine, was being repaired. I have noticed over the last several visits that Sammy's mood is tied closely with the fluctuating condition of any one of his many medical problems. Today he is fed up with County to the point that he wants to start getting his back injections at our hospital's pain management clinic, an idea that I have encouraged since our first visit. This week he even took the initiative to visit the anesthesiologist at our pain management clinic for an injection. However, the anesthesiologist informed him that he needed a copy of his MRI from County before he would be willing to inject him. So Sammy is left having to endure a constant gnawing pain in his lower back and legs. Although his mood is down, he states that his anger has subsided (my mental imagery suggestions having worked, I facetiously think to myself). We end the visit with my repeated encouragement for him to get physical therapy for his back.

January 24, 2000

An acute visit for Sammy today. He has been having bouts of nausea and vomiting, intermittent explosive diarrhea, and a poor appetite for one week. A quick look at his weight recorded on today's progress note reveals a five-pound loss from his visit two months ago. Sammy's abdomen, usually flat and thin, is now distended, and soft and painful when touched. He has good bowel sounds and does not guard his belly when I palpate it for signs of a mass. His rectal exam reveals no blood. He does not look to be suffering from any infection, but he does need to be ruled out for a bowel obstruction. I draw his complete blood count to check his hemoglobin, send his stool for culture and parasite analysis, and tell him to drink plenty of fluids and call me if he gets worse. I send him to the hospital for a four-view abdominal X-ray series, and make a note in the chart that he needs to schedule a colonoscopy at his next visit. I also note in Sammy's chart that I am concerned with his health. He is a frail gentleman with several significant disease processes. He is not someone with a lot of reserve if he were to get very sick.

January 31

I do not hear again from Sammy until today when he returns looking tired and drawn. He still has no appetite, and his diarrhea has not improved. His stool culture and stain from last week shows no bacteria, parasites, or white blood cells, which effectively rules out any infectious cause for his gastrointestinal problems. His abdominal X-ray, however, was not normal and read by the radiologist as a "possible partial bowel obstruction." In addition, his abdomen, which last week was soft and distended, has not decreased in size and has grown ominously firm. In light of his continual deterioration, I arrange for him to be admitted to the hospital in the morning for a colonoscopy, and further evaluation. The need to rule out a possible abdominal cancer is on my mind. I tell Sammy to take only clear fluids overnight and that I will meet him in the hospital in the morning.

February 1–3

When I enter Sammy's hospital room, it is obvious that he is not happy with me or with being in the hospital; he turns his head away from me and is silent. After several moments Sammy vocalized his displeasure with the colonoscopy he just had. I try to lift Sammy's mood with the good news that the gastroenterologist did not find any cancer, but he is feeling too violated from this procedure to be cheerful. Over the next two days, Sammy is not allowed to eat and receives his nutrition from intravenous fluids. This he also protests. After the colonoscopy, a small bowel follow through of his upper gastrointestinal tract is performed, and the result of this imaging study shows: "possible thickening of the stomach and duodenum." To rule out cancer in this region, we next perform a cat scan of his abdomen. This demonstrates a normal stomach, duodenum, and pancreas; however, the liver reveals several "echogenic spots." These "spots" might be the normal vascular pattern of the liver, but we still need to rule out cancer, this time with an ultrasound of his liver. It is scheduled as an outpatient procedure, welcome news to Sammy, who desperately wants to go home after being poked and prodded for three days.

February 7

It is Sammy's first visit since being discharged from the hospital; he greets me, expressing again his displeasure with his recent colonoscopy. He whimsically suggests that all doctors, and me in particular, should each receive one to help us appreciate what it is that we are ordering for our patients. I smile at his candor and tell him that in good time I, too, will have one done. A quick look at his abdomen reveals that his distention has improved. While he was in the hospital, we took the opportunity to repeat a twenty-four-hour urine collection with the result showing an elevation in the amount of protein slipping through his kidneys; his creatinine clearance has also decreased from 23 to 10 milliliters per minute. The deterioration in his renal function is a concern, and prompts a discussion about the need for Sammy to have an arterial-venous graft placed for his inevitable future dialysis. We stop his Celebrex and start Tylenol, a medication offering less pain relief but one which is not as harmful to his failing kidneys. This whole discussion is tough on Sammy for two reasons. First, he has several friends on dialysis, and he knows well the energy and mood swings that they experience before and after each dialysis; he even states that he would rather die than be on dialysis. Second, Celebrex has been giving him adequate pain control, and his apprehension about another medication change is understandable. We end the visit with Sammy insisting that he is not interested in dialysis, and he reminds me that colonoscopies are also off his list of acceptable procedures. I gingerly remind him to follow up with the gastroenterologist for the ultrasound of his liver and nervously note in the chart that Sammy has lost fifteen pounds in the last three months. We still await Sammy's free blood pressure medication from Merck Pharmaceutical. I fill out several forms for Sammy's application for Medicaid in my continued efforts to make our healthcare system work for him.

February 21

Sammy's abdomen distention continues to improve, and overall he looks better. His weight today shows a five-pound weight gain from his last visit; however, I do not believe this since he still looks as thin as a sapling. I imagine that the nurse has weighed him with his boots on this week—and he tells me as much when I ask him. Not surprisingly, his joint pain from his arthritis has increased since stopping Celebrex. I refer Sammy to our pain clinic once again for his back injections. I make a note in the chart to write an additional letter of support for Sammy's Medicaid application. We finish the visit with my encouraging Sammy to get the ultrasound of his liver that the gastroenterologist had requested when he was in the hospital three weeks ago.

February 28

Sammy returns today having had the ultrasound of his abdomen completed. Thankfully, it shows no liver masses, but in a continually frustrating manner, the image is not completely readable due to gas in his bowel, and the radiologist hesitated at reading it as free of pancreatic cancer. This inconclusive result leads the gastroenterologist to request an endoscopic retrograde cholangiopancreatography (ERCP) to completely rule out any malignancy of the pancreas. I explain to Sammy the procedure, which involves the visualization of his pancreatic duct by a fiber optic tube inserted into his mouth and snaked down into his intestine. Sammy politely reminds me that he is not having any more colonoscopies performed. I tell him that this is technically not a colonoscopy since we are using the other end of him. Sammy, his sense of humor still intact, finds this mildly amusing. His wife tells me that they will follow up with this procedure once his back pain is resolved. "One thing at a time, doctor," she reminds me. "One thing's all I can do at a time." Not surprisingly, County cannot find Sammy's MRI in their vast vaults of radiological images. Subsequently, our pain clinic's anesthesiologist has requested that Sammy get a new MRI taken before he performs the spinal injections. This is acceptable to Sammy, but he tells me that he is too claustrophobic for the narrow tube that they will image him in. I offer him sedation to ease the anxiety, but Sammy is not interested in being "knocked out" for this procedure. In our continual saga to get his back pain effectively treated, and with a new roadblock in the way, Sammy decides to continue with these treatments at County. He leaves in good spirits with yet another note from me in support of his claim of disability for Medicaid coverage.

April 7

It is Sammy's first visit in close to two months; he is here for a blood pressure check, and it is elevated. He states that he has been feeling well and from the relative ease in his gait, I know that he has recently received a back injection at County. Unfortunately, he has not seen the gastroenterologist, nor has he had the ERCP done. His wife states that she has spent all her time on his other medical problems. He also has not gone for physical therapy, but this is not as urgent as the need to rule out pancreatic cancer. For his elevated blood pressure, I increase his ace inhibitor, which has finally arrived from Merck Pharmaceutical's free medication program, but now that I have just increased his dose, I am forced to order him more free samples. The prospect of another three-month wait for this medication is aggravating. In addition, two applications and three support letters later, Sammy still awaits the decision on his Medicaid application. We finish by drawing routine labs to continue monitoring his kidney function. I encourage him to get the ERCP done with the gastroenterologist, to which he says, "Oh, you mean that colonoscopy on the other end!" Sammy looks better, but his continual delay in getting the final procedure to rule out a cancer in his pancreas worries me.

May 12

Today is Sammy's first visit in over a month. He comes to the clinic today for another quick blood pressure check and medication refill. He is still pain free from his last back injection and ambulating well. Also, his blood pressure has improved from his last visit. I remind him again to get his ERCP scheduled with the gastroenterologist, and I refill his medications. Sammy leaves in good spirits.

■ ■ ■

As the summer drew near and my intern year came to a close, Sammy hobbled out of the clinic in stable health and better spirits than when he stumbled in almost a year earlier. Like working on an old car, through which the constant repetition of tearing it apart and putting it back together teaches you the craft of mechanics, Sammy's multiple health problems began to teach me out-patient medicine. In his nine months of care with me, I had seen Sammy a dozen times and admitted him to the hospital for a three-day stay. During this short time together, we had managed all of his many medical conditions, some as mundane as his elevated blood pressure and chronic back pain, and others more unique and pressing, such as our ongoing search for a possible cancer. But, beyond the basics of medicine, I began to learn an important intangible aspect of healthcare, or as many of my attendings in medical school called it, "the art of medicine." In Sammy's case, this "art," was how to get by in a system that is failing its patients.

During my intern year, Sammy never qualified for Medicaid, so subsequently he did not have coverage for any of his medications. He and his wife earned a total of $30,000 a year, too little to pay for his medications that totaled approximately $10,000 annually, and too much to qualify for any Illinois state low-income medication help. With little to no money available to spend on this important part of his healthcare, he and I were left with obtaining his medications in a patchwork fashion from County and multiple pharmaceutical companies' indigent medication programs. As mentioned earlier, these drug companies' free medication programs, often limited to three months, necessitated our frequent changing of his medications. As anyone who has ever taken medication knows, it is difficult to be completely compliant with the dosing regimen of even one drug. I can only imagine that this problem was compounded for Sammy by the multiple changes that we were forced to make with many of his medications, all the while attempting to dodge the "medication expense bullet."[1] Another potential problem with frequent changes in a patient's medication regimen is the increased chance of a dosing error on the physician's or pharmacist's part, not to mention the difficulty guessing equivalent dosages of different drugs or the possible dangerous drug interactions that can occur with multiple medications.

Throughout the time I cared for Sammy during my intern year, one question that was—appropriately—never asked of Sammy was for him to pay his clinic and hospital bills. By my writing, "No charge," on his clinic bills and the hospital's underwriting of his three-day stay, Sammy was able to receive the best possible care at no charge. The cost of Sammy's care, however, came not from the many taxes that he had paid through the innumerable odd jobs he had held throughout his life, but rather at the expense of our underfunded, inner-city clinic and our financially strained community hospital.

If Sammy, a middle-aged and disabled citizen, forced to spend a large amount of his time and energy making our inadequate health-care system work for him—through a series of complicated steps—was an anomaly, I would not be concerned. Unfortunately, Sammy is not unique; he typifies all too many patients at the clinic where I work, and all too many people in the United States. Sammy, for me, became the soothsayer of what is amiss with our American health-care system.

Sammy remained my patient for the next two years as I continued in my residency. He, as a patient without health insurance but with serious medical problems, forced me to confront many challenges inherent to a healthcare system that is not accessible to all, and the challenges of working with a patient who is chronically ill. Sammy, more than any patient to date, had contributed to my education and growth as a family doctor. Sammy's many and varied physical aliments forced me not only to review my medical school texts, but also to seek the advice of specialists, thus assuring that I was properly managing his disease processes. A team approach to patient care is always desirable, and Sammy was a patient that taught me the importance of that.

Sammy's labile mood, often the result of his arthritic pain, reaffirmed in me the important connection between a patient's physical being and his mood. It was also instrumental in my understanding of the importance of patients having their pain managed properly. Our relationship also drove home the fundamental message of how important continuity of care is to a patient's health. The positive influence that a doctor and motivated patient can have on the patient's health—and the doctor's understanding of this important relationship—has been a valuable lesson for me. Finally, through the many obstacles that Sammy and I were forced to negotiate to secure him adequate care, I began to recognize some of the glaring inadequacies of our healthcare system.

Sammy, like most of my patients, had given me more than I was able to reciprocate. Perhaps this is inherent to medical training in the early years, when the learning curve is steep, and there is an imbalance between what the patient offers you in educational experience and what you can offer the patient in medical experience. But with this realization comes the awareness that the profession of medicine is one of lifelong learning, and I imagine that my future patients, similar to the many that I encountered during medical school and internship, will always give me, in certain ways, more than I can return.

THIRTEEN

The End of the Beginning

June 30, 2000

It is our last day as interns! Jay, one of the other eleven family physician interns, and I had been working for a full month in the ICU with our one senior and a unit full of very sick patients. The senior resident, in a show of confidence in our ability to handle difficult cases, left the managing of the patients to us. Being the only two interns on our service, Jay and I were forced to be on call every second or third night with an occasional drop-in intern to help space out the on-call schedule. The shifts were excruciatingly long; thirty-six hours for the intern on call and twelve-hour days for the one not on call. The end of the month came none too soon for both of us; we were near the breaking point from exhaustion, and our humor had long ago turned from light and airy to dark and morose. During this indentured servitude, we had no doubt learned an incredible amount, but the long hours had taken their toll on our spirits. We had worked over one hundred hours a week for each of the last four weeks with only two days off during this thirty-day period.

As I left the unit that afternoon, I took the elevators down to the first floor, walked past the exit door I had escaped through six months earlier after losing Harold Brown on Christmas morning, and then took the remaining flight of stairs to the basement level. I walked down the long hallway that I had entered 364 days earlier, passing several new interns coming into the hospital for their first night on call. Their nervousness and trepidation, like mine a year ago, was apparent.

As I walked out of the hospital, it did not occur to me that I had just stepped over the important medical training threshold of finishing my internship that very day and becoming a senior the next day. My mind was only on my pillow and the deep sleep that my body ached for. It would not be until the following week when,

on call again but this time in the role of senior to a new appre-
hensive intern, that I was reminded of myself one year ago, and
how far I had come in that year.

The end of every year is also a genesis; this holds particular
truth in medical training. It was not the end of my intern year, but
the beginning of a new year as a senior and the rest of my life in
medicine. As I drove home that last day, passing the same exits I
had contemplated turning around on one year earlier, my mind
drifted across the landscape of my last twelve months, each
thought, like that of the changing scene outside my car, remained
only briefly before melting into the next. And as my surroundings
floated by, I felt, perhaps due to my exhaustion, a surreal, almost
transcendental, sensation of being lifted into the air. The scene
below became a slow-motion, silent movie—each thought, like
each movie frame, momentarily discernible, then dissolving into
the next. And as I rose, all the individual memories—the long
days, the sleepless nights, the delivered babies, the lost
patients, the mind-numbing facts, and the hours spent enabling
our healthcare system to benefit all—crystallized into one lucid
and humbling impression: I was in the foothills of medicine. I had
walked a long, grueling path this year and gained significant
heights, and with this passage I had confirmed my purpose in life
and my commitment to the profession and working with the
underserved. And even though I felt physically able and mentally
ready, I knew there would be many more years of hard work
before I would ascend above the tree line and be able to look out
across the landscape of my profession.

■ ■ ■

April 2005

All of the chapters in this book began as letters that I wrote
home to my family. Several of the letters, about experiences I
had during my intern year as well as the medical trek in Nepal

during my second year of training, were actually written during the remaining years of my residency and my first year as an attending. Intern year, with its incredible workload and time requirements, did not afford me the leisure to write about all the memorable patients during that short twelve-month stint. It was not until my second and third years of training and my first year as an attending, with its more humane work hours, that I had time to put pen to paper in the hope of recording all that I had felt, seen, heard, and thought during my first year. To help rekindle my memory, I reviewed the copious personal notes that I had taken on each of these patients, and I reread their medical records. To protect the patients' and their family members' personal identities, I have changed their names along with several minor details. But the events surrounding each experience and all the medical information associated with each patient are as factual as possible.

Editing this manuscript over the last several months has been a powerful experience for me. Now an attending and several years removed from these experiences, I am struck by the intensity and emotional vulnerability that is unique to the intern year. Rereading the letters has made me realize that there is no other year in medical training or practice that is as intellectually, physically, or emotionally challenging as the intern year. There is something about severe sleep deprivation that opens up deep emotions. These areas of emotional vulnerability allowed me to find the words and expressions to describe what I recorded in this book. Occasionally I wonder if I could, or would need to, write about my present medical cases the same way I did as an intern. Writing for me is a tool to help make sense of my experiences. As an intern I needed that tool. As a senior resident during the final two years of training and now as an attending, due to the nature of being in a leadership position, I have had little time to be introspective. I have turned outward, concerned more with helping interns during residency and medical students who rotate through our clinic.

All the patients I write about I had worked with during my intern year of residency. The only exceptions are the patients described in the Prologue and Chapter One. These episodes occurred while I was in Nepal and during my final year of medical school on a one-month rotation at the Ventura County Medical Center in southern California. Because intern training consists primarily of hospital-centered rotations, these patients had come to the hospital for acute needs and, once discharged, resumed their care with their original primary care doctor. Subsequently, I lost contact with the majority of them, except for an occasional update I would receive in passing from their primary care doctor. In this manner I was able to follow Sheri's progress, and fortunately she is doing well. But I never saw Daphne and her infant, James Freeman, or Baby X again. Baby X's mother was scheduled to bring her daughter to our clinic for a checkup after her hospital discharge, but she never came for the appointment, nor did she ever appear on the clinic schedule during my remaining years of residency.

The two patients I did see were Ms. Jackson and Sammy Ellington. Ms. Jackson followed up with me for several months at my outpatient clinic for her wound and diabetes management. Once her wound completely healed, she stopped coming to see me, although I did hear that she occasionally comes to the clinic for her blood sugar checks. The other patient, Sammy Ellington, became my most regular patient during my three-year residency and would not see any other doctor at our clinic. Sammy's dedication to me and our ability to remain in such steady contact was partially the result of the increasing amount of time I spent in our outpatient clinic as I progressed through residency. More significant, however, was Sammy's concern for his own health that motivated him to come regularly to the clinic.

At the beginning of my second year of residency, Sammy finally did have his ERCP (endoscopic retrograde cholangiopancreatography) performed, and thankfully the result did not show any malignancies in his gall bladder, common bile duct, or pancreas. However, in light of Sammy's marked weight loss, and a subsequent blood test that showed an elevated cancer marker, the gastroenterologist requested that Sammy have yet another endoscopic exam, during which a small ultrasound probe would be inserted into his mouth and fed down into his stomach, imaging his liver and pancreas. If you are keeping score here, as Sammy was, you might ask, as Sammy did, if another ultrasound of his liver and pancreas—especially when the first one was negative—was really needed. What I explained to Sammy, who was quite incredulous, was that this ultrasound, with its probe position being much closer to his pancreas and liver, would finally (I said as convincingly as I could) give us the information we needed to rule out any cancer. Not surprisingly, Sammy did not get this test done immediately; in fact, the gastroenterologist and I held our breath when eight months later he finally came in for the test. And as the gastroenterologist noted, Sammy probably did not need the test now, for indeed if he had had pancreatic cancer, he would have died in the interim. The negative result on the ultrasound confirmed our prediction, and Sammy was declared free of cancer. He had rolled the dice and won.

Near the end of my second year of training, Sammy was finally approved for Medicaid. It took one and one-half years and multiple letters of support to get Sammy on Medicaid. For both of us, this was a high point in Sammy's care; he would now have coverage for his clinic appointments and medications, unburdening us from the immense amount of time and energy it took to navigate our healthcare system for his benefit.

During the middle of my third year of residency, as a result of Sammy's own continuing renal deterioration and my frequent nagging, he agreed to have an arterial-venous graft implanted, thus ushering in dialysis treatments that will last the rest of his life. Not long after these blood-cleansing treatments started, Sammy began to gain weight and feel better.

It might seem to the reader, as it did to me for a good part of my residency, that Sammy moved very slowly in completing many of his important tests and scans. Numerous doctors would call this type of patient "noncompliant," and no doubt these doctors have at least one story of a "noncompliant" patient whose tardiness in following medical instructions brought about an untimely end. Sammy made me fear the same for him, on more than one occasion. But in the end, Sammy taught me above all else—above my own wishes and desires as well as above the whole body of medical knowledge—the importance of allowing patients to have the time and space they need to make their own healthcare decisions.

As Sammy was leaving my examining room on the last day of my residency, I offered to continue seeing him at my new clinic on the South Side of Chicago. He stopped at the door, pondered the question, and, in a style I had come to respect, told me that he would need time to make the decision.

Although the patients that I cared for in residency and now care for as an attending are halfway around the world from the patients I treated in Nepal, there are two obvious similarities between these countries: neither the U.S. nor Nepal offers universal healthcare to all of its citizens, and both countries have populations who are in dire need of healthcare but have barriers to obtaining it. In Nepal these barriers are financial and in many cases geographic; many patients we saw in our medical camps had to cross 14,000-foot mountain passes to come to our clinic. In the U.S. the barriers are primarily financial. Nepal has an excuse for not offering healthcare to all of its citizens, since it has a long history of political unrest, challenging geographic terrain, and economic destitution (Nepal's per capita GNP is $210 per annum compared to the U.S. per capita GNP of $29,000 per annum).[1] It is a country that at present *cannot* offer healthcare to all of its citizens. The U.S., on the other hand, the richest country in the world, *chooses not* to offer healthcare to all of its citizens.

Out of all of the information I was exposed to during residency, including the tens of thousands of facts I memorized and the hundreds of lessons I learned, there is one truth, abundantly clear, that stands above the rest: my patients' lack of health insurance not only complicated my job as a physician but for many patients was a direct cause of an increase in their morbidity or mortality. From the many patients I have written about examples abound. First, there was the pregnant teenager without health insurance, who was so used to being turned away from clinics when she was not pregnant, she thought the same would happen when she was pregnant. Her lack of prenatal care complicated the delivery, and tragically her baby does not have the use of her right arm. Then there was Evelyn Howe, who, due to lack of health insurance and the fear of a large medical bill, stayed away from a doctor, resulting in the growth and metastasizing of her breast cancer. Evelyn died before the hospital was even able to print her bill! After Evelyn Howe, there was Sheri, the ICU patient with HIV whose Medicaid health insurance was not accepted by many of the physicians she went to. All Sheri needed was a primary care doctor to help her stay compliant with her medications, but being turned down for care countless times discouraged her from seeking help. Then there was Harold Brown, who had to become infected with HIV before he was able to get health insurance from the government (Medicaid) that would cover his many other medical problems. After Harold Brown, there was Ms. Jackson, who had to live with the stigma of not having health insurance and knowing that her free care was a burden to the hospital and medical staff. Finally, there was Sammy, for whom I was forced to make the system work, allowing him to get the best care possible.

Many who are aware of and concerned with the human condition have said that healthcare should be a human right enjoyed by all people, regardless of their ability to pay. Until this happens, the Sammy Ellingtons of the world—and the doctors concerned with their care—will be forced to do whatever it takes to make our dysfunctional and woefully inequitable healthcare system work for their benefit. But what about the other 40 million Americans without health insurance? Where and how are these people cared for, who unlike Sammy lack access to a clinic and a doctor willing to bend the rules? Unfortunately, the vast majority will forgo regular medical care with a primary care doctor and wait until their medical conditions become so advanced that emergency room care or admittance to a hospital is required—at considerable cost to society.

Since finishing my residency on the West Side of Chicago and continuing my work with the underserved as an attending physician at the Chicago Family Health Center on the South Side of Chicago, I have observed a significant increase in the number of patients who are applying for disability benefits

(Supplemental Security Income) and/or government-sponsored healthcare insurance (Medicare or Medicaid). Rarely a day goes by when I do not have at least one new patient in my examining room who has recently lost his job and healthcare insurance. These patients, of both genders and all walks of life, have found their way to our clinic (a Federally Qualified Health Center which serves the disenfranchised) for temporary respite from their medical, financial, and personal woes.

Neighborhood clinics like mine are the pulse, if you will, of the health of a community, and from my vantage point both the physical and mental health of the inner-city neighborhoods where I work have worsened over the last several years.

For example, some of my patients' blood pressure and glucose levels, which are influenced by the body's catecholamine and cortisol levels in response to physical and psychological stress, have been increasingly difficult to control, putting them at increased risk for serious complications such as diabetic neuropathy, myocardial infarction, and strokes. Other patients are visibly more anxious and depressed than they used to be. I have started prescriptions and increased dosages of antidepressants more frequently in the last few years than in the previous years. And some of my patients, because of the strain of unemployment, dwindling social services, and increasing difficultly feeding their families, come into my examining room and break down and cry, like the patient who was recently laid off from one of the steel mills that surround our clinic. This strong, proud gentleman, a man who does not talk easily about his troubles, sat in my clinic, told me how difficult it is now, and broke down.

Sitting in an inner-city clinic in the heartland of America, I do indeed have my finger on the pulse of this country. And that pulse seems weaker and less regular than it used to be. There is both a lack of hope and a feeling of despair that I have not seen previously. As the richest country in the world, and a nation that has a history of caring for its people, the U.S. has an obligation to continue that care, especially for the most vulnerable.

If we could change one thing in healthcare to right the wrongs of the system and to benefit the people we serve, it should be

to give everyone in this country adequate and affordable
health insurance. This noble gesture would honor human
beings and treat them with the dignity they deserve.

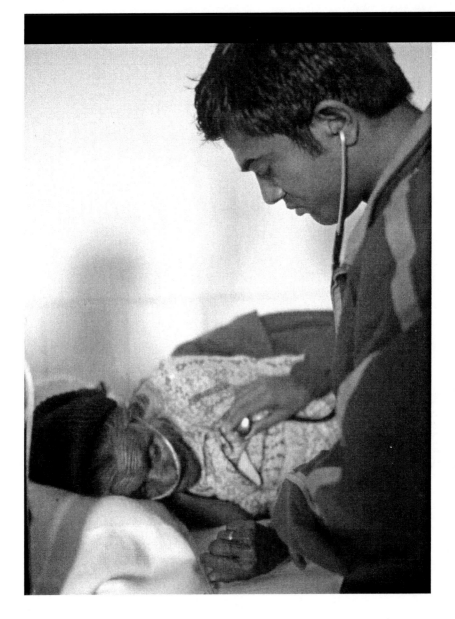

*Dr. Mahendra Poudel examines a patient with pneu-
monia at the Dr. Megh Bahadur Parajuli Clinic in
Ilam, Nepal, March 2005.*

A Return to Nepal

In March 2005, I flew back to Nepal to volunteer at the Dr. Megh Bahadur Parajuli Clinic recently built by Himalayan HealthCare (HHC) in Ilam, a sizable village in the eastern part of Nepal, bordered by India to the east and Tibet to the north. This was my fourth trip to Nepal in four years; the previous visits had been three-week medical treks: the first is recounted in the Prologue, the second was into the mountainous region above Ilam, and the third was to Everest base camp. Each of these treks had allowed our medical team to offer primary care to hundreds of Nepalese patients. During one of my return trips I had the good fortune of reuniting with the patients whose stories are in the Prologue. The malnourished Tamang boy from the village of Sertung, whom our medical team had taken back to Kathmandu for treatment, is healthy and resides in a boarding school in Kathmandu, where he is at the top of his class academically. His father has returned to their village and still battles alcoholism. The young Tamang woman from the village of Sertung, who went into septic shock and had to be flown to Kathmandu, is also doing well. She is back in her village with her husband, and she recently gave birth to a healthy baby. Himalayan HealthCare has lost contact with the woman from Tipling who had abdominal tuberculosis and the English gentleman who had acute appendicitis.

Since my first visit to Nepal four years ago, the political situation remains unstable and, from a number of standpoints, has worsened. The Maoist insurgency, begun in 1996, has claimed the lives of more than 12,000 Nepalese, many of them innocent people caught in the crossfire of the Maoist-government fighting. Although some of the goals of the Maoists are praiseworthy (healthcare for all, increasing the standard of living of the Nepalese people, and the end to the monarchy as a governing body), their means to obtain these goals are abhorrent. The taking up of arms, mass slaughter of police and army personnel, extortion (by way of a "war tax"), and the kidnapping and induction of young men from the rural areas into their army are all repugnant and detrimental to the country and the Nepalese way of life. Many of the rural areas in Nepal now have few, if any, teenage through middle-age males. These boys and men have either been inducted into the Maoist army or have left their villages, with many having relocated to Kathmandu for work or India for study.

The consequences of this mass exodus are significant. In the rural communities, terraces are not being planted and harvested at the usual self-sustaining rates; Kathmandu has become a congested, and increasingly polluted city, and many rural health clinics and aid projects have either been shut down or drastically scaled back. Children are not receiving immunizations and supplementary nutrition, such as vitamins and iron pills; pregnant women are not receiving prenatal care; the population in general is not receiving adequate primary care. No one has yet empirically studied the changing healthcare statistics of these rural areas, but I am sure that there will be—as in many war-torn countries—a rise in the infant and maternal mortality rates and a worsening in the overall health.

How this war has affected HHC (an organization of which I am now a board member) is also significant. HHC has had to pull its staff members from the clinic in Tipling, as well as canceling regular medical treks to two remote regions in Nepal: the Dhading region, which lies north of Kathmandu on the border of Tibet, and the mountainous region north of Ilam on the borders of Tibet and India. Furthermore, an HHC staff member was recently abducted and then released by the Maoists. Dal, the young health assistant (who had run through the pre-dawn light during my first medical trek to get to the solar phone to call the helicopter for our critically ill Tamang patient), was abducted during his two-day walk out of the mountains from the Tipling clinic to Trisuli Bazaar, the trailhead that would have taken him back to Kathmandu. Dal recounted the experience for me when I was at the Ilam clinic, where he is now stationed due to the presence of the Maoists in Tipling.

Dal reported that he was taken by armed Maoists to a camp in the hills outside of Tipling village. As a form of intimidation, he was forced to wear a chain of hand-grenades around his neck while he stood guard at the camp the first night. He was then subjected to several days of interrogation, during which time he was questioned extensively about the HHC organization. The Maoists then tried to indoctrinate him into their philosophy and army, which he bravely rejected. Fortunately, he was not harmed. Upon his release, the Maoists levied a $400 "war tax" on him and gave him and HHC thirty-five days to register with them—a form of endorsement—or to stop our healthcare programs. Anil and the HHC board decided not to capitulate to this demand and were forced to remove the medical staff from the Tipling clinic in the Dhading region.

There is no doubt that the current government's response to the Maoists, as well as some of the government's army's tactics—which have been condemned by many human rights groups—have added to the tension and bloodshed. Furthermore, the massacre four years ago of the Nepalese Royal Family by a family member and the uneasy sharing of power between the democratically elected parliament and King Gyanendra (brother of the slain King Birendra) have left Nepal in a tenuous political situation. Additional fuel was injected into this political "tinder box" on February 1, when King Gyanendra, in an effort to deal effectively with the Maoists and the country's "corrupt" politicians, declared a state of emergency. During this "power grab," as many Nepalese people have called it, the King placed a number of the elected politicians under house arrest, closed the airports to all flights, turned off all phone lines and internet connections, and severely restricted the press. It was a frightening period for those who had friends and colleagues in Nepal, eased somewhat when the airport was reopened after one day, and the phone lines and internet connections were turned on a week later. However, the tight control on the press and the Monarch's complete control of the government continue.

Despite the uncertain political situation in Nepal—and much to the concern of my family and friends—I heeded a call from Anil, the director of HHC, and headed back to help in the new HHC clinic. I landed in Kathmandu, now under a visibly higher degree of security since my visit one year ago. The number of army and police officers at the airport, as well as around the city, had increased markedly. I had one day to spend in Kathmandu with Anil, who appraised me of his feelings about the King's implementation of emergency measures, which were similar to the thoughts or other Nepalese with whom I had contact during my visit. With an amazing blend of uncertainty, courage, resolve, and humor, Anil stated that he would give the King a chance at restoring peace and prosperity. An ardent believer in democracy, Anil, like many others in his country, has put the democratic ideal on hold. Similar to U.S. citizens after September 11, the Nepalese appear to be willing to forego some of their civil liberties for the hope of peace.

While talking to Anil, an educated, successful, and articulate man, who has a brother living in the United States, I wondered if he and his family would consider immigrating to America. He touched on this thought during our conversation, saying he has considered it more frequently as the political situation in Nepal has worsened. However, he is passionately committed to the welfare of the Nepalese people, and I imagine he realizes that Nepal—albeit not the safest place to raise a family—is the best place for him to be to serve his needy countrymen.

Before I boarded a plane from Kathmandu to Ilam, Anil and I headed over to the Nepal Medical Council to get my medical license, essential for a visiting doctor in the country. This medical council resides in a rundown, low-lying cement building on a dusty lot in the heart of the city. Next to it is the medical hospital where some of the HHC pediatric patients have received heart valve surgeries at no cost, thanks to the hospital and its doctors.

Upon entering the Council, we met several international medical volunteers who were also applying to work in Nepal. I sat down beside two registered nurses from Scotland who were with a humanitarian organization whose volunteers service the villagers in the hills outside of Pokhara, a sizable city in central Nepal, known as the starting point for the fifteen-thousand tourists each year who trek the popular Annapurna circuit. The nurses described the one-week "full surgical camp" they run in the villages, recounting the abdominal surgeries their volunteer foreign medical doctors perform in a week of charitable healthcare. When Anil asked how they provide their surgical patients with the vital follow-up care after the surgeons have departed, they answered, "We have ophthalmology camps that follow the surgical camps and the ophthalmologists examine the patients." After we left the Medical Council, Anil and I questioned the appropriateness of having an eye doctor evaluate an abdominal surgical patient. However, one of the true motives of these medical camps became apparent after I learned that this organization is faith-based and given to proselytizing. The government of Nepal (a country that is 85% Hindu, 10% Buddhist, and 5% Muslim and Christian) has very clear and strict rules against humanitarian groups which proselytize. However, some religious organizations ignore this rule and offer the prospect of "health and the hope of heaven".

Healthcare providers who blur the line between their personal religious beliefs and their professional obligations do the profession and, more importantly, their patients, a disservice. There are very few professions similar to medicine in which one develops such intimate and privileged knowledge about another person. Moreover, the patient comes to the healthcare provider, often in a vulnerable state, and completely trusting that he will receive beneficial medical care. There is no place in medicine for healthcare providers who take advantage of patients' helplessness by recruiting them into a religious or moral belief system that is not their own. At present, it is a reality that the vast majority of charitable healthcare given throughout the world is by religious and faith-based organizations, but it is very troublesome that some of these organizations have another motive for the healthcare they administer. Additionally, medical professionals who proselytize denigrate the profession of medicine. We are trained to be objective, nonjudgmental, and fair. When a healthcare provider subjects patients to his or her own belief system, it lessens not only the sacred patient-doctor trust and the profession of medicine, but also ourselves as human beings.

As I sat down for the Council's interview, the head medical doctor, one of a half-dozen Nepalese doctors sitting across the table from me, studied my file intently. He then looked up and asked me to tell the Council members about myself. As I started a long-winded sentence about my life's work to date, he hastily cut me off and said, "Thank you, you're approved, bye, bye." As I left this interview—the quickest of my medical career—I thought to myself that if it was this easy to get approved to work medically in Nepal, I could understand why these faith-based groups can so easily offer healthcare in this country.

The next day I headed to Ilam. After an hour's flight from Kathmandu and a three-hour winding, bumpy, and dusty car ride into the tea-covered hills of eastern Nepal, I arrived at the clinic. I had the pleasant surprise of seeing not only Dal but also Kamal. Both of these HHC medical assistants had been the real heroes of the first medical trek that I was on and the reason that the young Tamang woman survived. I felt an instant renewed kinship with these two from the bond that had formed during our earlier, intense and emotional experience. Kamal, true to the lives of many Nepalese, has to earn a living separated from his wife and three children. His family resides in Tipling near the health post which HHC is no longer staffing because of the Maoist activity. For Kamal to see his family, he must travel nineteen hours by bus and then hike two days to his village. Consequently, he sees them only once every several months. Kamal is not the only young Nepalese man in this situation; there are many more who have been separated from their families in the villages for extended periods as a result of the present guerrilla war. Despite the fact that these two had been living under the strains of a decade of violence, they, like Anil, still maintain a sense of optimism and have retained their good spirits.

Dal and Kamal showed me around the impressive new clinic. Built with international funds and the hard work of the Nepalese people, the clinic is a noteworthy accomplishment. The aesthetically designed three-story building contains two examining rooms, an ER, three inpatient beds, a pharmacy and laboratory, and even a small OR. Painted white and sitting on a hill that overlooks a scenic valley and poor village, this modest clinic—as I would quickly learn—is a beacon of hope for the people in this region of Nepal.

After the tour, I met the clinic's two young Nepalese medical doctors with whom I would become close friends during the week. Mahendra and Tirtha had both been at the top of their Kathmandu medical school class, and both had come to this rural clinic to embark on an adventure, as well as to fulfill a calling—their desire to help the less fortunate in their country. I had come to Ilam for two reasons: the first was my responsibility to HHC as a board member; the second was to fill, at least for a one-week period, the clinic's still-vacant senior medical doctor position. Because my medical school and residency training had been eighteen months longer than Mahendra's and Tirtha's training, I was designated their senior.

Prior to my arrival, the clinic had announced to the village that an American doctor was coming. This had generated a large amount of interest, so much so that there were several patients waiting for me the evening I arrived, a day before I was scheduled to start to see patients. It reminded me of my first trek four years before when we had arrived at the Tipling clinic to find a long line of patients waiting to be seen. That trek, because of the severity of illness of the Tamang woman, had been the most medically and emotionally trying. My second and third treks to Nepal had been less intense and had allowed me to offer the basics in primary care and the time needed to instruct our patients in preventive medicine. No patients on these two treks were critically ill. But this volunteer experience at the Ilam clinic would change all that, casting me back once again into the role of an emergency and critical-care physician—a role accompanied by intensity and emotion.

So, on the evening of my first day we started to see patients. A few of the first patients we examined had what I had learned from my prior treks to be common ailments in Nepal, namely, gastritis, worms, anemia, and arthritis. In addition, in what I came to see as a regular occurrence that week, many patients came to me for a second opinion. Prior to my visit, these patients had seen either Mahendra or Tirtha and now had returned to inquire if I agreed with the initial diagnosis. One patient was even so bold as to ask me to read one of the doctor's notes and tell her what it said. I politely declined her request and, after examining her, I told her that I agreed with the doctor's assessment. Mahendra and Tirtha said that this would be a common occurrence now that the villagers knew that there was an American doctor at the clinic.

Until I arrived, the clinic had seen an average of twenty patients a day and had admitted only one inpatient. All this changed after I arrived. The next morning, as Mahendra, Tirtha, and I went for our early morning meal at the canteen, we noticed that the patients had already begun to line up. After our meal, Mahendra and Tirtha informed me that all of the patients wanted to be seen by me. To manage this in the most efficient manner, we had each doctor present his patients' histories to me and then we performed the physical exam together, thereby allowing us to get through the fifty patients we would see each day.

One of the first patients reminded me of the critically ill Tamang patient mentioned earlier. Like that patient she had come to the Ilam clinic with a fever and was complaining of back and pelvic pain. She, too, had had a spontaneous miscarriage (her fifth of six pregnancies) three weeks prior to this visit. Over the last week her condition had worsened. Her medical history and physical exam, which elicited pelvic pain, suggested a diagnosis of endometritis. Unlike the Tamang woman's, this patient's vital signs, fortunately, were normal, and she had not started to show signs of septicemia. To avoid any further worsening of her condition, we admitted her, and she became our first inpatient. We started her on two broad-spectrum antibiotics and began an IV for hydration. Her story became more interesting when we discovered that her hemoglobin was very low (5.1 g/dl instead of within the normal range 12–15), which meant that she was severely anemic; essentially, the oxygen-carrying capacity of her blood was one-third that of a normal person. Her anemia was clearly chronic in nature; a person with a hemoglobin level this low who is not complaining of dizziness—and is able to stand—has developed the ability to compensate for low hemoglobin over at least a several-month period. Furthermore, since she had lost five pregnancies in as many years—most likely as a result of her anemia—we surmised that she had been anemic for some time.

Her condition started to improve with antibiotics and IV fluids, but she would also need four units of blood. Interestingly, the village's Red Cross blood service, for lack of refrigeration, has to rely on volunteers to donate blood at the time a patient needs the blood. So the blood bank developed a list of all the names and blood types of the villagers willing to donate. After a small sample of the patient's blood is drawn, it is "typed and crossed" against a small sample of blood that is drawn from each of several villagers who share the same blood type. Once the best matches are found, the chosen donors each give one pint of blood. It was from the generosity of these villagers that we were able to quickly start her on two of the four units she needed, thus helping us avoid any further deterioration in her medical condition.

That first day, as with each day of the coming week, we saw a number of patients who came to the clinic for a "second opinion." As before, most of these patients had already been evaluated earlier that week by Mahendra or Tirtha, and some had even been examined by specialists in a number of Kathmandu's teaching hospitals. It struck me as peculiar that these patients would assume that I, a general practitioner, would know more about their specific disease than a specialist. For all of these second opinion cases, I reviewed each doctor's assessment and medical plan for each patient and found all to be accurate and sound. In each case, I went out of my way to inform the patient that I agreed with his or her doctor's diagnosis, and told all of them to trust these accomplished medical professionals.

Our most seriously ill patient came into the clinic after we had completed our schedule for the day. She was a sixty-four-year-old woman brought in by her daughter and son-in-law. Her family had waited two days after her initial onset of worsening respiratory distress to bring her to the clinic because the patient had emphatically stated to her family, "I'll wait until the American doctor arrives." When she sat down in front of us, we knew right away that she would be admitted to our inpatient ward. Her respiration rate of thirty-five breaths per minute and her signs and symptoms of respiratory distress dramatically indicated her need for hospitalization. She had a history of hypertension and gout, and a cardiologist in Kathmandu had recently discontinued her digoxin, a medicine that helps regulate both the pace and strength of each heartbeat. On examination, her lungs were clear, her heart rate of ninety beats per minute was in the normal range, and her blood-oxygen saturation was normal. The increased rate of breathing at this point was unexplained; we surmised from her pale conjunctiva that she was anemic and would need a blood transfusion to correct her increased respiratory rate. We admitted her to one of our inpatient beds, drew her blood, ordered a chest X-ray, and did an EKG. We read the EKG before going to dinner and were alarmed to find that it showed an occasional premature ventricular contraction (PVC).

PVCs, as the name implies, are contractions that happen in the heart's ventricles at an irregular or premature time. These aberrant contractions are usually triggered by an area in the heart's ventricle that is irritable. (This is opposed to a normal ventricle contraction that is triggered by the atrioventricular node, one of the heart's steady pacemakers.) The irritability in the heart's ventricle can be due to a number of reasons, but hypokalemia (low potassium) and hypoxemia are two of the most common causes. If her PVCs were due to hypokalemia we could correct the condition fairly easily with potassium supplements. However, if this arrhythmia was triggered from an area in her heart that was now hypoxic or, worst yet, ischemic (in other words she was having a myocardial infarction or heart attack), the laboratory, unfortunately, did not have the capability to analyze her cardiac enzymes—the crucial blood test that would allow us to monitor and treat her heart attack. At present she was having approximately seven PVCs a minute. This frequency was enough for us to be concerned, but we felt we did not need to intervene—at least not yet. However, if the frequency of her PVCs increased, or if they began to occur in couplets or triplets, we would have to intercede, for at this point her heart could easily go into ventricular tachycardia, and she, most likely, would die.

Since this patient's admission, her labored breathing and respiration rate had increased slightly, and we began to hear wheezing. We gave her an aerosolized albuterol treatment to help dilate her airway, and we continued oxygen. Based on the patient's difficulty with breathing, I knew that if we could not find and correct the underlying cause of her respiratory distress, she would need to be intubated, but the clinic did not have a respirator. So, if she went into respiratory failure, our best chance of saving her would be to manually oxygenate her with a resuscitation bag. Manually oxygenating someone is physically taxing, and needs several people, continually taking turns, to effectively perform the procedure for extended periods of time. However, that part would be the least of our worries, for we would still have to transport her to the nearest major hospital, a four-hour drive out of the mountains on a steep, winding, and uneven road. If she did not die from the lack of adequate ventilation, then the ride would probably kill her.

The other doctors and I were hoping that the laboratory results would show that she was anemic, a condition we could easily correct with the goodwill and donation of a pint of blood from each of two or three villagers. But, when Mahendra informed me that the Red

Cross lab technician was out of the village for the day, I began to worry. I wondered if there was anyone in town with type "O-negative" blood, the universal donor blood in an emergency situation. Much to my distress, the village's blood bank list was not available. At this time of the day it was still light, and the four-hour drive to the teaching hospital in the terai (the lowlands in southern Nepal) was still an option, although the drive out of the mountains would be extremely difficult.

After leaving my dinner untouched because I was so nervous about this patient's condition, I sat with the other doctors and reviewed a series of plans that we would take for each possible blood test result. At this point the blood work came back, and we were surprised to see that she was only mildly anemic (hemoglobin of 9.8 g/dl), not enough to explain her worsening respiratory state. But the blood work did show that she was hypokalemic with a potassium level of 2.5 mEg/l (normal is 3.5–5.1 mEg/l), a possible explanation for her cardiac arrhythmia, which now had ominously worsened with her PVCs having increased in frequency to twenty times per minute. What was more worrisome, however, was the fact that these PVCs were now coming in couplets. We quickly administered her potassium through the IV and went to review her X-ray.

The X-ray equipment at the clinic is rather rudimentary. Unlike the U.S. state-of-the-art digital X-ray equipment with images that can be transmitted over a phone line to any computer inside or outside the hospital, this X-ray machine, purchased in India for a few thousand U.S. dollars, still uses actual film. The technician develops each X-ray by hand and often gave us the films still wet, straight from the fixer and wash baths. Although the X-ray facility is antiquated, for this case it was more than adequate and it gave us some telling information about her—she had a massive heart. The silhouette of a normal heart on an X-ray film spans about one-third the distance between the patient's left and right chest walls. Her heart's silhouette filled more than three-quarters of this distance, which meant that she had massive dilated cardiomyopathy (DCM). In the majority of cases the etiology of DCM is unknown, but alcohol use and viral infections are fairly common causes. Her heart's ventricles had been enlarging for many years, and had finally reached the

point where they could not adequately pump blood to her body—
or even her own heart—thus putting her into heart failure.

Over the next several hours, even with the administration of
a strong diuretic (Lasix), IV potassium, continual aerosolized
albuterol treatments, and two broad spectrum IV antibiotics
given for a possible pneumonia, her condition deteriorated. She
became more hypoxic, her respiratory rate increased, and her
cardiac arrhythmia worsened.

By now it was early evening and the sun was setting. With her
condition declining and our only hope of getting her to a cardiac
unit in a hospital all but dimmed, we decided to consult by phone a
cardiologist in Kathmandu. He was a friend of Anil's and had been
both Mahendra's and Tirtha's medical school professor. He
informed us that even if we had wanted to take her to the closest
hospital, it was not an option; the Maoists, in one of their more
annoying anarchistic practices, had blocked the main road to the
town where this hospital was located. He suggested that we continue managing her as we had done and to add another blood pressure lowering medicine (ace inhibitor), nitrates to dilate the
coronary arteries, and heparin to help decrease the chance that her
failing and inefficient heart would form and release a life threatening blood clot. We gave her the ace inhibitor, but did not have
nitrates in the clinic. We could not give her the blood-thinning
heparin because we did not have the ability in our laboratory to
monitor her coagulation factors. Giving her heparin "blindly" would
have been too risky. If we had thinned her blood too much she
could have bled to death. Our conservative approach was the
proper path to take. In the event that she developed a blood clot,
we would manage it at that time.

In much the same way my critical care attending during my intern
year had guided me toward the realization that Shari, my patient
with AIDS, was going to die, I took Mahendra and Tirtha aside and
gently let them know how grave our patient's condition was. But
unlike my situation as an intern, Mahendra and Tirtha knew this
patient's worsening medical condition and did not need my suggestion that they should alert the family for the possibility that she
might not make it until the morning light. As I watched Mahendra, a
young, caring, and sensitive doctor, rehearse what he was going to

say to the family, I could see his eyes well up with tears. This moment took me back to my intern year and the deep and complex emotions that I, too, had felt so many times. His emotional investment in his patients was both inspiring to see and emotionally trying to watch. My heart went out to him.

One thought that had been going through my mind during this day, and was increasing as this woman's health grew more and more critical, was her words to her family two days prior, "I'll wait until the American doctor arrives." There is no doubt that in Nepal there is a mystique about foreign medical doctors, and perhaps even more about American doctors, but as I watched Mahendra and Tirtha carefully and skillfully handle every aspect of her care—with me only asking simple questions—I realized that these two doctors had done everything that I would have done for her, and perhaps even more. In addition, I realized that her decision to wait two days for care might have been the difference between life and death. If she pulled through, I would forget all about her decision to delay coming to the clinic. If she did not make it, it would have been one of the many indelible marks that this profession leaves on us caregivers.

The meeting between Mahendra, Tirtha, and the family went well, and Mahendra, with great sensitivity, explained the critical condition of the patient. The family's wishes at this point were not to try to transfer her to another hospital, but in the event that she went into cardiac arrest they wanted us to perform CPR. If this scenario ever transpired, we would then be obliged to transport her out of the mountains, encountering the Maoists' roadblock. The thought of managing her medically did not bother me, but negotiating with a Maoist guerilla at gun-point was disquieting.

With unease, we watched our patient closely throughout the evening. We administered serial aerosolized albuterol treatments, supported her with supplementary oxygen, and did frequent lung exams. In the early morning of the next day, remarkably, her lungs started to sound a little better; the Lasix, breathing treatments, and antibiotics had had time to improve her respiratory condition. During the next hours her condition decompensated several times, which necessitated our administering additional breathing treatments and keeping a close eye on her. Nevertheless, by the morning she had stabilized. Over the next day she showed slow but steady improvement, and with each passing day she sounded and looked better. Near the end of the week we weaned her off oxygen, and soon thereafter she began to sip homemade soup her family had brought. On my last day in Ilam, she took a short stroll around the courtyard of the clinic.

As with Shari, I was both relieved and surprised to see her survive. It reconfirmed in me the humble lesson that I have continually relearned: I, thankfully, am a terribly inaccurate predictor of death. Unlike Shari, this Nepalese woman did not have all of modern medicine available when we were treating her. We lacked some important basic medicines, were not able to follow certain laboratory results, and surely would have lost if we had been forced to perform CPR or manually ventilate her. However, she survived, and this fact reconfirms a lesson that I have known since intern year of residency: it is nature that heals people. Doctors and nurses can facilitate nature, but it is nature that does the healing.

This was the first of many difficult cases we managed during the week. The breadth of medical cases and diseases we saw in the clinic was impressive, including: diabetes, hypertension, anemia, pneumonia, prolapsed uteruses, infertility, gall stones, acute abdominal pain (which was diagnosed as an ovarian mass with the ultrasound by Tirtha), amenorrhea, depression, and congenital disorders, not to mention the common complaints of arthritis, gastritis, and worms—a far cry from my South Side of Chicago clinic where I normally see only diabetes and hypertension, and perform physicals on healthy children.

With this increased number of villagers coming to the clinic, inevitably there were a number who were sick enough to be admitted. Our inpatient ward, which had three beds, was filled the first night. By the second night we had six inpatients, which required use of the ER and ultrasound rooms to house them. The inpatients were also complex cases. We had a woman who presented to us with headaches, nausea and vomiting, increased blood pressure, and a low pulse rate. Mahendra quickly, and I think accurately, diagnosed her with increased intracranial pressure, a disease process that I had not seen since my medical school days. We also had one woman suffering from dehydration, a result of her nausea and vomiting from her chemotherapy for breast cancer, and two women with pneumonia. Our days were busy, and our nights were long and sleepless with the three of us taking turns checking on the patients.

As the week progressed, I continually witnessed the fine medical skills and knowledge that both Mahendra and Tirtha possessed. Both were accomplished medical doctors, with Mahendra excelling at the internal medicine cases and Tirtha adept on the ultrasound machine. I also quickly realized that we were functioning as equals; I was not their senior medical doctor. Their histories, examinations, diagnoses, and management of the patients were well done. And during this week, I found myself increasingly taking a back seat to their management of the patients, often relegating myself to my familiar role of informing the patient at the end of the visit that Mahendra's and Tirtha's plan for them was correct, and they should trust these fine Nepalese doctors—making my point as directly as possible.

Mahendra and Tirtha were quite aware of the patients' preference to see me during this week; nevertheless, it did not diminish their self-confidence or alter their interactions with the patients. In fact, they found it amusing at times. One case, which brought smiles, involved a patient who had come to the clinic with the complaint of pain in both knees. After a thorough lower extremity exam, Tirtha correctly diagnosed the patient with degenerative joint disease (arthritis) and gave him a prescription for a pain medication. Tirtha, with a twinkle in his eye, asked me, "Can you listen to the patient's heart and lungs before he leaves, or he will not be satisfied with his visit." I placed my stethoscope on the patient's chest wall and then back, hearing normal heart and lung sounds. "Sounds like arthritis to me," I said smiling at the patient. The patient then broke into a wide toothless smile, thanked me, and then left looking quite satisfied.

At the end of my last day at the clinic we had a farewell dinner with the whole medical staff. I commented how impressed I was with all of them, but especially how well trained I felt the Nepalese doctors were. I specifically mentioned that I was confident that this medical staff could handle almost any situation. This comment would eerily foreshadow an upcoming event.

I thought that, after dinner, the other doctors and I were going to have a relaxed evening and a chance to chat about our busy week, but as we were leaving the canteen the ambulance pulled up to the clinic. The attendant jumped out and, with the help of one of the nurses, quickly wheeled the patient into the clinic. As Mahendra, Tirtha, and I entered the ER and looked at the young, petite woman, we realized that she was one of the employees of the clinic. She lay on the gurney with her eyes rolled back and her teeth clenched—seizing. From the fact that her husband had found her at their home in this condition, we knew that she had been seizing nonstop for over thirty minutes. She was in status epilepticus, a true medical emergency. Most seizures last only a few minutes and then are followed by a postictal period when the patient is quite somnolent and sleepy. Status epilepticus can continue indefinitely, and therein lies the problem. Nonstop seizures can cause permanent brain damage or death. There is a real urgency to stopping a patient's seizure that is "status."

Our exam showed that her respiration rate was normal, her lungs were clear, and her blood-oxygen saturation level was within the normal range which gave us confidence that she had not swallowed her tongue. To ensure that this would not happen, we attempted to insert a tongue protector into her mouth, but her teeth were clenched too tightly. The next task, which we had to do as quickly as possible, was to stop her seizures. This meant inserting an IV into one of the veins in her arm and then administering her both a sedative (Ativan) and a loading dose of an antiepileptic medication (Phenytoin). Placing an IV into a small vein is tricky in any patient, but extremely difficult in a patient who is seizing. The nurse and Mahendra tried to get access into one arm, while I tried on the other; all were failures. Mahendra then tried to get access into a vein in her ankle, also without success.

By this time she had been seizing for at least forty minutes. It now became a dire need to get IV access. I offered to try to place a subclavian venous line, which entails inserting a large bore needle under the collar bone and into the large vein that runs just superior to the apex of the lung. When Mahendra heard this he looked up at me with surprise. "You can do that?" he asked. I had done many during residency training, but I had not attempted one in over three years. This procedure, if done inaccurately, can puncture the patient's pleura space, allowing air in between the lung and chest wall (pneumothorax) causing the lung to collapse, a major complication we wanted to avoid. Thankfully, Mahendra gained access to a vein in her ankle after we discussed the risks of the procedure. He then injected five milligrams of Ativan into her vein, but then, frustratingly, the vein ruptured, and we lost our IV access. We held pressure on the site and hoped that the Ativan was traveling up to her brain and would soon end her seizures.

We waited about ten minutes, all the while trying again to gain access into any vein in either arm. After it was apparent that the Ativan was not stopping her seizures, we knew that we needed to gain IV access again to repeat another five milligram dose of the same drug as well as load her with Phenytoin. While Tirtha frantically tried to insert a line into her hand, and all of us worrying that she might be suffering from anoxic encephalopathy, it crossed my mind that we might have to do a venous cut-down on her to get access. In this procedure you make a deep scalpel cut into the ankle and then isolate an accessible vein. In my medical school and residency training I had never seen this procedure done and had only read about it. The idea of attempting it made me pause with apprehension, but I was saved again when Tirtha announced that he had gained access into her hand. He then asked a nurse to tape the line securely in place. But, as misfortune would have it, at that instant the power went out in the hospital.

In Nepal, power outages are a regular occurrence, and in the mountains they are even more frequent. Sometimes the cause is a tree that has fallen on the line, but increasingly it has been the Maoists who have disrupted the flow of electricity. With luck, outages are short, but they can last for days.

As we stood in the darkness, there was complete silence momentarily. Then I heard Tirtha, a soft-spoken and mild-mannered Hindu exclaim, "God Bless it! This damn hospital!" Mahendra then yelled, "Get me a torch." I heard someone scrambling around me, and then a weak and fading neon flashlight was turned on and directed at the patient. Remarkably, Tirtha was able to hold the IV line in place throughout the darkness and while she was seizing. One of the nurses quickly secured the line to her hand, and we administered the additional dose of Ativan and the Phenytoin bolus to the patient, but this vein also ruptured while we were administering the final few milliliters of the second medication.

We had now given her all of the medications that we had available to us. Without IV access, we stood there exhausted and seemingly defeated. All we could do, once again, was wait and hope that these medicines were traveling up her arm and into her brain, and not sitting in the interstitial tissue around her ruptured vein. Perhaps the Hindu God Ganesh (good luck) was looking down on us at this moment, for in the faint, flickering light of the neon torch we saw her seizures start to wane slightly; then her arms, which had been tightly contracted against her chest, relaxed; finally, her jaw went slack. She had stopped seizing.

Soon the lights came back on. With the patient now motionless and in a deep sleep, the nurse was able to get an IV line into her cubitus allowing us to give her a bolus of glucose, on the chance that she had been seizing because of hypoglycemia. We then started her on a Phenytoin IV drip to maintain an adequate level of this antiepileptic medication in her blood. With her jaw now relaxed, we attempted to suction the secretions out of her mouth. This caused her to gag, a hopeful sign—neurologically at least—that her brainstem was intact. Later she aroused a bit from her groggy and postictal state and was able to follow the simple command of sticking out her tongue, also a hopeful sign that she had at least some higher cortical or cerebral brain functions intact. However, we would not know until the morning, after she had had time to sleep off the Ativan, whether she would have any enduring neurological deficits from the prolonged seizures. With her seizures now under control, we stepped out of the room to collect ourselves.

Working in emergency or critical care medicine often exposes the caregiver to an emotionally charged environment. When the patient whom you are trying to save is one of "your own," it, of course, increases the tensions. There were many moments during this frantic episode when everyone in the ER thought that we might lose her. Their frightened looks and adrenaline-dilated pupils gave away their innermost fears. I had not seen this emotional response in the staff at any other time. Despite the staff's fears, they were able to choke back the emotions which normally may have interfered with the execution of their duties. Indeed, they worked very well and effectively together. Now with the patient stable and her care in the able hands of Mahendra, Tirtha, and the medical staff—I took my tired body to my room and fell fast asleep.

I left Ilam early the next morning for the four-hour drive back to the terai and then to the series of flights that would take twenty hours and bring me back to my home in Chicago. I bid a warm good-bye to Mahendra and Tirtha. We had been through a lot in the last week, and we had grown to be good friends. I think that the ultimate compliment that one doctor can pay another doctor is to allow him to be his personal physician. If I had taken ill during my stay in Nepal, I would not have said, "I'll wait until the American doctor arrives," I would have placed my complete trust in both Mahendra's and Tirtha's ability to care for me.

As I traveled in the local minivan taxi down the steep, winding mountain road and watched the tea plantations glide by, I struck up a conversation with one of the locals in the cab. Having intimate knowledge of Ilam and the surrounding areas, he informed me that several people from villages outside of Ilam had told him yesterday that the government's army had begun a campaign in their villages to kill the Maoists and break their stronghold in this part of Nepal. (With a virtual clampdown on the Nepalese newspapers, news was carried by word of mouth.) Knowing this continual army-insurgent violence would inevitably, and regrettably, injure or kill innocent bystanders caught in the crossfire of this war, I wondered if some of the injured might be on their way to the clinic to be treated. If so, I knew the staff could handle the situation well. This thought of the clinic staff's competency provided a sense of comfort as I left this great country and wonderful people, who have had to endure so much pain and suffering.

Robbie Lawrence McKersie. Central Park, New York City, June 2004.

Shortly after opening the envelope that contained Katarina's child's paternity results, I stepped off the airplane in Seattle. I was there to do a month-long rotation in family medicine at the University of Washington. My sister Alison had arranged for one of her friends to meet me at the airport.

I remember meeting Michele as I exited the plane and being pleasantly surprised at how much she intrigued me at first sight. She was very attractive and athletic. She had a shy, yet warm smile, and a quick and charmingly funny, staccato laugh. And I found it very easy to talk with her.

This month in Seattle could have been quite gloomy. The continual Seattle rain, the frequent e-mails from Katarina, a cool and impersonal training atmosphere at the university, and Michele losing a dear friend to depression, all could have made this month dismal. But Michele's warmth and energy through it all brightened not only the gray days but my spirit as well. Over the month our friendship grew and blossomed into a wonderful relationship.

On my final day in Seattle, the sun broke through for the first time in thirty days, and we were treated to a magnificently clear view of Mt. Rainier. Its snow-draped peak and beautifully sloping contours were memorable. As Michele drove me to the airport to make my return trip to Chicago, I looked at her and realized how close we had become and how safe I felt; for the first time in a long while I had confidence in a relationship. The clouds that had settled over me during this last year had started to lift.

As I have grown older and experienced more of life, I have developed a belief that some events happen for a reason; perhaps it was not just coincidental that Michele came into my life at this time. Michele has been a very stabilizing and wonderful influence. She is very empathetic and compassionate toward others; this quality not only lends itself well for her work in nursing, but it also makes her an extremely good listener. She is kind in all her interactions—with the world in general and most importantly with me—resulting in a very supportive relationship. Being a nurse has also given her a fundamental understanding of the schedule that medicine demands, and for this I am immensely grateful.

Throughout the innumerable hours—and far too many days—that I have been unavailable while writing this book, Michele has been extremely gracious, and again I thank her.

We are now married and have two beautiful children who warm my heart every moment of the day. This book is tenderly dedicated to Michele, our son, Robbie Lawrence, and daughter, Mia Himalaya. May they always have peace in their hearts and happiness in their lives.

Abscess: A cavity or well-circumscribed area within the body that contains an infection.

Ace inhibitor: A cardiac medication that lowers blood pressure.

ACGME: Accreditation Council for Graduate Medical Education. The governing body for all medical residency programs in this country.

Acidemia: A state of the blood (pH level) when either the concentration of hydrogen atoms is increased or the concentration of bicarbonate atoms is decreased.

Adenosine-Tri-Phosphate (ATP): A molecule that is one of the main energy sources for the body's metabolic processes.

Adrenaline: Synonymous with epinephrine. A catecholamine structurally similar to dopamine that is a cardiac stimulant.

Afebrile: Denotes normal temperature, roughly 98.6 degrees Fahrenheit.

AIDS: Acquired immunodeficiency syndrome. A syndrome in which the body's immune system is deficient and susceptible to opportunistic infections and diseases. The etiological factor is the human immunodeficiency virus (HIV).

Albuterol: A beta-2 agonist medication that dilates bronchial tubes and can increase the heart rate. Used as a treatment in asthma and emphysema.

Alveoli: The air sacs of the lungs. The membrane of the alveoli is where the exchange of oxygen and carbon dioxide takes place between the blood and inhaled air.

Amenorrhea: Abnormal or absent menstrual cycle.

Anaerobes: A microorganism that does not need oxygen to live, grow or replicate.

Anemia: A condition in which the level of hemoglobin in the blood is below the normal range and there is a decrease in the production of red blood cells. Often causes fatigue and pallor.

Annapurna Range: Mountain range in north-central Nepal that is a popular trekking area.

Anorexia: Medical term for decreased appetite.

Anoxic encephalopathy: Brain damage due to a lack of oxygen.

Anticoagulant: A medicine that prevents blood from coagulating.

Apoptosis: The process by which a cell dies. Believed to be due to the cell's own programmed death.

Appendicitis: Inflammation of the appendix. Often causes abdominal pain, anorexia, nausea, vomiting, fever, and an elevated white blood count.

ARDS: Adult respiratory distress syndrome. An acute condition in which the lungs' air sacs (alveoli) fill with interstitial fluids and blood, severely limiting the exchange of vital gases. The causes are varied, but infection and multiple organ failure are two disease processes that have been associated with ARDS.

Arterial-venous graft: The placement of a synthetic (Gore-Tex) connection between an artery and vein in the forearm for dialysis access.

Ascites fluid: Serous fluid that accumulates in the abdominal cavity. Liver disease secondary to alcohol abuse is a common cause.

Asphyxia: The pathological changes due to hypoxia.

Asystole: The absence of heart contractions.

Ativan: A member of the class of drugs called benzodiazepines. A sedative that acts on the central nervous system. Helps reduce anxiety.

Atropine: A powerful cardiac stimulant.

Atrovent: Synonymous with Ipratropium. Used as a bronchial dilator in asthma and emphysema.

Attending: Colloquial term for the senior (non-resident) physician.

Axillary: Synonymous with armpit.

Bacteremia: The presence of bacteria in the blood.

Balint Society of England: "Michael and Enid Balint were psychoanalysts who started seminars for GPs (Family Physicians) in London in the 1950's. The aim was to help the doctors with the psychological aspect of their patients' problems—and their problems with their patients. The focus of the work was on the doctor-patient relationship: what it meant, how it could be used helpfully, why it so often broke down with doctor and patient failing to understand each other." (See References/Sources/Notes)

Basic Metabolic Panel: (BMP) A laboratory test that measures the blood's sodium, potassium, chloride, carbon dioxide, blood urea nitrogen (BUN), creatinine, calcium, and glucose levels.

Benzodiazepines: A class of sedatives, of which valium is an example.

Bicarbonate: HCO3-. A negatively charged ion that is formed when a hydrogen ion dissociates from carbonic acid. Bicarbonate is the main buffering agent in blood.

Biopsy: The sampling of tissue from a living person for diagnosing abnormalities, such as cancer or inflammation.

Blood clot: A collection of platelets and clotting proteins that inhibit bleeding by forming a fibrous meshwork at the site of injury.

Blood urea nitrogen: (BUN) A metabolic by-product from the breakdown of blood, muscle, and protein. Excreted in the urine and primarily used to evaluate kidney function.

Bolus: Colloquial term for quickly giving a large amount of fluid intravascularly.

Bowel obstruction: A blockage of either the small or large bowel. Common causes are a tumor, post-surgical anesthesia, adhesions, or a twisting or telescoping of the bowel.

Bradycardia: A heart rate less than 60 beats per minute. Sometimes used in the colloquial as "bradying down."

Brainstem herniation: The displacement of the brain downward into the foramen magnum (the opening on the base of the skull in which the spinal cord passes) when the intracranial pressure has increased secondary to a cerebral bleed. Can cause a coma and death.

Bronchial tubes: One of the smaller sub-division of the bronchus tubes that bring air from the trachea to the alveoli.

Buddhist Prayer Flags: Often placed on mountain passes and in villages for good luck.

Carcinoma: A malignant cancer of certain types of soft tissue, such as skin, large intestine, lung, prostate, and breast.

Carcinomatosis: Widespread dissemination of a carcinoma in multiple organs and tissue.

Cardiac arrhythmias: Any abnormal heart beat, caused by electrolyte imbalance, heart attack, thyroid problems, certain medications, or other factors.

Cardiomyopathy: Disease of the heart. Can be caused by many factors, such as alcohol, hypertension, toxins, and pathogens.

Catecholamine: Biochemical elements that are the body's major signals during the stress response. Epinephrine, norepinephrine and L-dopa are the main ones.

CD-4 cell: One of the white blood cells that is an integral part of the body's immune system and the cell that HIV infects.

Celebrex: A newer anti-inflammatory medicine. Generally thought to have less gastric side effects than the older anti-inflammatory drugs like ibuprofen and acetaminophen.

Cerebral cortex: The outermost part of the brain, gray in color and whose function it is to control voluntary motor function and receive sensory information.

Cerebral Stroke: A sudden deficit in neurological functioning. Caused by an ischemic or hemorrhagic process.

Cesarean Section: An operation to deliver an infant via the abdomen.

Chai: Tea. Often served with milk, sugar, and masala (spices).

Clonidine: An antihypertensive medication that acts on the central nervous system.

Coagulation factors: A series of proteins in the plasma that are part of the blood clotting process.

Code: Colloquial term to denote that a patient's heart has stopped.

Code blue: The call that goes out over a hospital's intercom to alert medical personnel that a patient's heart has stopped.

Colonoscopy: An endoscopic exam of the colon via the rectum.

Coma: A condition in which a patient's consciousness is deeply impaired. The patient is unable to be aroused.

Common bile duct: The tube that connects the liver and gall bladder to the small intestine.

Congestive Heart Failure: A condition where blood backs up into the lungs and enters the alveoli as a result of inefficient pumping of the heart.

Conjunctiva: The outer membrane of the eyeball and posterior surface of the eyelids.

Cortical brain: Synonymous with cerebral cortex.

Cortisol: A steroid hormone secreted by the adrenal glands. Regulates the metabolism of proteins, fats, and carbohydrates. Helps in the stress response.

Coumadin: An oral medication that is an anticoagulant. Warfarin is the generic name.

County: Cook County Hospital is the main public hospital in Chicago. In 2002 a new and smaller one was built that was named the John H. Stroger, Jr. Hospital of Cook County.

CPR: Cardiopulmonary resuscitation. The technique by which you restore the cardiac output and pulmonary ventilation of a patient who has suffered a cardiac arrest.

Creatinine: Derived from the metabolism of creatine in skeletal muscle. Creatinine is found in the blood and excreted in the urine.

Creatinine Clearance: The calculated or measured amount of creatinine that is filtered by the kidneys per minute. This quantitative value is a good estimate of renal function. With worsening renal disease the creatinine clearance decreases.

CT: Computer tomography. (Synonymous with CAT scan). An imaging technique that uses a computer to synthesize multiple X-rays of an anatomical region into cross-sectional views.

CTA: Chicago Transit Authority.

Cubitus: Synonymous with elbow. Usually denotes the anterior side of the elbow where IV lines are placed.

Daal: Lentil soup served with rice.

DCFS: Department of Children and Family Services. A state run organization whose mission is to protect children who are reported to be abused or neglected and to increase their families' capacity to safely care for them.

Defibrillation: The act of attempting to restore normal rhythm to the heart's atrium and ventricle through the use of an electrical shock.

Deurali: A small village in northeastern Nepal we passed through during our October 2002 medical trek.

DHHS: The Department of Health and Human Services is the United States government's principal agency for protecting the health of all Americans and providing essential human services, especially for those who are least able to help themselves. The Department includes more than 300 programs, covering such activities as medical research, preventing outbreaks of infectious diseases, assuring food and drug safety, Head Start, Indian Health Service, and Medicare to name just a few. HHS budget for year 2003 is $502 billion.

Diabetes mellitus: A metabolic disorder in which the body's utilization of carbohydrates is reduced, caused by a resistance to insulin by the peripheral tissue or a lack of insulin production by the pancreas, or both.

Diabetic neuropathy: Nerve damage due to elevated blood sugars from diabetes. Can result in pain or numbness in the effected nerve.

Dialysis: The process in which a patient's blood is passed through a machine and filtered. Waste components are removed and the blood's electrolytes are normalized. Patients with end-stage renal disease usually have to have dialysis three times a week. Each dialysis session can take up to four hours.

Diaphragm: The thin sheet of muscle at the base of the lungs, separating the abdominal and chest cavities. This muscle helps with respiration.

DIC: Disseminated intravascular coagulation. A condition in which there is uncontrolled clotting and hemorrhaging occurring at the same time.

Diffusion: The movement of small particles towards a uniform distribution. In respiration this movement happens across the membrane that separates the lung's blood vessels and air sacs.

Digoxin: A medicine that increases the force of contraction of the heart and regulates the heart rate.

Dilated Cardiomyopathy (DCM): Heart disease associated with the dilation, and subsequent inefficient contractions, of the heart. Etiology of most cases is unknown, but alcohol use and viruses can cause DCM.

Diuresis: The excretion of urine. Used colloquially to denote a large amount of urine excretion.

Diuretics: A class of medication that helps decrease blood pressure by promoting the excretion of urine.

Dopamine: A catecholamine in the body that stimulates the heart to beat faster and the body's vessels to contract, thereby increasing the blood pressure.

Echogenic: A differential in tissue density that can be seen on imagining studies.

EKG: (ECG) Electrocardiogram. The heart's electrical activity represented graphically.

Electrolytes: The ions that comprise the body's fluids. Sodium, Potassium, Chloride, Bicarbonate, to name a few.

Emergency Medical Technicians (EMT): EMT's are trained to care for patients on accident scenes and on transport by ambulance to the hospital. An EMT has the emergency skills to assess a patient's condition and manage respiratory, cardiac, and trauma emergencies. (Taken verbatim from the U.S. Dept. of Labor web site.)

Emphysema: A disease that slowly destroys lung tissue, inhibiting the exchange of oxygen and carbon dioxide during respiration. Cigarette smoke is a major cause of emphysema.

Endometritis: Inflammation of the endometrial layer of the uterus.

Endoscope: A thin, flexible tube with a tiny video camera and light on the end. Used to visualize the esophagus, stomach, and small and large intestines.

Endotracheal tube: A flexible tube that is passed through the mouth and into the trachea to assist a patient's respirations.

Epinephrine: A catecholamine structurally similar to dopamine that is a cardiac stimulant.

Episiotomy: An incision that is made into the perineum to facilitate the delivery of an infant.

Erb's Palsy: Paralysis of an infant's upper arm and shoulder muscles due to an injury of the brachial nerve plexus during delivery.

ERCP: Endoscopic retrograde cholangiopancreatography. An endoscopic examination used to visualize and image the pancreas and bile duct system. Gall Stones, tumors, and scarring can be diagnosed with this technique.

Everest: Highest mountain in the world. (8,848 meters)

Extubate: The process of pulling an endotracheal tube out of a patient's airway.

Federally Qualified Health Center (FQHC): Government subsidized healthcare centers that serve the underserved.

Foley catheter: A tube that is inserted through the urethra and into the bladder. Allows the drainage of urine.

Free fatty acids: One of the two bi-products of triglycerides, the main dietary form of fat.

Gall bladder: Organ that is part of the GI system. Secretes bile acids into the blood stream to help digest fats. It is prone to stone formation.

Ganesh: The name Ganesh is from the elephant-headed Hindu god of good luck, one of the most popular deities in Nepal and India.

Gastritis: Inflammation of the lining of the stomach.

Glucose: The colloquial name is sugar. The building block of cellulose, starch, and glycogen.

Gout: A metabolic disorder typified by a raised uric acid blood level, resulting in episodes of acute joint inflammation and pain.

Gurka: A caste of Nepalese that are hired to be mercenary soldiers. Britain has a regiment of Gurka soldiers.

Hemoglobin: The oxygen carrying protein that is located in the red blood cell.

Heparin: A substance that is naturally found within certain cells in the liver and lungs, and helps prevent platelets from agglutinating (adhering). Administered non-orally as a "blood thinner" to prevent the formation of blood clots.

Heroin: A street drug that is a derivation of opium. Gives a euphoric feeling and has strong psychological and physiological addiction potential.

Himal: Nepalese for mountain.

Himalayan HealthCare: An international, non-governmental organization established in 1992 that works to help enable rural Nepalese to achieve their own economic and social development.

HIV: Human immunodeficiency virus. An RNA retrovirus that is the etiologic agent of acquired immunodeficiency syndrome (AIDS).

Hospice: A comprehensive program of care to patients and their families facing the end of life. It emphasizes palliative rather than curative treatments, and usually takes place in the patient's home.

Hyperglycemia: Elevated blood glucose level, specifically above 115 mg/dl.

Hypertension: An elevated blood pressure. Normal blood pressure is 120/80.

Hypoglycemia: Low blood glucose level, specifically below 60 mg/dl.

Hypokalemia: A low concentration of potassium ions in the blood. Can be caused by an excess loss of fluids from the gastrointestinal system or kidneys among other causes.

Hypoxia: A decreased concentration of oxygen in the arterial blood that leads to a reduction in tissue oxygenation.

Ilam: A city in eastern Nepal that lies on the border of India, known for its tea and spice production.

Imipenem: Antibiotic with broad antimicrobial coverage.

Incubator: A container with a controlled environment (oxygen, temperature, and humidity) for premature infants.

Infant mortality rate: The number of children who die before their first birthday per one-thousand children born.

Infiltrating Ductal Carcinoma: A cancer of the epithelium cells in the breast's mammary ducts. This cancer at diagnosis has already started to infiltrate its surrounding tissue.

Intern: A first year resident.

Interstitial tissue: The space within a tissue. That which is not within a cavity, vessel or potential space.

Intra-costal muscles: The muscle layers between the ribs that help with respiration.

Intracranial pressure (ICP): Pressure within the cranium or skull. An increase in ICP can lead to herniation of the brainstem and death.

Intubate: The process of placing an endotracheal tube into a patient's airway.

Ischemia: Lack of blood perfusion to tissue.

JP: Abbreviation for Jackson Pratt drain. A surgical tube with one end placed in a body cavity (usually the abdomen) and the other end exiting the skin. The tube is attached to a suction bulb which allows for drainage of the wound.

Kalpokhari: A small village in northeastern Nepal we passed though during our October 2002 medical trek.

Kathmandu: Capital of Nepal.

Ketoacidosis: A state of metabolic acidosis caused by the incomplete breakdown of free fatty acids. Seen in diabetics and people who starve themselves.

Lasix: A medication to help one excrete urine.

Lavage: The washing out of a body cavity or organ (stomach) with the injection and then suctioning of fluid.

LR: Abbreviation for lactate ringers. An intravenous solution that is very close in ion concentration to blood plasma.

Lymph node: One of a series of collecting points along the body's lymphatic vessels, the system of vessels that returns lymphatic fluid that has collected throughout the body to the venous system. Lymphatic fluid is clear and mainly composed of white blood cells. During an infection these lymph nodes can become enlarged and painful due to the increased number of inflammatory cells that have collected in them.

Mabu: Village in northeastern Nepal where we had one of our medical camps in October 2002.

Mammogram: Imaging exam (X-ray, MRI or ultrasound) for screening and diagnosing breast disease.

Mani Stones: Large stone pillars built on many mountain passes. An offering to the gods.

Maoist: The Maoist in Nepal launched their "people's war" in 1996. They are fighting to overthrown the present Nepalese monarchy, which they claim is causing the present inequities and poverty in the country.

Mastectomy: The removal of the breast(s).

Medicaid: A joint federal and state funded health insurance program for certain low-income and needy people. It covers approximately 36 million individuals, including children, the aged, blind, and/or disabled, and people who are eligible to receive federally assisted income maintenance payments. Does cover certain prescription medications.

(Taken from the federal government's Medicare and Medicaid web site.)

Medicare: The federally run health insurance program for people 65 years of age and older, and people with end-stage renal disease who are on permanent kidney dialysis or have had a kidney transplant. Medicare covers approximately 40 million people for hospitalization and out-patient expenses. In the year 2006 Medicare will start to cover a portion of its recipient's prescription medications. (Taken from the federal government's Medicare and Medicaid web site.)

Metabolic acidosis: A process, usually due to infection, renal disease or exogenous factors, that causes a state of acidemia.

Metastatic: Having spread to a region distant from its original site.

Methadone: A synthetic narcotic that is used as a replacement for morphine and heroin addiction. Has analgesic action similar to morphine. As with morphine and heroin it is highly addictive.

Morphine: A derivative of opium. Produces a euphoric state (at low doses) and a depressive state (at high doses) in the central nervous system. Used as an analgesic and sedative in the medical setting. Has highly psychological and physiological addictive potential.

MRI: Magnetic resonance imaging. An imaging technique that, similar to the CT scan, recreates the anatomical region of interest into cross-sectional views. This imaging technique is superior to the CT scan when investigating disease processes in soft tissue, such as muscles, tendons, and organs.

Myocardial infarction (MI): Sudden insufficiency of blood supply to the tissues of the heart. Can result in damage and death of heart muscle.

Namaste: A Nepalese greeting that means, "I greet the god within you."

National Health Service Corps (NHSC): NHSC's mission is the commitment to improve the health of the Nation's underserved. The NHSC is presently comprised of more than 2,700 primary care clinicians/health care professionals who provide primary health care to adults and children in the communities of greatest need across the Nation. Since 1972 more than 23,000 health professionals have served with NHSC. Many of these clinicians have remained in service after fulfilling their initial NHSC commitments.

Nepal: A country of 23 million people with the land area roughly equal that of Illinois. It is nestled between China to the north, India to the south, and straddles the Asian Himalayan mountain range.

NG: Colloquial for nasogastric tube. A thin tube that is inserted into the nose and follows the esophagus into the stomach. Allows for feedings as well as gastric lavage.

Nitrates: A type of cardiac medication that dilates coronary arteries. Used during episodes of angina pectoris (chest pain).

Normal saline: Intravenous solution with sodium and chloride ions.

Obtunded: An impaired cognitive state.

O-negative blood: A type of "O" blood in the ABO blood typing system, considered the universal donor blood because it lacks the major surface antigens that the other blood groups (A, B, AB) have. This lack of antigens decreases the chance for agglutination (clumping) to occur with the recipient's blood.

OSHA: Occupational Safety and Health Administration. A department of the federal government whose mission is to prevent injuries and protect the health of America's workers.

Osmotic diuresis: The process by which the body can lose an enormous amount of fluid. Commonly seen in diarrhea diseases, as well as in diabetics whose blood sugar concentrated can become so high as to limit their kidney's ability to reabsorb fluid.

Palliative: Reducing the symptoms of a disease (pain, shortness of breath) without curing the disease. Palliative care is often given to people with end stage cancer.

Pancreas: Organ that is part of the digestive and endocrine system. Produces and secretes enzymes into the digestive track and insulin into the blood stream.

Pasteur, Louis: (1822-1895) The French chemist and microbiologist who had important discoveries in fermentation, pasteurization, and immunization.

Pelvic Inflammatory Disease (PID): Inflammation in the female genital tract. Caused by the accent of bacteria from the vagina and cervix into the uterus and fallopian tubes.

Perfuse: The movement of blood from arteries into the vascular bed of a tissue or organ.

Pericardium: The thick, fibrous membrane that surrounds the heart.

pH: The symbol representing the negative logarithm of the hydrogen ion concentration of a fluid. The normal pH of arterial blood is 7.4.

Phenytoin: An anticonvulsant medication. Decreases the rate that neurons are able to transmit a chemo-electrical signal.

Platelets: A component of blood that helps with blood clotting.

Pneumonia: Inflammation of the lung. Bacteria, viruses, fungi, and Mycobacterium tuberculosis (TB) are the main causes.

Pneumothorax: Air that is in the space between the lung and chest cavity which can collapse the lung.

Postictal: The period following a seizure. The patient is often quite somnolent and groggy.

Potassium: An ion and electrolyte in the body. An important component in the process of muscle contraction.

Potassium permanganate: Disinfectant solution for our hands that was used on the medical trek to Nepal. It is a cheap and effective way to sanitize one's hands in a developing country.

Premature ventricular contractions (PVC): An irregular or premature contraction of the heart's ventricles triggered by an irritable area within the ventricle. Major causes can be hypoxia, heart disease or abnormal electrolytes.

Primary care: Generally thought of as the following specialties: family medicine, general internal medicine, general pediatrics, and combined pediatrics/internal medicine. For the purpose of Federal designation of Primary Care Health Personnel Shortage Areas (PCHPSA) the above specialties as well as obstetrics and gynecology are designated primary care specialties. The National Health Service Corps considers all of the above specialties as well as psychiatry to be primary care specialties.

Prolapsed uterus: A uterus that has moved, due to laxity of its supporting muscles and tissues, downward into the vagina. In extreme cases the uterus can be protruding outside of the vagina.

Protein malnutrition: Synonymous with Kwashiorkor disease. Caused by a dietary deficiency in protein. Thin limbs, distended belly, and rounded face are several of the physical findings.

Pulseless electrical activity: (PEA) A condition when the heart is producing electrical activity but is not contracting.

Pyelonephritis: An infection of the bladder and kidneys.

Rales: The inspiratory breath sounds heard with a stethoscope in a patient with fluid in his lungs' air sacs.

Red blood cell (RBC): The blood cell that contains hemoglobin and carries oxygen.

Ryan White Care Act: Signed into law by Congress in August 1990 and recently extended. Named for Ryan White, the HIV positive teenager from Indiana, who made headlines with his fight against the ignorance and prejudice that he experienced from having HIV. The act provides federal funding to states to provide care (outpatient health care, case management, home health and hospice care, housing, nutrition services, and transportation) for HIV infected individuals. There is also funding with this act for drug assistance programs, education, prevention, and testing.

Sandakphu: This village in northeastern Nepal is situated at 11,800 feet and offers a magnificent view of Mt. Kanchenjunga (25,600 feet).

SIDS: Sudden Infant Death Syndrome. Unclear etiology, but it is most prevalent in infants between the age of one and six months. Risk factors include infants who are put to sleep on their stomachs and mothers who smoked during pregnancy, had a history of a sexually transmitted disease or urinary track infection, had poor prenatal care or anemia, or were pregnant before 20 years of age.

Sepsis: A bacterial infection of the blood that is often a complication of burns, surgery, infection, or illness. Patients developing sepsis progress from ill to seriously ill, onto organ dysfunction and failure (called severe sepsis) and then to septic shock.

Septic shock: The body's inability to perfuse blood to its vital organs. Caused by a systemic infection.

Septicemia: Blood poisoning. A disease of the whole body caused by organisms and their toxins circulating in the blood.

Serous fluids: Fluid that is of serum, which is the part of blood that has had the blood cells removed. The fluid is clear and watery.

Serosanguineous: Fluid that is composed of serum and blood. Thin and red in apprearence.

Sertung: Village in north-central Nepal where we had one of our medical camps.

Shaman: A medicine man.

Sherpa: Non capitalized sherpa in Nepal denotes the profession of a porter. Capitalized Sherpa denotes the Tibetan clan name. This clan is known for their high altitude mountain guiding and portering.

Shoulder dystocia: When a fetus's anterior shoulder becomes wedged behind the mother's pubis bone during delivery.

Small Bowel Follow Through (SBFT): An exam that follows barium (a thick, chalky fluid that shows up on X-rays) as it flows through the small intestine. Helpful in diagnosing tumors and obstructions.

Status epilepticus: Nonstop seizures that last longer than 30 minutes.

Streptococcus Pneumonia: A gram positive bacteria that can cause infections in many parts of the body, such as lungs, blood, and skin.

Stress response: The physiological and hormonal changes that help the body adapt to stress. For example, when you are frightened your pulse and blood sugar will increase.

Stupor: A condition in which a patient's consciousness is impaired. Usually the patient needs continuous stimulation to arouse them.

Sumbhek: Village in northeastern Nepal where we had one of our medical camps in October 2002.

Systolic blood pressure: The numerator of the blood pressure reading. It is the maximum blood pressure obtained during the contractile phase of the heart.

Tachycardia: An elevated heart rate, usually over 100 beats per minute.

Tamang: Caste from eastern Nepal.

TB: Tuberculosis. A disease caused by mycobacterium tuberculosis. In its active state the disease resides predominantly in the lungs, but can affect any tissue or organ in the body. The bacteria can lie dormant in the body for many years, reemerging when one becomes immune compromised.

Terai: The low-lying (elevation 600 feet) southern region of Nepal just north of India. This region is very fertile and produces rice, wheat, vegetables, and fruits.

Tika: A mixture of vermilion powder, rice, and curd that is placed on the middle of the forehead during auspicious occasions, such as religious ceremonies, festivals, marriages, and arrivals and departures of family and friends. It signifies a number of greetings, such as good wishes, congratulations, and thank you. The villagers of Sertung placed this red dot on our foreheads when we finished our second medical camp in Nepal.

Tipling: Village in north-central Nepal where we had one of our medical camps.

Tracheostomy: Synonymous with tracheotomy. An operation in which a hole is cut into the windpipe on the front of the neck, just below the vocal cords. A small plastic tube is then inserted into the trachea and sutured into place. The patient can then be hooked up to a ventilator, and if need be, supported indefinitely.

Trisuli Bazaar: A small village in north-central Nepal.

Twenty-four-hour urine collection: Analyzed for the total protein and creatinine excreted by the kidneys in 24 hours. These values give a good estimate to the patient's renal function.

Ultrasound: A diagnostic imaging technique using high frequency (>30,000 hertz) sound waves.

Vasodilators: Any substance that can dilate the body's vessels. For example, certain medications as well as toxins that are released from bacteria.

Ventricle: A cavity in the body. The brain and heart have ventricles. The heart's ventricles are the two lower chambers that pump blood to the lungs and the aorta.

Ventricular Fibrillation: A condition in which there are no organized ventricle depolarizations and the heart is unable to contract as a unit. In this state, the heart is said to be quivering and unable to pump blood.

Ventricular Tachycardia: Heart rate that is greater than 100 beats per minute and originates from a place in the ventricle.

VHF: Denotes Very High Frequency. Solar phones operate on this technology.

White Blood Cells (WBC): A series of blood cells in the immune system that helps protect the body from infection.

Yak: A member of the cow family that has adapted to living at high altitudes.

REFERENCES/SOURCES/NOTES

Prologue: Into the mountains

Kapoor VK, "Abdominal Tuberculosis", *Postgraduate Medical Journal.* 74(874): 459-67, 1998 Aug.

Parajuli, Anil., *Himalayan HealthCare Ganesh Himal Medical Trek Itinerary* (March 2001).

Himalayan HealthCare web site: http://www.himalayan-healthcare.org.

Introduction:

The Centers for Disease Control (CDC) publishes health statistics approximately monthly. These publications are excellent sources for vital health information.

1. Hoyert, D., Arias, E., Smith, B., Murphy, S., Kochanek, K., "Deaths: Final Data 1999," CDC's *National Vital Statistics Reports* 49, no. 8:11.

2. "Entry into prenatal care–United States, 1989-1997," CDC's *Morbidity and Mortality Weekly Report* (MMWR) 49, no.18 (5/12/2000): 393-398. See also Himmelstein, D., et al., *Bleeding the Patient, The Consequences of Corporate Health Care*, Common Courage Press, 2000, page 33.

   For an accurate and sobering quantitative evaluation of the detrimental effects that for-profit healthcare companies have had on our citizens' health, Drs. Himmelstein, Woolhandler and Hellander's, *Bleeding the Patient, The Consequences of Corporate Health Care*, is immensely informative.

3. Himmelstein, D., et al., *Bleeding the Patient, The Consequences of Corporate Health Care*, Common Courage Press, 2000, pages 153-155.

4. Ibid. Page 28.

5. *Insuring America's Health: Principles and Recommendations.* The National Academies Press, Washington, D.C., 2004.

6. Himmelstein, D., et al., *Bleeding the Patient, The Consequences of Corporate Health Care*, Common Courage Press, 2000, pages 12-13.

Chapter 4: Pam the RN

1. "Insulin deficiency prevents glucose from leaving the blood, and the result is the body loses fluids and electrolytes through an

217

osmotic diuresis, a process in which the filtering and re-absorption capacities of the kidneys are overwhelmed by the sugar-rich blood." For a detailed explanation of the metabolic pathology of diabetic ketoacidosis, as well as a description of the signs and symptoms of the disease, see Dr. Rudy's and Dr. Tzagournis' endocrine chapter in *Textbook of Family Practice*: Rakel, Robert. (Editor) *Textbook of Family Practice*, 5th Edition. Chapter 41: "Endocrinology," (Chapter Authors Rudy, David., Tzagournis, Manuel.) 1995. W. B. Saunders Co., Philadelphia. Page 1078.

2. For a good description of the signs and symptoms and treatment of drug withdrawal the following textbooks are superb: Schwartz, George, MD. (Editor) *Principles and Practice of Emergency Medicine*. Fourth Edition. Chapter 144: "Critical Care Medical Toxicology." (Chapter authors Mofenson, Howard, MD, et al.) 1992. Williams and Wilkins, Baltimore. Page 1710-1711; Grenvik, Ake. (Editor) *Textbook of Critical Care*. Fourth Edition. Chapter 13: "Drug Abuse, Overdose, and Withdrawal Syndromes." (Chapter author Schnoll, Sidney, MD). 2000. W. B. Saunders Co. Philadelphia. Page 198.

Chapter 5: Daphne Williams

Much of the data that the National Abortion Federation (NAF) uses in its Fact Sheets comes from The Alan Guttmacher Institute which is well regarded by both "Pro-life" and "Pro-choice" advocates for its objective information on female reproductive and abortion issues. The Alan Guttmacher Institute web page is http://www.agi-usa.org.

1. "Women who have abortions." National Abortion Federation (NAF) Fact Sheet, 1997.
2. "What is surgical abortion?" and "Women who have abortions." NAF Fact Sheet, 1997.
3. Paul, M., Lichtenbert, S., Boragatta, L., Grimes, D., Stubblefield, P., A *Clinician's Guide to Medical and Surgical Abortion*. Chapter 2: "Unintended Pregnancy and Abortion, A Public Health Perspective." (Chapter author Henshaw, Stanley, PhD). Churchill Livingstone, New York, 1999. Page 17. See also Torres, A. and Forrest, J.D., "Why Do Women Have Abortions?" *Family Planning Perspectives* 20, no. 4 (1988):169-176.
4. Paul, M., et al., A *Clinician's Guide to Medical and Surgical Abortion*. Churchill Livingstone, New York, 1999. Page 5. See also "Safety of Abortion." NAF Fact Sheet. 1997.

These statistics for the years between 1979 and 1985 are based on the following source: "Induced Termination of Pregnancy Before and After Roe-vs-Wade. Trends in the Mortality and Morbidity of Women." JAMA 268, no.22 (December 9, 1992): 3231-3239.

5. Ibid.

6. "Deaths: Final Data for 1999." CDC's *National Vital Statistics Report* 49, no. 8 (9/21/2001): 13.

7. "Teenage women, abortion and the law." NAF Fact Sheet. 1996.

8. "The sons of teen mothers are 13% more likely to end up in prison while teen daughters are 22% more likely to become teen mothers themselves." Source: Maynard, R.A. (Ed.). *Kids Having Kids: A Robin Hood Foundation Special Report On the Costs of Adolescent Childbearing*. New York: Robin Hood Foundation. 1996. For additional information on the consequences of teen pregnancy see Haveman, R.H., Wolfe, B., & Peterson, E. (1997). Children of Early Childbearers as Young Adults. In R.A. Maynard (Ed.), *Kids Having Kids: Economic Costs and Social Consequences of Teen Pregnancy* (pp. 257-284). Washington, DC: The Urban Institute Press. (A special thank you to Ms. Leila Darabi, Communications Assistant, at The Alan Guttmacher Institute for finding these sources.)

9. Adler, N., et al., "Psychological Factors in Abortion: A Review." *American Psychologist* 47, no. 10 (Oct. 1992): 1194-1204.

10. Paul, M., et al., A *Clinician's Guide to Medical and Surgical Abortion.* Churchill Livingstone, New York, 1999. Page 28.

11. For information on SIDS see the National Sudden Infant Death Syndrome Resource Center's web site, www.sidscenter.org. (Or contact the center at 2070 Chain Bridge Road, Suite 450, Vienna, VA 22182, (703) 821-8955). The Resource Center is an affiliate of the National Center for Education in Maternal and Child Health and is a service of the U.S. Department of Health and Human Services, Public Health Service, Health Resources and Services Administration, Maternal and Child Health Bureau.

12. Paraphrase of Stedman's Medical Dictionary definition. *Stedman's Medical Dictionary*, 26th Edition. 1995. Williams and Wilkins, Baltimore, MD. Page 1837.

13. Paraphrase of Stedman's Medical Dictionary definition. *Stedman's Medical Dictionary*, 26th Edition. 1995. Williams and Wilkins, Baltimore, MD. Page 405.

Chapter 6: Evelyn Howe

1. This often quoted figure of one in nine U.S. women who will develop breast cancer at sometime during their life is based on a life span of at least 85 years. A more understandable statistic is

taken from Dr. Pinto's "Breast Tumor" chapter in *Medicine*, "Approximately one of nine U.S. women who live to age 85 will develop breast cancer at some time." Fishman, M., et al., *Medicine*, 4th edition, Chapter 48: "Breast Tumor," (Chapter author Dr. Harlan Pinto), Lippincott-Raven, Philidelphia, 1996, Page 414. These statistics are based on the following source: Feuer, EJ., et al., "The Lifetime Risk of Developing Breast Cancer," *Journal of the National Cancer Institute* 85, no. 11 (June 2, 1993): 892-897.

2.   This figure of 35% of women who develop breast cancer who will not be able to say "I am a survivor," is based on a five-year survival rate of 65% for *all* breast cancer patients. Clearly some of these patients, such as the ones with stage 0 (zero) breast cancer, will most likely live their entire lives without recurrence, whereas patients with stage IV breast cancer ("metastatic breast cancer") have a medium survival rate after diagnosis of eighteen to twenty-four months, and a five-year survival rate that is roughly 5%. See Giuliano, A., "Breast," *Current, Medical Diagnosis and Treatment*, Appelton and Lange, 38th Edition, 1999, Chapter 16, Page 699.

3.   Fishman, M., et al., *Medicine*, 4th edition, Chapter 48: "Breast Tumor," (Chapter author Dr. Harlan Pinto), Lippincott-Raven, Philidelphia, 1996, Page 419-420. See also Robbins, S., et al., *Pathologic Basis of Disease*, 5th edition, Chapter 24: "The Breast," W.B. Saunders Co., Philadelphia, 1994, Page 1108.

4.   Spiegel D, Bloom JR, Kraemer HC, Gottheil E: "Effect of psychosocial treatment on survival of patients with metastatic breast cancer." *Lancet*. 1989 Oct 14;2(8668):888-91. The following is an abstract of Dr. Spiegel's study:

> "The effect of psychosocial intervention on time of survival of 86 patients with metastatic breast cancer was studied prospectively. The 1-year intervention consisted of weekly supportive group therapy with self-hypnosis for pain. Both the treatment (n = 50) and control groups (n = 36) had routine oncological care. At 10 year follow-up, only 3 of the patients were alive, and death records were obtained for the other 83. Survival from time of randomization and onset of intervention was a mean 36.6 (SD 37.6) months in the intervention group compared with 18.9 (10.8) months in the control group, a significant difference. Survival plots indicated that divergence in survival began at 20 months after

entry, or 8 months after intervention ended." (This abstract was taken from The National Library of Medicine's web site: http://www.ncbi.nlm.nih.gov.)

Additional information for chapter 6 was gathered from the following sources: American Cancer Society's web page: http://www3.cancer.org; Davidson, N., "Breast Cancer," *Scientific American,* 1999, Section 12, Chapter VII, Pages 1-23; Tierney, L, et al., *Current, Medical Diagnosis and Treatment,* Chapter 16: "Breast," (Chapter author Dr. Armando Giuliano), Appelton and Lange, 38th Edition, 1999, Page 682.

Chapter 7: Sheri

1. P. Champe, R. Harvey, *Biochemistry* (2 ed.; Philadelphia: Lippincott,1994), pp. 65-66, 92.
2. D. H. Taylor et al., "Effects of Admission to a Teaching Hospital on the Cost and Quality of Care for Medicare Beneficiaries," *New England Journal of Medicine* 340, no. 4 (January 28, 1999): 293–99; A. J. Hartz, "Hospital Characteristics and Mortality Rates," *New England Journal of Medicine* 321, no. 25 (December 21, 1989): 1720–25.
3. E. Dauer, L. Marcus, "Adapting Mediation to Link Resolution of Medical Malpractice Disputes with Health Care Quality Improvement," *Law and Contemporary Problems* 60, no. 1 (winter and spring 1997): 185–218.
4. Ibid. See also E. Lovern, "Teamwork University: Harvard Program Helps Healthcare Professionals Get the Skills They Need to Resolve Conflicts," *Modern Healthcare,* April 23, 2001.

   For additional information on mediation and medical malpractice, see E. Dauer et al, "Prometheus and the Litigators, A Mediation Odyssey," *The Journal of Legal Medicine* 21 (2000): 159–86.
5. M. Feinberg, "Retrovirus Infections," *Scientific American,* 1995, Section 7, Chapter XXXIIB, pp. 1–38;J. Kuby, *Immunology* (2d ed., W. H. Freeman and Co., 1991), pp. 47–83, 323–44. 348–66; R. Schooley, "Acquired Immunodeficiency Syndrome," *Scientific American,* 1999, Section 7, Chapter XI, pp. 1-14. See also Joint United Nations Program on HIV/AIDS web site: http://www.unaids.org and 2002 World Aids Conference in Spain, conference data, at: http://www.aids2002.com/.
6. Ibid.
7. Ibid.
8. Ibid.

Chapter 8: Harold Brown

For information on The Balint Society one can read: Salinsky, John., "Balint Groups: History, Aims and Methods." June 1977. This paper can be found at http://familymed.musc.edu/balint/.

Chapter 9: Dr. Martin Milioni

1. For information on residency work hours, see the web site for the Accreditation Council for Graduate Medical Education (ACGME): http://www.acgme.org.
2. Lynne Lamberg, "Long Hours, Little Sleep, Bad Medicine for Physicians-in-Training?" JAMA 287, no. 3 (January 16 2002): 303–6; Tait Shanafelt et al., "Burnout and Self-Reported Patient Care in an Internal Medicine Residency Program," Annals of Internal Medicine 136, no. 5 (March 5, 2002): 358–67; Jennifer Silverman, "Students Lobby OSHA for Work-Hour Limits," Family Practice News, July 1, 2001; Chester Sturnk et al., "Resident Work Hours and Working Environment in Otolaryngology," JAMA 266, no. 10 (September 11, 1991): 1371–74.
3. Amy Braverman, "End of the Medical Marathon?" University of Chicago Magazine, October 2002, pp. 34–39. (A special thank you to Dr. Kendra Sisserson for finding this source and Ms. Amber Mason, Alumni News Editor, at the University of Chicago Magazine for allowing me to quote this source.)
4. Ibid.; Melissa Halbach et al., "Effect of Sleep Deprivation on Medical Resident and Student Cognitive Function: A Prospective Study," Am. J. Obstet. Gynecol. 188, no. 5 (May 2003): 1198–1201; Stephen Cohen, "Hi. I'm Your Doctor. I Haven't Slept in 36 Hours," USA Today, March 22, 2000, p. 29A; Drew Dawson and Kathryn Reid, "Fatigue, Alchohol and Performance Impairment," Nature 388 (July 17, 1997): 235.

    The following sources were also used for the discussion on resident work hours: Buysse, D.J., et al., "Sleep, Fatigue, and Medical Training: Setting an Agenda for Optimal Learning and Patient Care," Conference Report, Sleep 26, no. 2 (2003): 218–25; Clever, Linda. "Who Is Sicker: Patients or Residents? Residents' Distress and the Care of Patients," Annals of Internal Medicine 136, no. 5 (March 5, 2002): 391–93; House of Representative and Senate bill locator: http://thomas.loc.gov; Kohn, Linda, et al., "To Err Is Human: Building a Safer Health System," Institute of Medicine, Committee on Quality of Health Care in America. Washington, D.C.: National Academy Press, 1999; Lewis, Diane. "Curbs on doctor's hours sought." Boston Globe,

May 1, 2001; Tarnow-Mordi, W., et al., "Hospital Mortality in Relation to Staff Workload: A 4-year Study in an Adult Intensive-Care Unit," *The Lancet* 356 (July 15, 2000): 185–89.

Chapter 10: *Cutting through stereotypes*

1. National Residency Matching Program data can be found at the following web sites: http://www.nrmp.org, http://www.aafp.org.
2. Ibid.
3. See the Robert Graham Center (Policy Studies in Family Practice and Primary Care) web site: http://www.graham-center.org. See also R. Kutob et al., "Declining Interest in Family Medicine: Perspectives of Department Heads and Faculty," *Family Medicine*, July-August 2003, pp. 504–9; Cindy McCanse, "Match Results Mixed across Primary Care," *Family Practice Report* 8, no. 4 (April 2002): 3; Janet Senf et al., "Factors Affecting Specialty Choice," University of Arizona study looking at factors that influence medical student's career in primary care, 2003; "2001 MATCH Information Sheet" March 22, 2001, p. 4 (see the American Academy of Family Physicians' web site: http://www.aafp.org/match/nrmpinfo.html).
4. Anne Barnard, "A Match for Life," *The Boston Globe*, March 22, 2002.
5. Immigration Attorney Robert D. Aronson's web site: http://www.Ingber-aronson.com.
6. "Distribution of Office Visits by Physician Specialty and Professional Identity: United States, 1999," 2001 *Facts about Family Practice*, Table 26 (see the American Academy of Family Physicians' web site: http://www.aafp.org/facts/).
7. Ibid. See also "Non-Federal Physicians in the United States by Activity, December 31, 1999," 2001 *Facts about Family Practice*, Table 2.
8. Paraphrased from "2001 MATCH Information Sheet," March 22, 2001, p. 4 (see the American Academy of Family Physicians' web site: http://www.aafp.org/match/nrmpinfo.html).
9. "Number of office visits by race/ethnic background of patient to all physicians and selected specialties: United States, 1999," 2001 *Facts about Family Practice*, Table 33 (see the American Academy of Family Physicians' web site: http://www.aafp.org/facts/).
10. "The United States Relies on Family Physicians, Unlike Any Other Specialty." Number 5. 4/14/00. The Robert Graham Center for Policy Studies in Family Practice and Primary Care. Can be found on the American Academy of Family Physicians' web site: http://www.aafppolicy.org.

11. The percentage of Americans without healthcare insurance can be found at the National Center for Health Statistics web site: http://www.cdc.gov/nchs. For the year 2000, 14.7 percent of all Americans were uninsured; this equates to approximately 40 million people without health insurance. (See CDC web site: "Percent of persons without health insurance coverage for all ages: United States, 1997–2001," Figure 1.1.) However, this quoted figure of 40 million Americans who lack health insurance are those individuals who did not have health insurance for all twelve months of the year 2000. A more telling statistic that the Congressional Budget Office recently released showed that between 60 and 75 million Americans lacked health insurance at some time during the year 1998. This higher number of uninsured is partly due to people who lose health insurance when they change their jobs or are laid off. *Physicians for a National Health Program Newsletter*, Spring 2003, p. 6. In addition, see Robert Pear, "New Study Finds 60 Million Uninsured during a Year," *New York Times*, May 13, 2003.

    Americans' increasing reliance on government insurance (Medicare and Medicaid) can be found at the following site: "Number and percent of persons aged under 65 years with private health insurance and with public coverage, by age group: United States, 1997–2001," Table 1.2. This and similar data can be found at the National Center for Health Statistics web site: http://www.cdc.gov/nchs.

12. "2001 MATCH Information Sheet," March 22, 2001, p. 4 (see the American Academy of Family Physicians' web site: http://www.aafp.org/match/nrmpinfo.html).

13. National Health Service Corps web site: http://www.nhsc.bhpr.hrsa.gov.

14. D. Gray, "Diabetes Mellitus, Type II," *Griffith's 5 Minute Clinical Consult* (Baltimore: Williams and Wilkins, 2001); John Karam, "Diabetes Mellitus and Hypoglycemia," in *Current Medical Diagnosis and Treatment*, ed. L. Tierney et al. (38th ed.; New York: Appleton and Lange, 1999), pp. 1118–60.

Chapter 11: James Freeman

1. The American Lung Association estimates that approximately 444,000 Americans die each year from diseases caused by smoking. The quote of 160,000 deaths in a year due to lung cancer was for the year 1997. Source: A. Skarin, "Lung Cancer," *Scientific American*, 1997, Section 12, Chapter VI, p. 1. (Incidentally, for the year 2000 over

155,000 Americans died from lung cancer.) "The American Cancer Society estimates that there will be 172,000 new cases of lung cancer in 2003." Source: "Trends in Lung Cancer Morbidity and Mortality," American Lung Association, June 2003, on the American Lung Association web site: http://www.lungusa.org.

Prognosis based on International System for Clinical Staging of Lung Cancer. Source: Skarin, A., "Lung Cancer," *Scientific American*, 1997, Section 12, Chapter VI, Page 9.

2. These dollar amounts are based on U.S. cigarette companies' 1997 expenditure on advertisement and promotion, totaling 5.7 billion dollars. This averages out to be approximately 15 million a day. Disturbingly, by the year 2001 (the most recent year data was available), the tobacco industry had doubled its marketing expenditures to 11.2 billion. Source: U.S. Federal Trade Commission Cigarette Report for 2001 (June 12, 2003). This information can be found at the following web sites: http://www.ftc.gov/os/2003/06/2001cigreport.pdf, and http://tobaccofreekids.org.

"And much of that marketing directly reaches and influences kids." Source: "Smoking And Kids," Campaign for Tobacco-Free Kids. Web site: http://www.tobaccofreekids.org. Original source: U.S. Federal Trade Commission Cigarette Report for 2001 (June 12, 2003). This information can be found at the following web sites: http://www.ftc.gov/os/2003/06/2001cigreport.pdf.

"A third of underage experimentation with smoking is attributable to tobacco advertising and promotion." Source: "Tobacco Industry Continues to Market to Kids," Campaign for Tobacco-Free Kids.Web site: http://www.tobaccofreekids.org. Original sources: R. Pollay et al., "The Last Straw? Cigarette Advertising and Realized Market Shares among Youths and Adults 1979-1993," *Journal of Marketing* 60, no. 2 (April 1996): 1–16; N. Evans et al., "Influences of Tobacco Marketing and Exposure to Smokers on Adolescent Susceptibility to Smoking," *Journal of the National Cancer Institute* 87, no. 20 (October 18, 1995): 1538–45; J. P. Pierce et al., "Tobacco Industry Promotion of Cigarettes and Adolescent Smoking," JAMA 279, no. 7 (February 18, 1998): 511-5.

"90 percent of all smokers start when they are adolescents." Source: P. Lantz, P. Jacobson, K. Warner, "Youth Smoking Prevention. What works?" *The Prevention Researcher* 8, no. 2 (April 2001):1. Data based on SAMHSA, HHS, 2001 National Household Surveys on Drug Abuse.

Moolchan and his colleagues estimate that 75 percent of teenage smokers will smoke as adults; see E. T. Moolchan et al., "A Review of Tobacco Smoking in Adolescents: Treatment Implications." *Journal of the American Academy of Child and Adolescent Psychiatry* 39, no. 6 (2000 June): 682–93.

"On average, adult men and women smokers lost 13.2 and 14.5 years of life, respectively, because they smoked." Source: CDC, "Morbidity and Mortality Weekly Report–Annual Smoking-Attributable Mortality, Years of Potential Life Lost, and Economic Costs–United States, 1995–1999." *Morbidity and Mortality Weekly Report* 51, no. 14 (April 12, 2002): 300-303.

It is projected that one-third of persons aged 0–17 years who will become smokers will die prematurely as adults because of a smoking-related illness. See CDC, "Projected Smoking-Related Deaths among Youth—United States," *Morbidity and Mortality Weekly Report* 45, no. 44 (November 8, 1996): 971-74. See the web sites http://www.cdc.gov/mmwr and http://www.lungusa.org.

3.   "Each day nearly 4,800 adolescents (age 11-17) smoke their first cigarette: nearly 2,000 will become regular smokers, totaling to almost one million new smokers annually." Quote from the American Lung Association web site: http://www.lungusa.org.

C. Ahern, S. Batchelor et al., "Youth Tobacco Surveillance," CDC MMWR, U.S. 1998-1999, October 13th, 2000, Vol 49, No. SS-10, Pages 1–92. Between 1999 and 2001 (the most recent data available) the percent of high school students who smoke decreased from 35 percent to 29 percent. Source: CDC, "Trends in Cigarette Smoking among High School Students-United States, 1991–2001," *Morbidity and Mortality Weekly Report* 51, no. 19 (May 17, 2002): 409–12. Web site: http://www.cdc.gov/mmwr.

"It is no secret that cigarette advertisements emphasize the themes that many teenagers struggle with: youthful vigor, sexual attraction, and independence." Source: Paraphrased from the American Lung Association web site: http://www.lungUSA.org.

4.   M. Grippi, "Pathophysiology of Respiratory Failure," *Pulmonary Pathophysiology* (Philadelphia: Lippincott,1995), p. 275.

5.   R. D. Hurt, D. P. L. Sachs, E. D. Glover et al., "A Comparison of Sustained-Released Bupropion and Placebo for Smoking Cessation." *New England Journal of Medicine* 337, no. 17 (October 23, 1997): 1195–1202.

Chapter 12: Sammy Ellington

1. Since the writing of this book, the U.S. Congress and the Bush administration have passed the Medicare reform bill. This bill, among other things, earmarks $400 billion over ten years to help offset the high cost of prescription drugs for senior citizens. The bill is set to take effect in the year 2006. The average senior will save approximately 30% on prescription medications. Although this bill is a good start in addressing one aspect of our failing healthcare system, it does not address the prescription drug costs of the 40 million Americans without healthcare insurance, one of those being my patient Sammy.

Chapter 13: The End of the Beginning

1. GNP per capita data (in U.S. dollars) is based on 1998 World Bank data. Can be found at http://www.worldbank.org. As another comparison, Nepal's healthcare expenditures were approximately $4 per capita compared to the U.S., which spent $5,035 per capita on healthcare in 2001. See Diwakar Chand, *Essays on Development of Nepal* (Lazimpat, Kathmandu. Chandni Publications, 2001), p. 160 (A special thank you to Ms. Anu Kumari Lama, Tourist Officer, at the King Mahendra Trust for Nature Conservation in Nepal for finding this source.); *Physicians for a National Health Program Newsletter*, spring 2003, p. 7 (based on data from Office of the Actuary, CMS; Heffler et al., Health Affairs Web Exclusive, 2/7/03).

See also Lauralee Sherwood, "Peripheral Endocrine Glands," in *Human Physiology* (2d ed.; Minneapolis: West Publishing Co., 1993), pp. 649–94.

Glossary of Terms:

The following books and web sites were indispensable in helping define all of the terms and definitions in this book:

Department of Health and Human Services: http://www.hhs.gov/

Lonely Planet, *Nepal*, 4 ed., 1999.

Medicaid: http://cms.hhs.gov/medicaid/

Medicare: http://www.medicare.gov/

National Health Service Corps web site: http://www.nhsc.bhpr.hrsa. gov/

Parker, Antin, et al., *Himalayan Odyssey*. New York: Dell Publishing, 1990.

Salinsky, John., "Balint Groups: History, Aims and Methods." June 1977. Can be found at http://familymed.musc.edu/balint/

Sherwood, Lauralee, "Peripheral Endocrine Glands." *Human Physicology*. 2d ed.; Minneapolis: West Publishing Co., 1993.

Stedman's Medical Dictionary. 26 ed.; Baltimore: Williams and Wilkins, 1995.

U.S. Department of Labor, Bureau of Labor Statistics, Occupational Outlook Handbook. Can be found at http://www.bls.gov.

PHOTO CREDITS

Front cover photo of Mount Kusum Kanguru (20,887 feet) in Nepal was taken by Robert McKersie. Front cover photo of the baby in the incubator © Louie Psihoyos/CORBIS. Title page photo of Tamang woman with septicemia was taken by Robert McKersie. Prologue page photo of Tamang boy on a scale was taken by Robert McKersie. Introduction page photo of author was taken by Anil Parajuli. Chapter 1 photo of ER entrance at Ventura County Medical Center was taken by Dr. Geeta Maker-Clark. Gallery photo of Dr. Maria Brown at the Pilsen homeless clinic was taken by Ms. Jean Clough. The photographers of the gallery photos of Ms. Meade Palidofsky and Deangelo Horton, the young man with a tattoo on his hand and face, and Dr. John May are unknown. Gallery photo of the women performing the Temporary Lockdown play was taken by Giau Truong. All gallery photos of Nepal were taken by Robert McKersie. Epilogue page photo of Dr. Mahendra Poudel was taken by Robert McKersie. Dedication page photo of Robbie McKersie in Central Park was taken by Robert McKersie. Back cover photo of the author was taken by a nice gentleman at a passport photo studio in Kathmandu.

978-0-595-36368-1
0-595-36368-7